FOR

HILAIRE
BELLOC

FOR
HILAIRE
BELLOC

ESSAYS IN HONOR OF HIS 71st BIRTHDAY
EDITED BY DOUGLAS WOODRUFF

NEW YORK
SHEED & WARD
1942

FOREWORD

THE ESSAYS which are here assembled were written independently of one another for this volume. They are the work of men of a younger literary generation, the oldest among whom found such books as the *Path to Rome* waiting for them as soon as they were of an age to appreciate them, and the book is offered as an expression of admiration and gratitude to a great writer by men who, however they would discriminate and differ from each other about where they would place the emphasis or what has been most valuable, stimulating or enjoyable in Mr. Belloc's wide range of literary wares, are at one in desiring to pay him some special mark of honour.

These are historical essays, because for half a century Mr. Belloc has maintained the liveliest interest in historical studies, and in the volumes bearing his name, now well over a hundred in all, historical writings, whether monographs, biographies or histories, are much the largest single division. In no field that he has entered has his impact been more stimulating, or his influence more marked. He has presented, often with carefully provocative overstatement, unfamiliar and unfashionable views, seeking to correct not details but the large outlines in which the past is seen and taught.

We print at the beginning of our volume a general appraisal, from the pen of Mr. Douglas Jerrold, of Mr. Belloc's influence, but we did not think a birthday volume such as this the suitable place for any extended appreciations or critical estimates of his writing in prose and verse. The theory of a birthday volume is that it should treat of topics likely to interest and divert the recipient, and while there are many literary men who find no topic half as interesting as their own work, he is not at all that kind of literary man.

In the Dedicatory Ode which was placed at the beginning

of Lambkin's Remains, some forty-six years ago now, the youthful Hilaire Belloc wrote

> The plan forgot, I know not how,
>   Perhaps the refectory filled it,
> To put the chapel in, and now
>   Were mortgaging the rest to build it.

It was to prove a very prominent part of the final structure, and there was to be, as he developed, more and more about the Catholic Church in his books; and whatever other lack of unity there is in the essays in this volume, it seemed to us appropriate that they should come from men who all share with him the great bond of the same Catholic faith.

D. W.

Hilaire Belloc and the Counter-Revolution

by DOUGLAS JERROLD

THE SEED of the counter-revolution in Protestant Europe has yet to fructify. Its germination and growth is the major political event of our time, yet most people are unaware of it, even as a movement below the surface of events. By some it is confused with, and condemned as, Fascism. By others, even more absurdly, it is confused with, and applauded as, Liberalism. We shall see how deep the confusion is if we ask whether, in the present war, England is fighting for or against the doctrines of 1789. Is ours a revolutionary or a counter-revolutionary offensive?

On the one hand we are told that we are fighting for democracy—a political conception which derives directly from the doctrines of the Enlightenment. On the other hand, we are told that Nazism and Communism are indistinguishable, and that we are fighting the forces of world-revolution, which also unquestionably derive from the doctrines of 1789. If we say that we are Crusaders who have rejected the Cross, fighting demagogues who have deserted the people, we shall perhaps not be far from the truth, which is why this war, though it would assuredly lead to the destruction of Christian civilization if Germany won, will not necessarily lead to its renaissance if Germany is defeated. The hour of the counter-revolution has not yet struck. And its issue is, therefore, not yet determined.

The reason is simple enough. Throughout non-Catholic Europe the ideas of 1789 struck so deep that it is still difficult (twenty-five years ago it was impossible) to gain attention for any political doctrines aiming at reform which

I

do not pay at least lip-service to these ideas. This is partly because the belief in an automatic progress, deriving by a law of nature from the natural goodness and wisdom of man, is a psychological necessity to men who have lost their faith, and are not willing to follow Mr. Bertrand Russell in building their *Weltanschauung* on "a firm basis of unyielding despair." There are, however, two other important contributory causes.

Firstly, the outcome of the ideas of 1789 has not been the tolerant "negative" state of the last century, but the powerful political state of the present century. In such a state, be it democratic or the reverse, political power, being supreme over economics, becomes the vested interest of the dominant class. Be that class the new aristocracy of the pen and the desk, as in England, or the political gangsters who control the Communist and Nazi political machines, it will, as surely in plutocratic England or in divided France, as in Germany or Russia, control the Press, the platform and the schools. It will also, however foolish it may appear to be in its public antics, possess, as all ruling classes possess, an uncanny instinct for detecting ideas likely to destroy the source of its own power.

Secondly, the Revolution itself has been so slow in coming to a head that its doctrines have acquired an intense respectability. All through the nineteenth century it was common form for Liberals, Whigs, and Young England Conservatives to pay lip-service to the Rights of Man, and the whole corpus of political doctrine associated with them. That century of unparalleled material progress appeared to derive from the revolutionary doctrines, to be the rare and refreshing fruit of the assault on privilege and property. Yet, for all that, privilege did not cease to be a necessary prerogative of sovereignty, nor property cease to be the inalienable right of the common man.

It was, indeed, apparent to some that the relatively solid fabric of society inherited from the eighteenth century was being steadily undermined. The people, promised the moon by their betters for a century, would, in the end, insist on joining personally in the search. But, in the nineteenth century scramble by the popular politicians for the support of the people, only the most hard-bitten reactionaries ventured a discussion of fundamentals. We blundered into unrestricted democracy, into secularism, and into State Capitalism, without defining our aims and, in most cases, without intending to achieve them. There was never a "programme" for destroying the faith of the people, for creating a vast urban proletariat, for ruining agriculture and aggregating the wealth of a nation into a few hands. This only meant, however, that by the time these consequences of the age of reform became apparent, the principles from which the consequences had derived had become, in default of any open challenge, sacrosanct. Was it not evident, said all men of good will, that any deficiencies still left in our society resulted from the influence of property which is reflected in a society still, even in 1910, predominantly middle-class, and, in certain aspects, still aristocratic? The natural reaction of such men was to demand more and more State interference. The need was urgent: the instruments of reform ready to hand.

The rise of Socialism was not merely disastrous in itself, in that it harnessed many fine and disinterested minds to a false philosophy, but it also manœuvred into the defence of the capitalist regime, almost the whole of those forces which should have been led in the attack on it. By the time the Socialist-Capitalist controversy took its decisive turn, and the two Front benches agreed, after the last war, on the compromise of State-Capitalism, the possible opposition was hopelessly divided. On the one hand were the die-hard, and hopelessly belated, defenders of free capitalism, and on the other, those who stood for the full Socialist programme. Supporting (*faute de mieux*) one extreme, were to be found many true lovers of liberty, and supporting the other (also *faute de mieux*) many true lovers of humanity. The great majority of the people were nominal supporters of one or other of the two great Front

4   *For Hilaire Belloc*

Bench Parties, and therefore, in practice, supporters of
both.

This state of affairs persists largely to this day. Nevertheless, the counter-revolution is today afoot, and is, at long
last, gaining ground. This is largely, if not entirely, due
to Hilaire Belloc: partly to Hilaire Belloc the man of
genius, who alone of his contemporaries foresaw and defined the servile state, but partly also to Hilaire Belloc
the radical politician, whose denunciations of the parliamentary system were even more immediate in their influence than his inspired prophecies.

It is impossible for anyone except Mr. Belloc himself,
and probably impossible also for him, to say precisely how,
and in what logical sequence, his ideas about parliamentary
government in this country were formed. What is certain
is that, sensing instinctively that tacit agreement on fundamentals between the two great Parties (which is, indeed,
essential if a Parliament is to govern under a two-party
system), Mr. Belloc diagnosed a corrupt bargain for the
defence of privileged or personal interests. It must be
difficult indeed for those of the war and post-war generations, and impossible for the youth of the present day, to
imagine how revolutionary this suggestion appeared to the
Edwardian world. I do not want to conceal my view that
the diagnosis was incorrect rather than inspired. It was,
so it has always seemed to me, an attempt to translate
English politics into French: it was motivated also, I
fancy, by the time-honoured suspicion of the Radical for
the Whigs, then at the height of their power.

What matters to the historian, however, is something
quite different. The writings of Hilaire Belloc between
1909 and 1914 formed a challenge so unexpected, and so
fortunately supported by the disclosures of the Marconi
scandal, the silver scandal, and one or two relatively minor
affairs, that it not merely compelled public attention but,
for many months, almost monopolized it. The prestige of
the Parliamentary system was dealt a blow from which it
has never wholly recovered here or elsewhere. Not even

the combined efforts of Hitler and Stalin have restored it
to the pinnacle on which it rested so securely in the early
years of this century.

We are here considering proximate causes, not ultimate
truths. The consequence of this challenge offered to British
complacency by the attack on the Party system, and the
political integrity of its leaders was, in the small sphere
of English politics, as striking as Luther's denunciation
of the sale of indulgences. The one denunciation may
have been as ill-founded as the other (though to say that
would be a grotesque exaggeration) but the effect (always
remembering that we are comparing very small things
with the very greatest) was similar. The profound psychological consequence was this. Men no longer blamed
their political opponents for the evils of the times: they
began to blame the politicians. In so doing they were
blaming themselves and thus acquiring a healthy doubt,
by now intuitive throughout the Western world, of their
own natural wisdom and virtue, which their fathers and
grandfathers had been taught to regard as axiomatic.

Yet if the challenge to the Party system was thus an event
of importance, many of Mr. Belloc's warmest admirers
regard the importance as political rather than intellectual. It was far otherwise with his indictment of the Servile State, the most penetrating and prophetic piece of
political pamphleteering of the century. In this book, Mr.
Belloc foresaw and foretold the development of Liberal
capitalism into State capitalism and thence into the slave
community, exactly and precisely as it is occurring all over
Europe today. Being wise before the event (for *The Servile State* was being written while Mr. Lloyd George's
Insurance Bill was still under discussion in the House of
Commons) the book had small influence at the time. It
has, however, had a growing influence ever since, reinforced by twenty-eight years of writing giving the necessary historical, political and economic basis for the counter-
revolution.

Maine has said truly that the change worked by civiliza-

tion is the change from status to contract. Belloc pointed
out that the contractual basis of civilized society was, in
the name of social progress, being steadily undermined,
that property-less man was not a free moral agent, and
that the true basis of enjoyment was not use but ownership. These ideas appeared to contemporary England
revolutionary. They were, in fact, the starting point of
the English counter-revolution. The challenge offered to
the force of big business in the name of really private
enterprise, the challenge offered to radical humanitarian-
ism in the name of the real rights of man, slowly began
to strike roots in a country averse from philosophic speculation but very much alive to practicalities. The ideas of
Joseph de Maistre and his successors in France, from
Chateaubriand down to Péguy and Maurras, aroused few
sparks of interest in England, but the plight of the land-
less labourer, the small shopkeeper and the unwanted
craftsman was familiar.

What was remarkable was that the Servile State was
prophesied so long before the event. It is indeed curious,
by contrast, looking back on the post-war years, to recall
the adulation extended to H. G. Wells, whose prophecies,
however inspired, were invariably wrong. Mr. Wells first
saw in the Naval Agreement at Washington the dawn
of a new era of universal peace. He then chose the decade
when the world was visibly drifting to bankruptcy under
the leadership of the banks to advocate an open conspiracy
of super-business-magnates as the path to Utopia. In his
Outline of History he saw the inevitable progress towards
the World-State just when the twin forces of exclusive
political nationalism and economic autarchy were entering
the stage of history. Finally, Mr. Wells promised the
eclipse and proximate dissolution of the Church of Christ
just when the Church was being universally recognized
as the only possible bulwark of freedom against reaction.
On the other side of the argument, almost alone except
for G. K. Chesterton and some of the younger Catholic
writers, stood Hilaire Belloc, who challenged the whole

corpus of nineteenth century history, sociology and science, and whose prophecies have all been proved right as quickly as those of Mr. H. G. Wells have been proved wrong. Mr. Wells swept the majority of the English student public (for the first time, since the new franchise, an important if not decisive factor in English public life) from one folly to another. But, for the first time since the Reformation, there was a growing counterpoise to the deceptive fallacies of humanitarian positivism. No longer were there one or two voices crying in a wilderness, but a growing volume of reasoned opinion increasingly alive to the real nature of Christian civilization and to the conditions on which alone it can survive.

Edwardian England was still, in essence, nineteenth century England, our England that was "chosen," set apart from the Continent, wholly divorced from the European concert and actually unaware of the nature of the Catholic tradition. Mr. John Murray and his fellow Guides were still drawing relieved attention to the number of Protestant Churches and Protestant inhabitants ("all of the better sort"[1]) in France: the procession of the Blessed Sacrament was forbidden in London. We still wore top hats to go to Church, and the Continental Sunday was in deep disrepute. These were, indeed, trivialities, but the new movements were of a piece. We were learning to take broader views, but our expanding horizon revealed nothing of Europe or the Faith. Anti-clericalism in France and Italy, Liberalism in Spain and Nihilism in Russia were on the fringe of the picture, while the centre was filled by an ever-expanding view of British wealth, British credit and British middle-class virtue giving to the working classes (so long as they worked) a helping hand. Our vision had the qualities of its defects. We still thought one Englishman worth two foreigners in the field, and half-a-dozen on the tennis court. We were still a quarter of a century distant from the days when "Austin's heroic struggle" on a newspaper placard meant that an English lawn tennis player

---

[1] *Guide to South Eastern France.*

had taken one set off a foreigner at Wimbledon. At any rate we were not a frightened people, nor yet a servile people. We were rich and secure and complacent, for our God was an English God, extremely jealous of foreigners. Behind the comfortable virtue of the middle-class was the commonsense of the British people, and in front of it an incorruptible phalanx of public men, nursed in the parliamentary tradition, just, capable and wise.

Had you told the England of those days that a nation which determined its policy by the free play of human volition would inevitably go bankrupt: that freedom is only possible within the framework of a closed moral system: that if you so rig your economic system as to destroy the economic independence of the family, you make State worship inevitable and thus pave the way for the gangster tyrannies: that the concert which held Europe together was not the balance of power or any other political device, but the common habits of life derived from a common faith, and that if and in so far as the Faith weakened, unrestrained nationalism would destroy civilization: if you had told that England that the great menace overhanging the world was not the German Fleet, the Yellow Peril or the growing power of organized labour, but the growing scepticism about the fundamental values and decencies, not one of these things would then have been understood, let alone believed.

Today, as we know, these things are said everywhere, and if they are still not yet generally believed, there is at least a fundamental division of opinion about them. And the change is decisive thus far, that there is no one today who believes that we can halt half-way between the Christian order, based on the independent Church and the free family, and the materialist secular State, which takes over both these institutions, and with them the responsibility for individual prosperity and national discipline.

There are many who think that the restitution of property is fraught today with insuperable difficulties, that the powers and influence of international finance are so great that the sacrifice of productive efficiency which is necessary if we are to re-create a widely-distributed system of ownership, would never be tolerated. Above all the restoration of agriculture in this country, without which no close approach to a Christian social order is possible, would be bitterly opposed, not only by the financial and shipping interests, but by organized labour also, whose leaders, at any rate, are prepared to acquiesce in a permanent loss of status for trade unionists in return for a guaranteed minimum wage and a low price level for necessities.

It is not my purpose here to discuss how far this line of argument is justified. What is noteworthy is that these fundamental questions are being discussed today by men of all shades of opinion in terms of conceptions which would have been quite unfamiliar to Englishmen before Mr. Belloc and his friends and followers, G. K. Chesterton first and foremost among them, began teaching and preaching. The Distributist State is not yet recognized as the only alternative to the Collectivist, but the movement is set that way, and that time will come. Already the British Foreign Secretary sounds a call to arms on behalf of the Christian civilization of Europe, not of England, and *The Times* leads a demand for the teaching of dogmatic Christianity in schools. Both these things would have been impossible a quarter of a century ago. Both are the consequences of the infiltration into all classes and churches of the classical ideas of European Catholicism, first translated into the English idiom by Hilaire Belloc. These ideas are the seeds of the counter-revolution. If they fall on good ground, they can bear no other fruit.

The writings of Joseph de Maistre inspired generations of French Catholic thought without even seriously threatening the political control of the anti-clerical parties. But they have kept alive a vast body of Catholic opinion which has always been able to prevent the destruction of the soul of France, which is the teaching Church, or of her body, which is her peasantry. It is, perhaps, most likely that the counter-revolution in England will also work this way, slowly and, for a generation or more, negatively. It would be ridiculous in any case to expect any swift and decisive change. But the battle is joined and the Christian cause will not go by default. For that, the debt which this country owes to Hilaire Belloc is very great indeed.

The Man Who Tried to Convert
the Pope

by R. A. KNOX

MOST OF US are aware that, at intervals during the last three centuries, efforts have been made by well-meaning persons to realise the pathetic dream of a re-united Church, something not quite Protestant and not quite Catholic, based upon those principles of compromise which are so dear to the English heart. But none of them, I suppose, has ever been made with so little appreciation of the facts, so quaint a misunderstanding of values, as that described by its author in a book entitled "Journal of a Tour in Italy in 1850," by George Townsend, D.D., Canon of Durham, published by Messrs. Rivington in 1851.

I am suspected, I do not know why, of being infected with that April Fool's Day spirit which delights to palm off literary frauds on the public. Let me explain, then, that the volume really exists, and that my quotations are all genuine. Nor let it be supposed that I am the victim, any more than I am the author, of an imposture. Canon Townsend has his niche in the Dictionary of National Biography; he is no fiction of a Tractarian humorist, he is solid fact. A visit to Durham might even supply us with his portrait, but I have felt the pilgrimage to be unnecessary. I think I see the old gentleman well enough as it is; white-chokered, well-tailored, earnest, whiskered after the fashion of his time. He had got his canonry, I suppose, before 1840, and was not therefore affected by the findings of the Ecclesiastical Commission, which cut down its value to a beggarly thousand a year; he liked, clearly, to do himself well, and was not infected with the enthusiasm of the Evangelicals. But the Oxford Movement had equally passed him by; he was a low Churchman of the old school, a complete fundamentalist in his attitude towards the Bible—as who was not, in his day?—and an Englishman *à l'outrance*. How did such a man condescend to take an interest in the corrupt politics of the Vatican, or the insanitary population of the Seven Hills?

I think it was due to an odd streak of logic in his composition, which drove him on from strength to strength, regardless of prudent counsels and shaking of heads in high places. He realised, it seems, that the numerous prayers which an Anglican has to offer up in the course of his ministry for the welfare and guidance of the Universal Church cannot be said with any real meaning when your practical interest is centred entirely in the national church of one people, sparsely represented even in its dominions overseas. He wanted to do something about it; to establish an effective contrast between the Christianity of his own country and Christianity on the other side of the channel; and his sublime confidence in the rightness of his own position convinced him that there was only one course open—he must persuade the erring Christians of the Continent to change their minds. How he took the first steps in this direction had best be described in his own words:

"Ten years have elapsed since I commenced a laborious work on the Pentateuch, entitled 'Scriptural Communion with God.' The sixth and final part was completed at the end of last year (1849) immediately before I left England for Italy. As the reunion of Christians, or the establishment of the truth, unity and concord for which we pray, by unpoperizing the Church of Rome, was the frequent subject of my private prayers to God, the meditations on which those prayers were founded were embodied in various dedications, prefixed to the last four parts of that work. The third part was dedicated to Pope Gregory the XVIth. It related to the mode in which the work of the reunion of Christians might be commenced . . . . that as laws must be rescinded by the powers which enact them, and as the

bulls of Popes have frequently been rescinded by their
successors, the bull, therefore, which decreed that twelve
doctrines be added to the Nicene Creed, as Articles of
faith, may be rescinded by the present Pope, or by any
of his successors, without propounding any condemnation of the articles themselves. If this was done, the
propositions which the Council of Trent commended
to the approbation of the Roman Catholic Church
might be reconsidered in another Council, summoned
under the authority of Christian temporal princes, of
whom the Bishop of Rome might be one; and in this
mode the hope of a better state of Christianity might
dawn upon the world."

The fourth part of the book was dedicated in the same
sense to the sovereigns of Europe, the fifth to Queen Victoria, and the sixth to the Universal Episcopate. "And the
Dedication is concluded with the words of the despair with
which I was conscious that I might as well have spoken
to the dead themselves, for the present time at least"—he
was addressing the Archbishop of Canterbury—"Can your
Grace do nothing—nothing to remove the mutual hatred
of Christians?"

It does not appear that either Gregory XVI, or Queen
Victoria, or Dr. Sumner, made any reply to these over-
tures. The Pope must have been on his death-bed, I
imagine, when his volume appeared. Queen Victoria was
much occupied at the time with the cares of the nursery,
and the remaining secular princes of Europe were mostly
hurled from their thrones by the revolutions of 1848.
Archbishop Sumner did not want to hear the word Rome
mentioned at all; it was but a year or two since Newman
had made his submission, and a storm was already brewing over the Gorham controversy which was to determine
the ecclesiastical career of Archdeacon Manning. In fact,
there could hardly have been a less opportune moment
for Canon Townsend's activities; but the more distracted
the state of Europe, the more confident he felt that the

summoning of a new Council, to supersede and undo the Council of Trent, was the only remedy for every disorder.

At this point fate intervened. The labour of educing six volumes of spiritual consolation from the sometimes arid material of Leviticus and Deuteronomy could not but tell upon the constitution of the writer, though he were a man so tough of fibre as Canon Townsend. A change of scene and climate was the doctor's ultimatum—we are in the period when it was fashionable to recommend the Grand Tour. At first, the patient demurred; then a salutary thought struck him. Why not consent to travel, and make this the excuse for a personal interview with the head of the corrupt Roman Church?

> "I would proceed to the Vatican," he says—Canon Townsend is always sonorous in his phraseology—"and seek an audience of the Pope, whom I had so often addressed from a distance, as an almost imaginary personage; I would appeal to him . . . . to begin, and to commend by his great authority, the reconsideration of the past. In proportion to my magnificent independence, should be my extreme and deferential courtesy. In proportion to my zeal to serve the cause of peace, on the basis of Truth, should be my caution never to offend. The very attempt to gain admission to the Vatican would subject me, I well knew, to the charge of enthusiasm, fanaticism, and folly . . . . I well knew, that disinterestedness is always folly, in the opinion of the selfish, the formal, and the dull."

A man who could thus imitate the style of Gibbon was not likely to be put off, it is clear, by any ordinary dissuasions.

But one curious difficulty he did experience. A stickler for the methods of primitive Christianity, as exemplified in St. Paul's epistles, he felt it would not be etiquette to demand an audience at the Vatican without a recommendation from some bishop nearer home. And this, he complains, was prohibited by the laws of his country. I find it difficult to believe that if Dr. Sumner had furnished the Canon with letters of introduction, either of them would have been prosecuted under the act of King Henry VIII in restraint of appeals. I fancy the true difficulty lay rather in the Archbishop's attitude towards the journey; I cannot resist quoting Dr. Townsend's account of it, because it is so beautiful a model of the attitude adopted by all Archbishops of Canterbury on all similar occasions.

"My venerable friend the Archbishop of Canterbury, though he declined to comply with my request that I might use his name, in the most general manner, as one desirous of the peace of the Church, when I should see the Bishop of Rome; and though he discouraged rather than encouraged my persevering, expressed to me, in his answer to my request, every kind and friendly wish."

That was all very well, but it was hardly a Pauline recommendation. Thereupon, Canon Townsend devised a scheme which does remarkable credit to his ingenuity. He would go over to Paris, call on the British Ambassador, get an introduction from him to the Cardinal Archbishop, and so extract from the Cardinal Archbishop the fortifying documents he needed. He realised, like others who have undertaken similar errands before and since his time, that an Englishman who goes round leaving cards, instead of sitting about in the lounge of his hotel, always goes down well on the Continent. Canon Townsend had little honour in his own country; Monsieur le Chanoine would carry all before him in the polite society of France.

There was a further difficulty which does not seem to have daunted him as it might have daunted the modern peace-maker. He had received, no doubt, an excellent public school education; but in those days there was no school certificate; he could not speak a word of Italian, or a word of French. But he had a resource here of which neither the Archbishop of Paris nor the Pope of Rome could boast. Mrs. Townsend must have been a remarkable

woman; I am sorry that her husband's reticence makes it
so difficult to form a distinct picture of her. But though
there was no Somerville in those days, and no Girton, it
is clear that she talked both French and Italian without
difficulty. Had not Canon Townsend a right to carry about
with him a sister, a wife, like the apostles? Certainly he
had, and I think it is quite possible that he would have
found it difficult to organise the expedition without her.
As she had got to go, she would come in very handy as an
interpreter.

For the rest, her husband rightly argued that, if he
talked his best school Latin to foreign ecclesiastics they
must at least show a polite affectation of understanding
him. It is clear that he used this method a good deal. Between Valence and Avignon, for example, he travelled
with a priest who, to his evident surprise, was "neither
vulgar nor slovenly in his appearance, nor sheepish in
his looks or demeanour," and he opened up at once with
the phrase "Intelligisne Latinam, Domine?" The only
trouble was the difference of pronunciation. Canon Townsend gives it as his opinion that "the Continental pronunciation of the Greek is better, and of the Latin worse,
than our own." But, whether it was better or worse, it
was inevitable that a man who read Latin "as spelt" should
tax the patience of his Continental interlocutors. However, he seems to have got on well enough. He did not,
I think, make the mistake of adopting unnecessarily
Ciceronian turns of phrase; his Latin was of a more pe-
destrian order. Thus, when his cabman pursued him into
the cathedral at Naples, complaining that he had not
received his full fare, the Canon ordered payment to be
made, and explained to the priest who was awaiting him
"Ecclesia non locus est controversiae," a sentiment which
was excellently received.

It was, then, in the guise of an ordinary English tourist,
anxious to learn what these damn foreigners look like when
they are at home, that Canon Townsend set out on his
memorable journey. To the last, his friend Dr. Gilly, the

historian and advocate of the Vaudois, tried to dissuade him. He records, under January 22nd, the day of his sailing, the ineffectiveness of these protests.

"If God could make Saul the persecutor Paul the Apostle, God can make the Bishop of Rome himself the opponent of the old Popery. Modern experience shall not destroy my faith that, in spite of all present appearances, men shall be one fold under the one great Shepherd. I will never sacrifice Truth, but I will persevere to speak peace, as the will of Christ, and of God. Wednesday, the 23rd. Arrived at Meurice's Hotel in Paris, where we had previously ordered apartments."

It must be confessed that our hero did not emulate the unkempt appearance or the fanatical deportment of earlier agitators, like Peter the Hermit. He travelled in style, with at least two servants—I am not certain of the exact number —to wait upon himself and Mrs. Townsend. And from the first he used, and found himself justified in using, the methods of a feudal class. Lord Brougham was staying at Meurice's, and Canon Townsend was well dug in with Lord Brougham. For Lord Brougham, it appears, had made some utterances in the celebrated case of King *v.* Williams, which were unacceptable to the clergy; when he came to Durham, therefore, on circuit, the other Canons did not ask him to dine; but, with a Providential broadmindedness, Canon Townsend did.

"At eleven o'clock, the earliest hour permissible by the customs of society, I called upon Lord Brougham. The conversation was animated and interesting."

What Lord Brougham thought we do not know, but he promised to provide letters. And at eleven the next morning Canon Townsend was round again.

"At eleven I was with him, and, while he breakfasted, renewed the conversation of the preceding day. After a lively and interesting conversation on Wycliffe, and the ecclesiastical history of the Middle Ages . . . . his Lordship gave me some letters of introduction to his friends at Rome." "I am not acquainted," he added, "with Pio Nono nor with the Archbishop of Paris, but here is a letter to the Marquis of Normanby" (then Ambassador in Paris) "and most sincerely do I wish you success in your (and he added some words of eulogy) mission."

Next day, the Canon is at Lord Normanby's. He "observed that he read Lord Brougham's writing with some difficulty, as it was very peculiar, but that he saw something in the letter that referred to my going to Rome." Poor Lord Normanby! He should have been more careful. As it was, he got a long allocution, in which the Canon explained his intentions in full detail. Under this treatment, like every body else who met Canon Townsend, he succumbed; he would write a letter of introduction to the Archbishop of Paris. But he warned our hero to be careful.

"He informed me that at the present juncture there prevailed at Rome a great deal of jealousy on the subject of conversion; that any attempt in that direction would be looked upon with much suspicion."

Canon Townsend remained unperturbed.

"I told his Lordship that my object, in one sense, was not conversion; that, in the commonly understood sense. I did not intend to put myself forward as the opponent of Popery . . . ."

and so on, and so on, till Lord Normanby hastily agreed to see the Archbishop of Paris himself, and let Canon Townsend know the result.

The next day was Sunday. Lord Brougham called, with eye bandaged as the result of an accident, to say good-bye; it was due to this accident, he explained, that he was forced to travel on the Lord's Day. "We wished him a pleasant journey, and a useful life." Let it not be supposed from this that Canon Townsend was lax about Sunday observance. Here are his impressions of the Continental Sunday:

"If we had not been grieved and shocked, we should have been amused by the vivacity of the people in the streets, whom we passed on our way. They seem to imagine that religion being a very dull, uninteresting matter, they must chase away its dulness by external and most intense gaiety. They seem to be utterly ignorant of the delightful fact that a Christian's duty is a Christian's privilege, and that to keep the Lord's Day holily is only to keep the Lord's Day happily, to increase inward felicity, and to anticipate the pleasures of the immortality that is before us."

"If we had not been grieved and shocked, we should have been amused"; what more appropriate description of the Englishman in Paris? But I must not linger too much over Canon Townsend's impressions of Travel. It is enough to say that he faithfully admires every building, picture and view which his guide-book recommends to his admiration, but seldom without some melancholy reflections upon the local representatives of the human species, their ignorance of the Bible, and their superstitious veneration for the Virgin Mary.

The interview with Mgr. Sibour, then Archbishop of Paris, took place on the following Saturday. The interpreter was a gentleman not named, but described as "the former Roman Catholic correspondent of the *Times*." Canon Townsend appears to have been particularly careful on this occasion to observe his own principles of "caution never to offend." He wanted letters to the Pope, he said, that he might converse with him on the expediency of summoning, in conjunction with other Sovereigns, another General Council. No word is spoken of the interdicted Bible or of the twelve articles added to the creed by the corrupt Council of Trent. The Archbishop, however, seems to have scented an equivocation about the term "Council," and asked on what principle Monsieur wished to see it assemble? The Canon talked vaguely about common Christianity and a common danger from the infidels; he referred to the negotiations in Queen Anne's time between Dupin and Archbishop Wake. Mgr. Sibour's next question was an unexpected one. "And," said he, "is Monsieur a Puseyite?" Canon Townsend has vividly depicted for us his annoyance.

> "I was sorry," he says, "to be thought to have touched that pitch, and to be defiled with the touch; I was sorry to be regarded as one of those imbeciles, who imagine that either Christian peace or Christian holiness can be restored to the universal Church by bringing the Church of England into conformity with the Church of Rome," etc., etc.

But he does not seem to have expressed his horror in very outspoken terms. All he said was "I am an Episcopalian Christian, and I can assume nor bear no other appellation." It is doubtful whether the Archbishop was much enlightened; however, he promised the letters of recommendation to the Holy Father, and, sure enough, on the following Tuesday they arrived. In a fortnight Canon Townsend was off to Rome, with the key to the Vatican in his pocket.

By diligence all the way to Lyons, by steamer from Lyons to Avignon. At Valence he finds a golden inscription to Pio Nono; "this marble monument," he says to himself,

> "with its inscription, shall be to me an omen of the reception I shall experience, and of the probability of the useful or useless results of my mission. I read the inscription. It was the memorial of the gratitude of the canons of the cathedral of Valence to Pio Nono; for what, I exclaimed, for what reason is the gratitude? I could with difficulty believe the evidence of my senses, when I read that the gratitude of the Canons of Valence to Pio Nono was here commemorated, because he had

permitted the bowels of his predecessor, who had died at Valence, to rest here, while the body was conveyed for its burial to Rome! . . . . What would be thought or said in England, if the Canons of Winchester had raised a memorial to Bishop Sumner, because he permitted them to retain the bowels of Bishop Tomline, while his body was buried at St. Paul's? If this act would be deemed absurd in England, why not in Italy?"

Quite so, quite so; only somehow Bishop Tomline does make it funnier.

Undeterred by the sinister omens which the entrails provided for him, Canon Townsend pressed on for Rome. He went from Marseilles to Genoa by sea; for the rest, he was dependent on the diligence, and it was not till the twentieth, after four weeks of travel, that he set foot in the city. The time of his arrival was hardly propitious. For more than a year Pius IX had been absent from the city, owing to a popular insurrection, and it was not many months since French troops had entered the capital to restore order there. The Pope was still in Naples, and the date of his return uncertain. The English Consul recommended that Canon Townsend should proceed to Naples at once, without communicating his plan or his desire to anyone at Rome. This was too much to expect; nor did our hero's good fortune desert him. He made friends with Father Mesaheb, a Maronite Jesuit from Mount Lebanon —so at least he is described—was taken round by him, argued freely with him on theological points, and secured an introduction from him to the antiquarian, Cardinal Mai. The interview proceeded on the now familiar lines. Latin was spoken, with interpreters present in case Italian were needed.

"He bowed, and permitted me to proceed, as I had done with the Archbishop of Paris, I fear at some length, to submit to him the object of my visit to Rome," etc.

The Cardinal seems to have insisted chiefly on the prac-

tical difficulties of summoning an international council
to discuss the danger of infidelity and Socialism in the then
state of affairs. But he took all the Canon's views in good
part, and, when, before leaving, his visitor pointed to some
English books with the observation, "it could not be expected that the nation which had produced such works
could ever again be submissive to Rome," contented himself with replying *Paulatim*.

> "He was evidently . . . . impressed with the convic-
> tion, which seemed indeed to be general among his
> brethren, that England was returning to the adoption of
> the Papal additions to the faith of Christ. I sighed at the
> mistake, and again expressed my conviction and my hope
> that this could never be; and he said again with em-
> phasis, *Paulatim*."

There is something pathetically typical, in that troubled Rome of 1850, about the Canon's haste for action
and the Cardinal's readiness to wait upon the future.
They parted good friends, with a warm invitation to
Cardinal Mai to come and stay at Durham any time when
he was evicted from his country. They exchanged letters,
on which Canon Townsend comments, "The only stum-
bling-block between us is this steady, invincible determination never to be reformed." He found, as others have
found before and since, how difficult it is to arrive at a
complete agreement with a man who will not adopt your
own point of view.

It is actually on record that our Canon visited St. Peter's
on a Sunday morning. "Can I keep the Sabbath, or Lord's
Day, holy, by going there? Yes. I wish to see how the common Lord of the Sabbath is honoured by those who assume
to be more peculiarly His servants." The sermon was
"upon the whole, unobjectionable," but the line must
be drawn somewhere. "I could not kneel at the elevation
of the Host." It must not be supposed that his sturdy
Protestantism was ever stampeded by its alien surroundings. He was visited by one of the English converts—I

wonder which? He was not impressed: "Discussion in conversation, when there is but little or no previous reading, becomes tedious." He is invited to attend the consecration of Cullen as Primate of Ireland; "I refused to sanction the insult to my Church and country." More profitably, he consents to perform a wedding service in the Lutheran chapel.

> "One of the princesses of Prussia had given a very beautiful covering for the Altar, and had adorned it, in the most elaborate gold embroidery, with a grouping of the Cross, an anchor, and flowers. I congratulated the company present . . . . and reminded them that the flowers of life most abounded in beauty and fragrance when they were blended with a good hope of the future and entwined round the Cross . . . . Much enthusiasm was kindled by a few observations of this nature, and the Lord's Day was not desecrated, though all was cheerfulness, and joyousness, and smiles."

But he remained true to his purpose of working for reunion, and, when taken to task by some gentlemen of the Scottish Free Church, represented to them that, though some supporters of Popery might justly be called serpents and a generation of vipers, "this could not be said of all." On Friday, the twelfth of April, the Pope returned to the City, amid the eager expectations of a large crowd, which knelt to receive his blessing, and of Canon Townsend, who bowed. On the 13th, an audience was solicited; on the 25th, word was received that the Holy Father would receive Signor Townsend the following day in private audience, *"unitamente alla Consorte."* In just over three months the indomitable peace-maker had triumphed over every obstacle, and stood on the threshold of his great enterprise. There were minor regrets; the Italian gentleman who was to have interpreted was unable to be present, but Mrs. Townsend readily volunteered to supply his place; and again

"I was sorry that I had not with me my academic dress. My wearing the robes of an English clergyman would have been but the more proper observance of the courtesy which was due to the Pope as a temporal Prince, and as the Bishop of the greatest of the Western Churches. I assumed the usual evening dress required by society in England."

At half-past five they were ushered into the presence. Why Pio Nono should have been dressed in "the long white fine cloth Dominican robe" or wearing the "Dominican cap on his head," I am unable to discover. He received them alone with the utmost graciousness, asked Mrs. Townsend whether she had been to Italy before, whether she admired the country, what objects in Rome had interested her most, in what language her husband desired to converse? Then the Canon was let loose; not, he hastens to assure us, in a speech, but in answer to the Pope's questions. He asked for a General Council of Christians, at which the Pope was to have precedence, though not jurisdiction. The usual practical difficulties were urged in reply. There was no discussion of details.

"It has been said, I know not why, that I alluded to the celibacy of the clergy, and the giving of the cup to the laity. I said nothing of the kind."

We learn from another passage that Mrs. Townsend understood Latin; apart from that, it is quite clear that the Canon did not mean to suggest any programme of reform for the Roman Church until the Council should be already in session. He presented a document for the Pope to read, enshrining his appeal.

"I am a Protestant," he explained, "and I have always been an enemy to your Church, but there will not be found in this document any expression which will be personally offensive."

Mrs. Townsend hastened to reassure the Holy Father about this: "No, no, mio marito è troppo buono" and so on.

Many Christians in England, the Canon explained, would rejoice in the hope of the reunion of the Churches. I cannot find that he had much authority for this remark, for it appears that all his friends had discouraged the expedition. But it did service on this occasion as on others. "Yes," said Pio Nono, "there are in England many persons of good will." "There are many good men there who would rejoice in peace," replies the Canon, and explains in a footnote that the Pope was quoting from a false text of the New Testament when he talked about "men of good-will." All modern scholarship, I fear, is against Canon Townsend and with the Pope on this point. Asked whether he knew Dr. Wiseman, our hero cautiously explained that he lived in retirement, and was not personally known to him. Then, after a forty minutes' interview, the intrepid couple took their leave, bowing themselves out as if from the presence of the Queen. Some Cubans who were admitted after them "both knelt down, as to God . . . . We had not done so. We had rendered every respect to the Pope as to an earthly sovereign; we could not venerate him as our God."

The text of the memorandum left with the Pope is then given. It defines the object of the Council, "restoring to the Catholic Church the ancient discipline and the primitive union," but says nothing about the Council of Trent, or the twelve popish additions to the Nicene Creed. In fact, it is a document which Dr. Pusey might have written, and I suspect that Pio Nono took the Canon for a Tractarian. We learn, on the authority of an English gentleman who had an interview soon afterwards, that he thought the *Canone di Durham* an excellent and good man, but found his Latin difficult to follow; "he did not think the proposal of summoning a Council would lead to the desired effect." And here a misunderstanding seems to have arisen. The Canon had a visit next day from Monsignor de Merode and Dr. Grant, of the English College, who told him that "his Holiness had read my memorial, and desired to converse with me further on the subject of its contents."

It would appear, from what followed, that a mere polite expression of interest was somehow misconstrued into a summons for a fresh audience. It was with that hope that Canon Townsend left for Naples, promising to wait on the Holy Father on his way home.

I have no space to describe that splendid visit to Naples; how they were shewn round the Cathedral sacristy, and Mrs. Townsend was not allowed to touch the chalices, though her husband was, on her assurance that he was a Canon too; how they attended the liquefaction of St. Januarius's blood—the Canon, under the impression that Mr. Neumann, a chemist of Berlin, had reproduced the alleged miracle in his own laboratory, saw the liquefaction perfectly, and bears witness to it. When they returned to Rome they found that the Pope was not expecting a fresh discussion with them, and did not like, on their side, to press for a second interview, since there was naturally a great press of business at the Vatican. Accordingly, on the 27th of May, they set out from Rome on their homeward journey.

Did Canon Townsend feel that he had failed? I think not, at the time. It is clear that there was one Catholic doctrine of which he had no appreciation—he did not realise that the decisions of a Council are irreformable. He thought of a Council—he uses the parallel himself— as if its decisions could always be changed later on, like the decisions of an English Parliament. And he believed, or at least tried to persuade himself, that a new General Council would find no more difficulty about repudiating Transubstantiation, than a Labour Government might have about dropping the artificial silk duties.

But there are other passages, scattered throughout the book, which talk the language of despair. I do not like the methods of those critics who profess to find traces of different documentary strata in Canon Townsend's be-

loved Pentateuch. But I confess that I am inclined to apply
the method to his own Journal, and suggest that these
defeatist passages were put in later, when the book was
preparing for the press, in the light of subsequent events.
Both at Rome and at Naples he observes the volcanic
character of the soil, and speculates whether Dr. Cumming
is not right in supposing that the whole of the south of
Italy, from Rome to Naples, is shortly to be destroyed by
fire.

"Oh for that warning voice, which he who saw the
Apocalypse heard cry in heaven, that I might be heard
in my appeal to the Bishop of Rome when I say, Repent, Repent, rescind your additions to the religion of
Jesus Christ!"

But Dr. Townsend *had* seen the Pope, and did not say
anything of the kind. Again, as he looks back on Rome
on leaving it, he breaks out into a tremendous denunciation of Rome, and of the traitorous spirits in England who
encourage its pretensions.

"Go on, Church of Rome. The divisions of England
strengthen thee! The traitors of England love thee, and
give thee power. Fill up the measure of thy ancient
iniquity. Send out the unrequired bishops to insult us,
the unrequired priests to mock us. Go on! The government is indifferent, the people are torpid, the Church
is silent."

And much more to the same effect. Now, why should
a clergyman who has gone out to Rome to promote unity
in Christendom, who has been received with the utmost
kindness by an archbishop, two cardinals and the Pope
himself, all of whom are content to point out that the
time is not ripe just yet for the summoning of a general
council—why should such a man feel, as he leaves the
city, so deep-rooted a grievance against its inhabitants?
The answer is that he did not feel it at the time; he
put that part in afterwards. He went back to England

with the consciousness that his memorandum lay on the table in the Vatican, wondering what reply it would provoke. On September 29th, little more than two months after his return, a bull was issued restoring the English hierarchy, and on October 7th Wiseman issued his pastoral from the Flaminian Gate. Poor Canon Townsend! Here was his journal, I take it, already advertised and undergoing its final process of polishing, with all the nice things he said about Popes and Cardinals, and all the nice things Popes and Cardinals said about him; and then suddenly, this official insult to Lambeth, this gratuitous affront to the feelings of Protestant England. He did the best he could; he put his journal into shape, let in a few passages to emphasise the hard-heartedness and all-but irreformability of Rome; then he sent it to the press, tacking on at the beginning a preface in which he lets himself go.

It is a strange preface to such a work. He explains that the journal was written, with the exception of a few sentences, "long before the promulgation of the late unscriptural, absurd and insolent bull of the Pope, whom I visited at the Vatican." He expresses the hope that the Papists of the Continent will be brought to their senses by a fresh reformation. But how is this to be secured? By resisting Papal aggression in England. The resistance, he assures us, must be of three kinds, Political, Christian and Ecclesiastical. First, by way of political resistance, we must repeal the Acts of Catholic Emancipation. Next, by way of Christian resistance, we must maintain our protest; our motto must be, No peace with Rome. I do not understand what he means by ecclesiastical opposition, and I am very doubtful if he did himself; the fact is, Canon Townsend was rattled.

> "If I could have imagined the possibility of the folly
> and crime which the Pope has committed, I would
> never have entered Rome."

It would be possible to point or at least to suggest,

all sorts of morals as a tail-piece to Canon Townsend's story. I prefer to leave it without comment, as the story of an honest Englishman who really did set out to do great things on his holiday, really did think that he could turn the Grand Tour into a grand slam, and failed so unexpectedly. He lived to 1857; he was not permitted, therefore, to see the summoning of the Council which he recommended, or to mourn the definition of Infallibility which was its principal result. And somewhere, I suppose, in the debris of the Vatican archives lies his memorandum to the Pope, all written fair in Italian, a document of our mortality, and a warning, should it ever be needed, to some new generation which has forgotten it.

On Newman, Chesterton, and Exorbitance

by DOUGLAS WOODRUFF

THE TWO chief apologists for Catholicism in the last hundred years in England were men as dissimilar as men can be. Both came from the homes of London professional men, both had some rather distant French blood, both were in their middle forties before they were received into the Church, after a long and public period of transition. But such accidental points of resemblance, like the fact that one was the teacher and the other the friend of the man in whose honour these essays have been written, are among the minutiae of literary history. Essentially Newman was a profoundly religious man whose religion illuminated and redeemed an otherwise deeply pessimistic outlook. He saw men as implicated in a vast calamity and the spectacle of their living death was one to dizzy and appal. Chesterton was also profoundly religious; but he found that same world a fairyland, and

> if, as says the Saint,
> The world is but a painted show,
> Oh, let us lick the paint.

He marvelled that his contemporaries were not more surprised and pleased to be alive; and he came to the religion of the Cross by the most extraordinary of paths, the search for a rational foundation for an instinctive and exuberant optimism.

It is the purpose of the pages which follow to find the point at which the thought of Newman and the thought of Chesterton meet and merge; in the doctrine of exorbitance.

I

We are very much more familiar with the adjective *exorbitant* than with the noun *exorbitance*; because we think and talk more about concrete situations, such as feeling overcharged, than about abstract ideas. In the writings of Cardinal Newman, the word exorbitance is common, and the idea central in his thought. Exorbitance is a going beyond or outside one's proper sphere and limits, with consequent disorder. It is excess, and it is the common consequence of pride. The fields in which Newman principally observed and described exorbitance were the groves of Academe, the fields of organised secular knowledge and intellectual activity. In our own day exorbitance has been more inescapably selfevident in the field of politics. In both the intellectual and political fields, the cause of this exorbitance, of the conflicts and exaggerations of the different branches of learning and of the ever expanding claims of the State is that same arrogant secularism and that extrusion of theology which it was the lifelong activity of Newman to oppose.

Newman was not primarily a man who abandoned the Church of England for the Church of Rome. The great event of his conversion in 1845, the triumph of his Apologia in 1864, the stir and argument which through six decades, to the very end of the last century, made the controversy over the nature of the Church so prominent as well as so lively, have inevitably dominated the general view of Newman's lifework. He was the man, the leader, who decided against the claims, of which he had himself been the foremost champion, of the Church of England to be considered an authentic part of the Catholic Church. That was startling hearing in Victorian England, where the Universities were still mainly ecclesiastical in structure and activity. The arguments, and the parties to them, were clear and concrete, and historical. But Newman's interest and importance as a contemporary topic, his historical importance in the history of the religious communions he left and joined, are not at all the same as his work and his place in the speculative thought of his time. And from that point of view there is so great a unity binding the Anglican and Catholic phases that the dividing line of the conversion, exactly in the middle of his long life, is not a line cutting anything into two. Alike as an Anglican and as a Catholic, Newman was concerned to oppose the dominant trend of his time, the movement which gathered strength from decade to decade, towards an ever more complete emancipation of all human activities from the claims of religious authority.

The nineteenth century was the supreme century of liberalism, and Newman was the greatest enemy modern liberalism has ever had to meet. He was the enemy of liberalism because liberalism was the enemy of revelation. The liberals believed that freedom was in itself good, not seeing that all freedom is freedom to do something, and whether it is good or bad depends on what is done. It is a neutral condition, a power of action. When good men are free the resulting activity is good. When bad men are free the resulting activity is bad; and as soon as we see they are bad, we bring their freedom to do harm to an end, as far as we can. The panegyrists of freedom were the panegyrists of mankind, who believed that good could only come of the freedom because those who were to exercise it were good. They wanted more power for mankind, and therefore more knowledge. They accordingly wanted to see each branch of learning pursued thoroughly and independently of any religious bearing reins. Give men more power, they exclaimed, let each subject of enquiry and branch of learning be enquired into thoroughly and fully, leaving to one side during these enquiries all question of whether or no there has been a revelation about the purpose and meaning of life.

In the years, just over a quarter of a century, which Newman spent in or near Oxford before 1845, this process of secularising and transforming the University was in full vigour. The first experimental Chair of Political

Economy, the Drummond Chair founded by the Banking House of Drummond, was accepted in the early thirties. Twenty years later, when Nassau Senior re-occupied it, his inaugural lecture was to provide Newman with a most strikingly clear illustration of what he meant by exorbitance in learning, and the extrusion of theology.

Nassau Senior began, as professors commonly do in their inaugural lectures, by saying what he understood by the subject he was to profess, what was its range and why it was important to mankind. Men do not devote themselves to some one particular field of knowledge unless they believe that it is of real importance; and they have every human incentive to think and to say that it is much more important than it is. So Nassau Senior said of political economy, not that it was the study of the laws governing the creation and distribution of wealth, while the effects of that wealth upon the virtue and happiness of mankind were outside its scope; he said, on the contrary, quite categorically that the increase of wealth is the chief means towards the moral improvement of mankind. And Newman commented upon that judgment that two propositions seemed to him incontrovertible about that assertion, that it was a judgment in morals and not in political economy, and that it was a judgment flatly at variance with the teaching of the Church, of Our Lord and His Apostles.

Political Economy was the supreme field in which the evils of exorbitance manifested themselves in the early part of the last century, as academic activities were in the later part. Dr. Malthus of Cambridge who was in private life a humane enough clergyman, was a capital instance of this disorder, when he told the working classes that the out-of-work man must not repine, but must understand that nature intended him and his family to starve. In the year in which the Oxford movement began, 1833, debates took place on the Poor Law reform, in which Lord Althorp explained that the laws of political economy forbade the practice not only of public charity but of private charity as well.

It is well known that the men of the Oxford movement, and Newman conspicuously, were but remotely interested in social questions, although they lived through an exciting and determining time, the days of the Chartists, of the Factory legislation, of the final establishment of Free Trade. Their private correspondence shows that they followed these events closely and warmly enough; but they were events of a different order to the great eternal issues to which all energies had to be devoted. Social questions made most appeal to men who did not think that the condition of man was, as it appeared to the profound intelligence of Newman, to be the prophet's scroll, "full of lamentations and mourning and woe," and as he wrote, in perhaps the most famous passage of the *Apologia*, "if there be a God, since there is a God, the human race is implicated in some terrible aboriginal calamity." No progress in the standard of life, in the arts and sciences, in culture and grace and pleasure, could do anything to change that dilemma, "either there is no creator, or this living society of men is in a true sense discarded from his presence." The business with social conditions and reforms was well enough provided it did not serve to distract men from their real preoccupations, and above all with the preservation of their one lifeline, the revelation made in and through the Incarnation. Newman is the great modern Apostle of the First Commandment.

He did not succeed in his own day. His success is the posthumous success of the justified prophet. I do not think any man can turn the pages of those old controversies between Newman and his liberal clerical adversaries without at once acknowledging that on the fundamental issue he was altogether right, and men like Benjamin Jowett altogether wrong. They contended that they were not less full of zeal for religion and the Church than Newman, but that religion itself would be strengthened by withdrawing from a false position of excessive authority. The motto of the University of Oxford is *Dominus Illuminatio mea.* Is the Lord to be the light of men, as those who first took the motto meant it, in the sense of *Credo ut intelligam,* belief as the prelude to understanding, of St. Anselm? Oxford, like all the medieval Universities of Europe, was a place where men believed before they studied, and studied that they might see further into the great truths of faith. All sciences were ancillary to theology. Theology allotted to each its sphere and boundaries. A host of subjects which today have all the apparatus of organised study were not studied, because they were considered trifles, irrelevant to the high purpose for which Christian clerks studied at all. Although the Renaissance made a great inroad, and established the great pagan poets and historians in niches of dignity as fitting objects of meticulous study, and invented the characteristic Oxford school of Litterae Humaniores, more humane letters, more humane than the schoolmen, yet it is true to say that the Oxford of Newman was more like the Oxford of the Middle Ages than it was to the Oxford of a hundred years later.

The place was still marked with all the marks of its origin and purpose, as a place where men in holy orders prepared young aspirants for the same life. The holy orders had sat lightly on the Fellows for many generations but they were considered necessary, and the University was still primarily a place of learning for Christian clergy. It was fourteen years after Newman had been received by Father Dominic that the University admitted Roman Catholics; and it admitted them as part of the substitution of a liberal for a Christian ideal as the aim of the education it offered. The limits of an essay preclude a discussion here of the arguments for and against the great change, arguments which appeal according to a man's view of religion. But those who would defend the transformation would do so today from a very different point of view from that which inspired the clerical liberals like Jowett in helping to effect the transformation.

If Newman and Jowett returned to modern Oxford, Newman would be very sad but not very surprised; Jowett
would not be sad, but he would, I think, be secretly very
surprised and mortified to find what a very diminished
place was enjoyed by the theologians and the Church,
which even at his death in the eighteen nineties had held
so very much more of the forefront of the stage.

In language which modern politics have made familiar,
Jowett was a great example of theological appeasement,
making perpetual surrenders to the claims of the secular-
isers, in the hope that a Church which showed itself so
reasonable and so free from imperialism towards other
fields of activity and knowledge would be left in possession of its own territories. He did not expect to be invaded
and annexed.

"Revealed truth," wrote Newman, "enters to a very
great extent into the province of science, philosophy and
literature, and to put it on one side in compliment to
secular science is simply under cover of a compliment, to
do science great damage. I do not say that every science
will be equally affected by the omission; pure mathematics
will not suffer at all, chemistry will suffer less than politics, politics than history, ethics or metaphysics; still, that
the various branches of science are intimately connected
with each other and form one whole, which whole is impaired, and to an extent which it is difficult to limit, by
any considerable omission of knowledge, of whatever kind,
and that revealed knowledge is very far indeed from an
inconsiderable department of knowledge, this I consider
undeniable" (The Idea of a University, Discourse IV).
The extent proved indeed difficult to limit. The philosophers and historians proceeded to part among themselves
the garments of theology. No man can understand the
change unless he sees it as an alliance of all the secular
subjects with theological frontiers and implications, against
the traditional Christian teaching. It was a war. The motive which made Gibbon set out to trace the triumph of
barbarism and religion was displeasure at seeing in Rome

that while antiquity with all its urbane polish was so very dead, a baroque and unaccommodating Church of Rome was so very much alive.

It was Dr. Arnold's main objection to the Tractarians that they made the Church a caste apart, and therefore excited hostility against religion, whereas it was the whole nation which should be considered as the Church. The Tractarians replied that their movement took its rise because it was only too self-evident that the England of William IV was committing the nation to apostasy, was falling away and guiding its legislation more and more by principles derived from other sources than the Catholic Faith. To us it seems a belated discovery, made at the end of the four Georges when it might have been made at the beginning of their dynasty. But it was a real discovery to the Tractarians, and it forced them to look for the title deeds of the Church elsewhere than in its close connection with the State. They revived the idea of the Church as an independent and authoritative society, just when the main stream was running away from all ideas of authority. If anything were needed to increase the bias of the exponents of secular subjects against the claims of religion, it was just this revival of the idea of the authority of the Church.

John Morley, writing in his memoirs of the Oxford of the early sixties, said that already, to his great content, the star of Newman had set and that of Mill had risen. John Morley had little belief enough in the orthodox creed, yet he was able to feel quite at home in the Lincoln of Mark Pattison, and through his long life he saw nothing but the progress from strength to strength of the offensive against theology; until in his last years, in the nineteen twenties, the very existence of a theological Fellow was disputed in a number of the old Oxford foundations, and it was urged by groups of natural scientists and sceptical humanists that theology was a specialised activity, to be carried on in one or two specialised foundations without claiming to have standing or relevance for the main current of University life.

There have been few swifter vindications of prediction than the history of modern Oxford in the light of Newman's forecasts. Yet he would tell us today that it needed no more than little knowledge of mankind to understand that men do not devote themselves to particular studies unless they think such studies are important, and that if they are left to estimate their own importance they will not err on the side of modesty or understatement. Some may be modest, but the pretensions of the study will be what its bolder champions claim. And the philosophers and historians claimed to be establishing reality, on the assumption of the irrelevance of theological knowledge, which was represented as a sort of debased pseudo-philosophical knowledge, or more generally as not knowledge at all, but a form of human activity itself the proper field for enquiries by the historian and the psychologist. All the secular sciences with theological implications or frontiers might fight among themselves, but they were all agreed in their common interest in making of theology the King Lear of the academic world; an outcast at the hands of the daughter studies he had fostered; and only attended by a poor fool or two.

II

There is a military operation of particular difficulty, which is sometimes attempted by heavily outnumbered and hard-pressed troops. It consists in forming a great quadrilateral, and retreating without losing formation. There is another military activity which consists in retreating without any formation at all. Newman, who liked military history, might have considered that the second activity was the apter metaphor for what has happened to theology as a branch of knowledge in the period, now nearly a hundred years, since he was lecturing on the idea of a University. There was vigorous counter-attack from the Catholic Church, in the restoration of Thomistic studies; the new confident secular studies, so busily dissecting and appropriating the old corpus of theological learning among themselves, were in their turn classified and arranged in the light of the perennial philosophy. But each generation of the Oxford clergy found itself surrendering territory, and making its restatement of what it invited its own contemporaries to consider the essentials of the Christian faith in more modest terms. The process appeared to those who conducted it to be a laudable and necessary reconciliation with what they knew as the latest scholarship of their day. But it was a vain labour because that scholarship was an activity which proceeded from the assumption that the religious activity of mankind was part of nature, to be studied and estimated by scholars rejecting any Christian framework of explanation just as they would have rejected a Buddhist framework. They were not appeased as successive surrenders were made over the character of the Bible, because their interest was not in seeing the Church made palatable but in establishing the authority of their own methods and studies.

The first great jettisoning of the traditional cargo in Oxford came in 1860 with *Essays and Reviews*. As well as Benjamin Jowett, the authors included a future Archbishop of Canterbury, Frederick Temple, and the father of the late Lord Baden-Powell. They met with a great deal of hostility, which culminated in legal proceedings and the famous judgment of the Judicial Committee of the Privy Council when Lord Westbury dismissed Hell with costs. As far as the law was concerned, and it remained the ultimate authority over the Established Church, the Broad Church party and the Latitudinarians were to enjoy the benefit of the fullest doubt. The Church was meant to be comprehensive, the lawyers could argue, and therefore it was right to see not how closely the meaning of the Church's governing formulations could be defined, but within how wide boundaries all sorts of meanings could be allowed.

It was an irony that Newman, as in Tract 90, had prepared the way, and made smooth the broad path, arguing
that articles which were obviously not ambitious of paradoxical interpretations might yet be patient of them.
And the men who had been prominent in the opposition
to the Tractarians and in the various proceedings to stop
them were now in their turn driving their own coaches
through the same articles of belief.

In seeking to find a new basis for the Church of England, Newman and his friends had shown how much
subtlety could do to create fresh standards of interpretation. It was not surprising if his opponents followed suit,
or showed themselves the bolder from the Tractarian
example. It was the Tractarian difficulty that to give the
Church of England a sense of independence of its connection with a nation rapidly assimilating all sorts of
quite unChristian ideas and standards, the reason act-
ing as a verifying faculty, had to go over all the doctrinal
and institutional ground. Newman saw with immense
clearness that the essence of the Christian revelation was
that it was not subject to such an inquest to find out and
establish whether it was true. But he had to argue that
the nature of the Church had been misconceived, over-
laid, seen in distortion; and although his conclusions,
like the personal conclusion of his own history, were im-
mensely orthodox, his movement was itself a dissolvent
influence; and the *Tracts for the Times* prepared the
ground for *Essays and Reviews*.

When the next major collective work of Oxford theological revision appeared, in 1889, *Lux Mundi* of which
Charles Gore was the leading spirit, it was a work which
inherited from both the *Tracts* and the *Essays*. For all
its High Church conclusions, its methods were of greater
significance, and its methods caused Dean Liddon to with-
draw, realising that reason as a verifying faculty was
again sitting in judgment. It seemed to him as wrong
as it was shortsighted for men to recognise the jurisdic-

tion of an illegitimate Court merely because on the first occasion the verdict was on the whole favourable.

Just such an interval as separated *Lux Mundi* from *Essays and Reviews* elapsed again, and *Foundations* appeared. This third famous volume of collective Oxford essays might have been more aptly named *Ruins*, for the foundations it exposed were not the first stones of a new edifice, but the exposed remains of a very old one. But Newman had been dead twenty years, and the day was still far off which he had foreseen when in extreme old age he wrote to Principal Sharp and told him of his belief that after the tide had gone right out it would return again.

In the meantime, the process went steadily forward of organising secular knowledge on the assumption that the revelation was untrue, and then applying what were announced as the results of impartial and objective enquiry and asking the apologists of Christianity what they proposed to do to make their doctrines fit the conclusions of the day. It was a process which commonly went on inside the same man, anxiously accommodating his religious belief to the results which seemed to follow when, making the assumption that religion had nothing to say in the enquiry, he proceeded to ask himself what date to assign to the Gospels, or whether God and the devil are active agents in human history. If the Christian religion is true, historical enquiries pursued on the assumption that it is not will be increasingly erroneous as they concern themselves with its immediate environment. But only too many well meaning clergymen divided themselves and then distressed themselves, from a wholly false expectation that they ought to be able to reconcile what they believed as part of the Christian faith with what they believed when they thought and concluded as sceptics.

There was obviously no reason to expect a reconciliation and the wonder has been the genius for negotiating compromises. At the bottom of this procedure lay something very simple, the uncritical acceptance of the idea that the scholarly approach had by definition to be the unbelieving one. That idea was sedulously planted by unbelievers, it was forced as conjurors force cards, but it really assumed the very thing under enquiry. Men could often see the truth of the matter when it was the dates of the Gospels that were in dispute, when they found critics using miraculous stories as evidence of a late date and then urging the late date as a conclusive reason for disbelieving the miraculous stories. But they did not so often see the same truth in the larger setting of their general prepossessions, studies and way of life as all giving them their definition of experience, by which they then judged what they could agree to be credible or not, and therefore what way of life, studies and prepossessions they ought to adopt.

It was one of the secrets of Newman's hold in Oxford in the eighteen thirties that he had been tremendously tempted to approach religion along the path of the narrower rationalism, that he knew all the ways such an attitude ministers to the self-esteem of men with acute intelligence, and that he had had the grace to maintain a humble acceptance towards the mysteries of revelation. His sermons were mainly concerned not with arguments with sceptics but with drawing out the immense consequences, which followed on the acceptance of the Creed. He showed believers who were in the main inclined to be nominal believers and givers of notional assents the immense vistas of the Gospel, and the immense claims it made.

III

The men who would not listen to Newman were filled with a secular optimism which made them primarily interested in taking effective possession of the earth. They behaved like eager new tenants, rushing to explore every room, and promising themselves a most enjoyable home. The Deity was bowed politely but firmly off the premises; they were His no longer. In the glad confident morning of belief in progress, men felt able to pay genuine tribute to the genius and the sincerity of Newman as an earlier age would not have done. The *Apologia* appeared in 1864, five years after the *Origin of Species* had come to give a massive backing to the ideas which had been current in up-to-date conversation for at least twenty years before. *Vestiges of Creation,* the book which made it smart drawing-room talk to say, with the character in Disraeli's novels, we have been fishes and shall be crows, had been published in 1844.

What did not affect Newman's work, and dominated Chesterton's, was the disillusionment of the new tenants. No sooner had Man been established as the supreme and only mind in the universe than a chill sense of discontent and loneliness crept in. And Chesterton began his literary life at a time when men were writing books asking Is Life Worth Living? In *Orthodoxy, The Ballad of the White Horse* and *The Everlasting Man* between 1908 and 1922, Chesterton moved forward from an appreciation of the Christian religion as a salt and preservative of natural good things, to an increasing realisation that the Faith and Hope which are the prerogatives of the Christian man are themselves the greatest goods of all.

Chesterton encountered excess in late Victorian London, in men like the gloomy man in the *Daily News* who lived at Clapham, and when Chesterton produced an essay which began, "Clapham like every other town is built upon a volcano," changed Clapham in the copy to Kensington, where Chesterton lived, being sure there was some insult, and that Clapham could only be mentioned to be insulted. Such was the sprawling development of London under the free play of economic laws, not checked or balanced by anything else. The pessimism Chesterton had to fight was much more than the literary pessimism of men who had got rid of religion only to find themselves wandering as "masterless men." It was also the pessimism of a fatalist acquiescence in being part of a vast inhuman process. The emancipation from Chris-

tian theology had meant immediately a new servitude
when men thought of themselves as a part of nature, and
no more, bound without hope of escape or change, to
pass through an allotted course of activity, acutely aware
of transience, dissatisfied by it, and unable to see any
escape. This was the despair that followed a proud, "I will
not serve."

> And they shall see what is written
> So plainly in clouds and sods
> Till they shall hunger without hope
> Even for evil Gods.

The pursuit of wealth and the pursuit of power are
the two great pastimes with which men, created for pur-
poseful activity, have distracted or entertained themselves.
Chesterton grew up in a world given over to the pursuit
of wealth. It was that appetite which showed him exorbitance in its clearest form, and in revulsion against
it he wrote much of his most effective prose, notably
What's wrong with the World? What was wrong was the
absence of positive standards by which to measure and
control developments in society; and the positive standards were lacking because men had discarded the religious
doctrines from which such standards could be deduced.
Chesterton saw his society rooted in injustice and sacrificing humanity to the creation of wealth; and found
that if he was to vindicate the claims of humanity he
must show that men were made for something else, that
they had a service to perform.

The Ballad of the White Horse, the greatest celebra-
tion in English letters of the theological virtue of Hope,
is throughout alive with this sense of the livery of the
Christian, equipped and busy about the service of his
Lord. In 1911 when it was published—he had been working on it over several years—the world was less familiar
than we are today with the joyless destructive warriors
who love violence and dynamism as an excitement.

> Death blazes bright above the board
>   And high above the Crown
> But in that heat of battle
>   We seem to tread it down
> Therefore I am a great King
>   And waste the world in vain
> Because man hath not other power
>   Save that in dealing death for dower
> He may forget it for an hour
>   To remember it again

And by contrast King Alfred and his followers, with more heart to run than the Danes to pursue, the men signed with the Cross of Christ, go gaily in the dark. And they preserve even such a monument as the old White Horse of Uffington, a symbol of all the human inheritance of the past,

> "because it is only Christian men
>   Who cherish heathen things"

The thought is closely parallel to that earlier extraordinary book, *The Man who was Thursday*. The dedicatory poem at the beginning of *The Man who was Thursday* —to the friend whose influence prevented Chesterton from going to Oxford—explains that the tale is a tale of the despair and pessimism against which the youthful Chesterton's cap and bells were heard. In every man there are the two principles, the Christian principle of preservation, symbolised by the policeman, and the pagan principle of destruction, symbolised by the anarchists. The book is a work of progressive optimism, as the lonely soul who imagines himself to be singlehanded, and the only policeman among the anarchists, finds that one after another his enemies are really his friends, and have misjudged him as he had them, and that the Universe is a friendly place after all.

Chesterton declares in his autobiography that he felt in youth the great temptations of despair, but *The Man who was Thursday* is "a tale of old fears and emptied

Hells," banished very early and triumphantly. Heretics were given to us, wrote St. Augustine, that we might not remain in infancy: and we may feel that Chesterton needed that there should be Swinburne and the others singing an emancipated but disillusioned and sad note, or he would not himself have considered necessary any religious sanction for existence. He lived, however, and grew up among a peculiar and virulent form of excess and exorbitance, and as his thought deepened, he saw the Christian revelation more and more as the condition of natural health and happiness; but he also came to see it as something much more than a sovereign protection, more than the unicorn's horn which the beasts wait' for, refusing to drink until they have seen dipped into the pool. Edward Lyttelton's observation that the less we think about the next world, the uglier we make this, commanded his full assent, provided men understand that they cannot cultivate religion for its aesthetic or political and social by-products. When he came to conclude the great work of Christian apologetic of his maturity, *The Everlasting Man,* he crystallised into an enduring epigram the thought of thirty years. He hailed the Christian revelation as "the lightning made eternal as the light," contrasting the fantastic strangeness of the historical story with the extraordinary saneness and wholesomeness of those societies in which it' had been embraced and believed and obeyed; and he concluded that if the Incarnation was strange, the human race also was strange, an extraordinary thing in nature, and that history showed that this strange revelation was in truth his necessary and natural food. And what Chesterton saw and loved in the Middle Ages was their sense of ordered proportion under religion.

It was the secret of medieval civilisation that it never consecrated its deviations into exorbitance or excess. There was plenty of the exorbitance of the passions. The knight who prayed, "Let me take this castle, if it be Thy Holy Will; and if it be not Thy Will, still let me take this castle," his kinsman who judged hell on the whole a price worth paying for the castle he wanted to take, these were violent men being violent inside a code and a system which continually tended to the repression of such passions. Looking at the men who had power in Europe for nearly a thousand years, we shall do well to recognise that the really remarkable thing is that there was so much legality, and so much orderly growth.

The great evil that came with the breakdown of the medieval doctrine, was the growth in particular of parodies and exaggerations of secular tendencies already well represented in the medieval time. Thus Kings had been given great dignity and authority in the conception of the Christian State and its executive officer the Christian King. The State and the King did matter profoundly, but it was a main source of the later troubles of mankind, when their demands became exorbitant, as they did with the rise of the post-reformation absolute monarchies, who fashioned the theory of absolute sovereignty which the later oligarchic or democratic regimes have all inherited and vaunted. So again, the commercial life, the growth of the free cities of Europe, was hardly less important in the building of a civilisation; but there was no side of life which more needed, as it grew, a continual subordination to theology. The rising Middle class, the merchants, making alliance with the Kings, achieved by their alliance their emancipation from the authority of the Church. The queer shapes, the vast amoral "isms," among which modern men live and breathe, the Capitalism and Communism, Nazism and Fascism, all flow from that successful aggression, that declaration of independence for certain fields of life, the political and the economic, from the authority of theology and the judgment of the Church.

The form in which both Newman and Chesterton encountered this release was the form peculiar to the eighteenth and nineteenth centuries, the era of the ascendency of economic doctrine of the need, not for a balance, but for the maximum of individual freedom.

Newman witnessed the routing of theological supremacy from its last stronghold in the Universities. Chesterton was filled with a noble indignation at the spectacles continually to be seen in the England of his lifetime, of the elevation of the search for profit into an idol, the dogma of a religion as cruel to humanity as it was false in itself.

Most of our modern controversy oscillates between the two poles of the supremacy of politics, or the supremacy of economics; men suffering terrible things from these two great exorbitances, seek to balance and moderate one by the other. All forms of socialism and fascism seek to control economics by political action; and the upholders of the free market seek to confine the bureaucracies within bounds and make them obey economic laws if they will not admit the authority of theological ones. Both Newman and Chesterton have essential wisdom for contemporary men thus distracted. From Chesterton the world of tomorrow can learn to find in the historic creed the only basis for that progressive and optimistic outlook which can no longer, save among the very simple, be found in the mere progress of man's power over nature. To enjoy the earth we must not consider it as our own.

And from Newman modern men can learn the later and harder lesson that these evils of disproportion and exorbitance are themselves but the revelation of the real condition of man, needing God not as an insurance for the just balance of a natural life, but desperately; it is not that something is salvaged and restored when men live as Christians, but that all is progressively and remorselessly lost if they fall away. Newman, who lived before Chesterton, should today be read after him, that men who have come to see how necessary the Christian religion is, shall then come to see how relatively indifferent nearly all social matters are in its eyes; and where those eyes are fixed.

Alpine Mysticism and "Cold Philosophy"

by ARNOLD LUNN

Do not all charms fly
At the mere touch of cold philosophy?—KEATS.

SUDDEN CHANGES in æsthetic fashion are often difficult to explain. Our ancestors, as we know, were all but unanimous in regarding the mountains with mild distaste or active disgust. There were outstanding exceptions, such as Petrarch and Gesner, but it is not in their works but in the writings of men like John de Bremble that we discover what mediæval man thought of the mountains. "Lord, restore me to my brethren," exclaimed de Bremble on the St. Bernard, "that I may tell them that they come not to this place of torment." Now, of course, it is easy to understand why de Bremble, who crossed the St. Bernard in 1118, should have felt less at ease than a modern tourist who is driven over this classic pass in a charabanc, but there is no necessary connection between detesting mountain travel and disliking mountain scenery. The Alpine passes, which were often infested by brigands, may well have seemed "places of torment" to the early travellers, but there is nothing alarming in a distant view of the Alps, and yet there is no mediæval tribute to the ethereal beauty of the Oberland as it appears from the Jura or Bern.

The Alpine dawn as seen from the roof of Milan Cathedral inspired the loveliest quatrain that Tennyson ever wrote:

> How faintly flushed, how phantom fair
> Was Monte Rosa hanging there,
> A thousand shadowy-pencill'd valleys
> And snowy dells in the golden air.

Generation after generation of the gifted and artistic race

49

which inhabited the North Italian plain saw what Tennyson saw, not once but many times, and left no trace in
prose or poetry to prove that they were not blind to the
enchanting loveliness of Monte Rosa rising beyond the
foothills of Lombardy.

The dome of Mont Blanc reversed in the blue of Lake
Leman challenges comparison with Monte Rosa from
Milan, but Calvin, Voltaire and Rousseau, who lived for
years in Geneva, never mention Mont Blanc. It would be
unreasonable to criticise Calvin's indifference to the
scenery which surrounded him, for we should not expect
the prophet whose disciples destroyed with such gusto
the glories of mediæval stained glass and sculpture to be
sensitive to beauty in any form, and we need not be surprised that Voltaire, whose æsthetic standards were those
of his century, never refers to Mont Blanc and its Gothic
aiguilles. Rousseau's failure to praise this glorious view
is more surprising, and casts some doubt on his sincerity
as the high-priest of Nature worship; but in spite of this
lapse, Rousseau must be regarded as the forerunner of the
Romantic revival, whereas Calvin and Voltaire were, in
their attitude to the mountains, as characteristic of their
respective periods as John de Bremble was of his century.

The standards of taste which determine our attitude
to scenery fluctuate with æsthetic fashion. The eighteenth-
century humanist who enjoyed the artificial extravagances
of Baroque gardens regarded natural beauty as uncouth.
The fashion for mountain scenery makes its appearance
with the Gothic revival. The æsthetic fashion which provides a criterion for the appreciation of scenery is itself
very largely determined by the dominant philosophy of
the age, for every culture is the expression of a creed.
From the humanism of Greece is derived the bodily per-
fection of the Hermes of Praxiteles, the earthbound Doric
temple, massively set upon the landscape, and an attitude
to Nature which finds Nature attractive in proportion
as Nature is disciplined by man. To the neo-humanist
of the eighteenth century, "Gothic" was a term of abuse,

mountains were uncouth, and religion faintly ridiculous.
The æsthetics of the century were moulded by the pre-
vailing philosophy of an age in which institutional religion was fighting a rear-guard action. It was "an agreed
point," wrote Bishop Butler of his contemporaries, "that
Christianity should be set up as the principal subject of
mirth and ridicule." Man cannot rest content with nega-
tions, for he requires some integrating principles to give
significance to life. The inevitable reaction against the
arid deism of the eighteenth century was the pantheistic
nature-worship of Rousseau, Wordsworth and Shelley.
The Gothic revival, the discovery of mountain beauty
and the Oxford Movement were different aspects of the
same Romantic movement.

It was no accident that the Gothic revival coincided
with the new-found enthusiasm for mountain scenery.
The trite comparison between a Gothic spire and an
Alpine *aiguille* is not so shallow as it seems, for both spire
and peak suggest that upward soaring movement of the
spirit from which the Greek humanist shrank. The en-
tablature of the Greek temple binds the column firmly
to earth. The Gothic spire and the Chamonix *aiguille*
rise from the earth into the blue infinity of heaven. If
the Gothic revival coincided with the discovery that mountains were beautiful, why did not the men who built the
great Gothic cathedrals love mountains? Perhaps because
the old cathedrals expressed in stone a supernatural faith
so secure against doubt that it did not require to be
buttressed by the revelations of God in nature. Petrarch,
the first of the Romantic mountaineers, tells us that he
opened the Confessions of St. Augustine on the summit
of Mont Ventoux. "The first place that I lighted upon,
it was thus written: 'There are men who go to admire the
high places of mountains, and who neglect themselves.'
. . . I shut the book, half-angry with myself that I, who
was even now admiring terrestrial things, ought to have
learned from the philosophers that nothing is truly great
except the soul."

The greatest exponent, in its later phases, of the Romantic revival was John Ruskin. He had more influence than any of his predecessors (or of his successors) in converting contemporary England to a love of mountains and to a love of Gothic architecture. Few people realise how much the new attitude to mountain scenery owed to Ruskin, and how completely he revolutionised architectural taste. Gibbon visited Venice on April 27, 1765. "Old and, in general, ill-built houses," he wrote, "ruined pictures, and stinking ditches, dignified with the pompous denomination of canals, a fine bridge spoilt by two rows of houses upon it, and a large square decorated with the worst architecture I ever saw." This view prevailed until Ruskin wrote his *Stones of Venice*. "The architecture of St. Mark's at Venice," wrote the *Daily News* reviewer of Ruskin's book, "has, from of old, been the butt for students . . . but Mr. Ruskin comes and assures us, etc."

Few men have loved mountains more passionately than Ruskin, and few have attacked mountaineers more bitterly.

"The Alps themselves, which your own poets used to love so reverently, you look upon as soaped poles in a bear-garden, which you set yourselves to climb, and slide down again, with 'shrieks of delight.' When you are past shrieking, having no human articulate voice to say you are glad with, you fill the quietude of their valleys with gunpowder blasts, and rush home, red with cutaneous eruption of conceit, and voluble with convulsive hiccough of self-satisfaction."

The love of mountains, of which Ruskin was the greatest prophet, developed as an important phase of a general revolt against the narrow humanism of the eighteenth century. The beginnings of systematic mountaineering, which Ruskin hated, date from the decade in which Darwin published *The Origin of Species*. The devastating effect of the materialistic philosophy, which had deduced from Darwin's hypothesis conclusions which Darwin had explicitly disowned, was described in a notable passage by a great scientist, Romanes.

"I am not afraid to confess," he wrote, "that with this virtual negation of God, the universe to me has lost its soul of loveliness, and though from henceforth the precept to work while it is day will doubtless but gain an intensified force from the terribly intensified meaning of the words 'that the night cometh when no man can work,' yet when I think, as think at times I must, of the contrast between the hallowed glory of that creed which once was mine, and the lonely mystery of life as I now find it, at such times I find it impossible to avoid the sharpest pang of which my nature is capable."

Many of the early mountaineers were orthodox Christians, but there were many more who in a greater or lesser degree recovered among the mountains that "soul of loveliness" which the universe appeared to have lost, and of these the greatest was the mountaineer who had left the Church of his baptism, in which he had taken Orders, to write *An Agnostic's Apology*.

"If I were to invent," wrote Leslie Stephen, "a new idolatry (rather a needless task) I should prostrate myself, not before beast, or ocean, or sun, but before one of those gigantic masses to which, in spite of all reason, it is impossible not to attribute some shadowy personality. Their voice is mystic and has found discordant interpreters; but to me at least it speaks in tones at once more tender and more awe-inspiring than that of any mortal teacher. The loftiest and sweetest strains of Milton or Wordsworth may be more articulate, but do not lay so forcible a grasp upon my imagination."

This confession will surprise readers who only knew Leslie Stephen as the high-priest of a somewhat arid and unimaginative agnosticism, and Leslie Stephen himself would certainly have disclaimed any attempt to base conclusions, however tentative, on his own emotional reactions to mountain scenery. Leslie Stephen was a mystic *malgré lui*. A man's half-beliefs are often not only more interesting but more illuminating than the beliefs which he is prepared to defend at the bar of reason. *Die Aberglaube,* as Goethe somewhere says, *ist die Poesie des Lebens.* Leslie Stephen's Victorian agnosticism is already a little dated, but his essay on Wordsworth and his *Playground of Europe* have outlasted the mental fashion of the Victorian Age.

The interpretation of Alpine mysticism has been the work of poets, using the word in its widest sense. It would be easy to compile an anthology of essays and long passages which deal either explicitly or by implication with such themes as "the religion of the mountain" or the "philosophy of a mountaineer," and so forth, but I have not yet discovered a serious attempt to formulate a scientific explanation of our reactions to mountain beauty, or to discover a philosophic basis for mountain mysticism. The diagnosis of mountain emotion is often inhibited by the distaste for the emotional, for we forget that emotion can be discussed unemotionally. The limestone of which the Wetterhorn is composed and the emotion which that limestone inspires have at least this in common. Both the limestone and the emotion are facts of which philosophers and scientists may be invited to offer an unemotional explanation.

So far, however, the philosophers and the scientists have not come to the assistance of the mountaineer, and the Alpine poet has had the field to himself. I have no desire to belittle their achievements in this field, for the intuitions of the poet provide the philosopher with valuable data. There is no reason why those who try to explain the things which the poets feel, but make no attempt to explain, should not collaborate with the poets in a common enterprise. *"J'ai remarque,"* writes Anatole France, *"que les philosophes vivaient généralement en bonne*

*intelligence avec les poètes. . . . Les philosophes savent
que les poètes ne pensent pas; cela les désarme, les at-
tendrit et les enchante."*

I shall use the words "mystic" and "mysticism" in their
popular rather than in their technical sense. The Greeks,
to whom we owe the word "mystic," described as *mystæ*
the initiates of the mysteries who believed that they had
received a direct vision of God. To the *mystæ* God was
not an object of academic belief, but a Being experimen-
tally known by direct intuition. The great mystics were
fully conscious of the immense difficulty of communicating what is incommunicable—one remembers St. Augustine's: "Si nemo me quasvat scio . . ." "If nobody asks me
I know. If I desire to explain, I do not know"—but, none
the less, they never ceased in the attempts to illuminate
the obscure, and to discover the apt word, phrase, analogy
or metaphor which at least suggests that which can never
be accurately described.

In Alpine literature, on the other hand, the word
"mystic" is often used as if it were the equivalent of
"misty," and as if obscurity rather than illumination were
the essence of mystical experiences. The vagueness of
Alpine mysticism is partly due to those paroxysms of shy-
ness which overwhelm the average Englishman in any discussion of religion. The Greek *mystæ* claimed without
embarrassment that he enjoyed a direct vision of God,
but this useful monosyllable is unfashionable today—
excepting as an expletive—with the curious result that
Alpine mysticism might be described as an attempt to
construct the corpus of Alpine theology without mention-
ing Theos. It is significant that the only passage in the
literature of the mountain which has found a place in
Alpine anthologies, and which could equally well be
quoted in any representative anthology of mythical literature, is a passage which we owe, not to a mountaineer,
but to a mountain worshipper, who did not climb because he was "afraid of slipping down." This is what Mr.
Belloc saw from the heights of the Weissenstein:

"I saw between the branches of the trees in front of me a sight in the sky that made me stop breathing, just as great danger at sea, or great surprise in love, or a great deliverance will make a man stop breathing. I saw something I had known in the West as a boy, something I had never seen so grandly discovered as was this. In between the branches of the trees was a great promise of unexpected lights beyond. . . .

"Here were these magnificent creatures of God, I mean the Alps, which now for the first time I saw from the height of Jura; and because they were fifty or sixty miles away, and because they were a mile or two high, they were become something different from us others, and could strike one motionless with the awe of supernatural things. Up there in the sky, to which only clouds belong and birds and the last trembling colours of pure light, they stood fast and hard; not moving as do the things of the sky. They were as distant as the little upper clouds of summer, as fine and tenuous; but in their reflection and in their quality as it were of weapons (like spears and shields of an unknown array) they occupied the sky wth a sublime invasion: and the things proper to the sky were forgotten by me in their presence as I gazed.

"To what emotion shall I compare this astonishment? So, in first love one finds that *this* can belong to *me*.

"Their sharp steadfastness and their clean uplifted lines compelled my adoration. Up there, the sky above and below them, part of the sky, but part of us, the great peaks made communion between that homing creeping part of me which loves vineyards and dances and a slow movement among pastures, and that other part which is only properly at home in Heaven. I say that this kind of description is useless, and that it is better to address prayers to such things than to attempt to interpret them for others.

"These, the great Alps, seen thus, link one in some way to one's immortality. Nor is it possible to convey, or even to suggest, those few fifty miles and those few thousand feet; there is something more. Let me put it thus: that from the height of Weissenstein I saw, as it were, my religion. I mean, humility, the fear of death, the terror of height and of distance, the glory of God, the infinite potentiality of reception whence springs that divine thirst of the soul; my aspiration also towards completion, and my confidence in the dual destiny. For I know that we laughers have a gross cousinship with the Most High, and it is this contrast and perpetual quarrel which feeds a spring of merriment in the soul of a sane man.

"Since I could now see such a wonder and it could work such things in my mind, therefore, some day I should be part of it. That is what I felt.

"That it is also which leads some men to climb mountain-tops, but not me, for I am afraid of slipping down."

Every poet, Hilaire Belloc among others, accepts, consciously or unconsciously, the Platonic distinction between αὐτὸ τὸ καλὸν (beauty itself) and τὰ πολλὰ καλά (many beautiful things); that is, between beauty as a universal and beauty in its particular manifestations. The loveliness which Hilaire Belloc saw from the Weissenstein is a reflection in time and space of that timeless loveliness which is uneroded by change. "Natural beauty," as St. Thomas Aquinas says, "is but the similitude of divine beauty shared among things." On these great issues there is a generous measure of agreement among poets. "These, the great Alps, seen thus, link one in some way to one's immortality" can be compared with Baudelaire's "It is the immortal instinct for beauty which is the liveliest proof of immortality."

Leslie Stephen would have rejected, perhaps with regret, Hilaire Belloc's interpretation of mountain beauty. "The mountains," writes Leslie Stephen, "represent the indomitable forces of nature to which we are forced to adapt ourselves. They speak to man of his littleness and his ephemeral existence." This is true, but that is only part of their message. *"La nature a des perfections,"* says Pascal, *"pour montrer qu'elle est l'image de Dieu; et des défauts pour montrer qu'elle n'en est que l'image."* Mountains only "speak to man of his littleness" if he is so foolish as to accept a yard measure as the criterion of his status. Shakespeare's mind is neither greater nor smaller than the Wetterhorn, for mind and matter are incommensurable. "All our dignity," says Pascal, "is born of thought." What, then, is the origin of the thoughts which mountains inspire in the minds of mountain lovers? Can science and philosophy add anything to the intuition of the poet?

Scientists assure us that there was a period when life was non-existent on the surface of the planet, from which it follows that life was potentially present in the molten crust and gases of the primeval planet, or alternatively some cause external to the planet must be invoked to explain the origin of life and the origin of a sense of beauty. Darwin's attempt to meet this difficulty was characteristically evasive. He assumed the existence of the sense of beauty, and, instead of explaining its origin, discussed its influence on evolution. According to Darwin's theory of sexual selection, beauty has a survival value. The female is attracted by a beautiful mate, with the happy result that beauty is passed on to the next generation, whereas the uglier examples of the species fade away and pass their days in forlorn bachelorhood. No doubt; but our problem still remains unanswered. I am prepared to believe that the peahen's reaction to a peacock's gay colouring influences the evolution of peacocks, but what we want to know is why the peahen thinks the peacock beautiful, and whence is derived the æsthetic sense which manifests itself throughout the animal kingdom. This is a question to which the materialist has no reply. "When the materialist," writes J. B. Mosley, "has exhausted himself in efforts to explain utility in nature, it would appear to be the peculiar office of beauty to rise up as a confounding and baffling *extra*."

The impotence of the scientist to reconcile a sense of beauty with a purely mechanistic interpretation of evolution provides a negative argument in support of the Platonic doctrine of beauty. The philosopher reinforces these conclusions with the positive argument that nothing can be present in an effect which was not present in the cause. It is fantastic to suppose that our reaction to mountain beauty could be potentially present in the lifeless rock, sea and mud of the primeval planet. You cannot get plus out of minus:

> *Quis cælum posset nisi cæli munere nosse,*
> *El reperire deum nisi qui pars ipse deorum.*[1]

It is not necessary to climb in order to accept the Platonic interpretation of mountain beauty, but the mountaineer has a great advantage over the non-mountaineer. He has chosen the ascetic way to mountain understanding, and among the hills, as elsewhere, asceticism is the key to the higher forms of mystical experience. One need not question the sincerity of Ruskin's condemnation of those who had transformed the mountain cathedrals into arenas for athletic feats, but I have sometimes suspected that the peculiar venom of his attack may have been due to the fact that the mountaineer provoked an uneasy and unformulated doubt as to the quality of his own life, which was essentially non-ascetic and soft. He had been privately educated and thus deprived of the ascetic experiences which the Victorian public schools so generously provided. He played no games, took part in no sports. He inherited a comfortable income from his father, which insured him against the necessity of uncongenial work. His life from birth to death was a stranger to the discipline of pain, danger or discomfort.

---

[1] These lines of Manilius may be paraphrased: "What can man know of heaven save by the grace of heaven? How can man discover God unless he is a creature of God?"

Asceticism is often confused with puritanism. The Puritan condemns pleasure as wicked, and the ascetic abstains from certain pleasures, which he admits to be innocent, as the price to be paid for the higher forms of happiness. An ascetic may confine his drinks to water, but he does not deserve to be branded as a Puritan so long as he makes no attempt to prevent other people from drinking wine. An ascetic might be defined as one who sacrifices pleasure to happiness, for pleasure and happiness are not identical. A candidate for the Oxford "Greats" Schools was once invited to comment on Aristotle's dictum, "A good man can be perfectly happy on the rack." He answered: "Possibly, if it were a very bad rack, or if he were a very good man." Good men have been happy even on good racks, for, as that puzzled pagan Seneca observed, men have been known to laugh, and "that right heartily," under torture.

The greatest thinkers, Roman, Greek, Muslim and Jew, agree that pain and happiness are not necessarily opposed. Whymper aptly quoted on the frontispiece of *Scrambles in the Alps* a sentence from Livy: "Though pain and pleasure are in their natures opposite, they are yet linked together in a kind of necessary connection."

"How singular is a thing called happiness," exclaimed Socrates, "and how curiously related to pain, which might be thought to be the opposite of it; for they are never present to a man at the same instant, and yet he who pursues either is generally compelled to take the other: their bodies are two and they are joined by a necessary single head. . . ."

The famous saying of Mohammed, "Hell is veiled with delights, and heaven in hardships and misery," finds an echo in all great philosophies, Christian and non-Christian.

Indeed, the very word "ascetic" comes to us from the pagan world, and once meant no more than "exercise." To the Greek the athlete was the typical ascetic, for he exercised his body by sacrificing the pleasures of self-indulgence to the happiness of self-discipline. He was, as

St. Paul said, temperate in all things to win a corruptible
crown. No illustration, as St. Paul knew, was more calculated to impress his hearers with the reasonableness of
Christian asceticism; for where institutional religion de-
clines, as in the pagan world, the ascetic instinct finds expression in strenuous sport. If it were not for this peculiar
form of happiness, which is the reward of the ascetic, there
would be no boat-racing and no rock-climbing and no
ski-racing. No ski racer can reach the international class
unless he is prepared to risk fall after fall when practising
or racing, at a speed which often attains to sixty miles
an hour. There is no pleasure in such ski-ing, but there
is a queer kind of happiness.

"The racer's mind must overcome the physical reactions, which shrink from the fastest line on steep
slopes, and must keep the body under the control necessary for performing turns with complete precision.

"When the racer is ski-ing well there come moments
when he knows that his mind has won, and for a few
brief seconds he has complete control over his body.
Such moments are rare, but it is for them that men endure the physical discomforts attendant upon all ascetic
sports, for they then experience a happiness, almost
an ecstasy, which has nothing in common with pleasure
or enjoyment as these terms are normally understood.

"It is this spiritual, perhaps almost mystical, thrill,
this fleeting glimpse of the paradise of Eden, which
causes men to encounter gladly the dangers and hardships of mountaineering, to endure the acute physical
agony of rowing and long-distance running, and to overcome the physical difficulties attendant on all sports."[2]

The happiness of the rock-climber is derived from the
same source as the happiness of the racer—from the
dominion, that is, of the mind over the body.

"The great peaks," says Mr. Belloc in the passage I
have quoted, "made communion between that homing

[2] From *High Speed Ski-ing*, by Peter Lunn.

creeping part of me which loves vineyards and dances and slow movement among pastures, and that other part which is only properly at home in Heaven." Had Mr. Belloc been a climber, he would have discovered that the dominant theme of mountaineering is not the communion but the contrast and perpetual quarrel between "the homing creeping part" and the part which is "at home in Heaven."

It is the part which is at home in heaven that forces the creeping part which loves vineyards up the steep and rocky mountain side, and with every foot of ascent the protest of the creeping part becomes more pronounced. For though the result is the same whether one falls two hundred feet or two thousand, the downward drag of the earth below varies with the aerial distances which separate the body from its natural habitat, the gross and comfortable security of the horizontal. There is no sport which illustrates more perfectly the ascetic principle that happiness must be paid for by pain, and that the degree of happiness is in proportion to the price paid. Few sports offer their devotees a wider range of disagreeable moments. The agony of the half-slip when one is leading on an exposed climb, the desperate struggle to regain balance, a struggle which is a matter of infinitely small readjustments on a battle-ground measured in inches, are the price which the cragsman pays, not only for the exquisite relief of safety after peril, but also for the quasi-mystical happiness of those moments when his mind has established complete dominion over his body, moments when the effortless rhythm of the upward movement transforms the accident of crack and ledge into an ordered sequence of harmonious movement.

Many mountaineers who have lost all contact with institutional religion have discovered among the hills the satisfaction of certain aspirations which others have fulfilled within the framework of the religious life. They have caught the reflection of eternal beauty in the temporal loveliness of the hills. They have been initiated into the secret of the ascetic, and have found the happiness which is the by-product of pain and danger. But when we have said this we have said all that can usefully be said on the relation of mountaineering to religion. Points of contact do not suffice to establish their identity. Boxing involves asceticism, but no one has yet claimed that there is a religion of the Ring. It is a pity to make exaggerated claims for our sport.

There is something to be said for the view that the better type of young men gravitate naturally towards the ascetic sports, such as mountaineering, which involves the discipline of danger; but though the individual mountaineer is entitled to claim that he is a better man than he would have been if he had never climbed, he should not imply that he is a better man than those who do not climb, or even than those who detest all forms of active and dangerous sport. Samuel Johnson was no ascetic. He disliked mountains and detested solitude, and was seldom happy outside the congenial atmosphere of London, but he was a better man than most mountaineers. "If there is one thing worse," wrote Mr. Chesterton, "than the modern weakening of major morals, it is the modern strengthening of minor morals. Cleanliness is not next to godliness nowadays, but cleanliness is a convention and godliness is regarded as an offence. . . . A man can get used to getting up at five o'clock in the morning"—as mountaineers do—"a man cannot very well get used to being burnt for his opinions; the first experiment is commonly fatal."

Is the man who detests crowds necessarily more spiritual than Samuel Johnson, who detested solitude? Epictetus, the greatest of the Stoics, addresses the same admonition to those who hate solitude as Johnson hated it, and to those who hate mobs: "If you are fated to spend your life alone, call it peace . . . if you fall in with a crowd, try to make holiday with the crowd." If we could acquire this Stoic detachment we should all be serenely unaffected by our environment, whether this environment were a bank-holiday crowd or the severe loneliness of the Arctic regions. The Chinese proverb reminds us that "noise is not in the market-place, nor quiet in the hills, but in the ever-changing hearts of men."

The man who despises the routine of office life, and who escapes into unexplored mountain ranges to find his soul, may be less successful than some mystic of the suburbs who catches the 9.5 train to his office and the 6.10 train back to his home. Mountain worship began when institutional religion declined. It is the "estrangèd faces" that need the dramatic stimuli of mountain beauty. The true mystic hurrying from his office to the tube can see

> The traffic of Jacob's ladder
> Pitched between Heaven and Charing Cross.

It is not a sign of a spiritual but of a materialistic nature to over-emphasise the importance of material environment. I remember a discussion on this point with a great modern sculptor, Eric Gill. I was charmed by his picturesque hand-made smock. "It has many conveniences," he remarked. "My nice friends feel ashamed of me, and therefore don't ask me to lunch in their clubs." The talk then turned on the ugliness of our machine-made civilisation, and the supreme importance of surrounding oneself with hand-made furniture. I conceded that it would be easier to live a good life if one dined off a table carved by one of Eric Gill's disciples, but this seems to me evidence of the frailty of human nature. The true mystic could enjoy the beatific vision while sweeping out a latrine.

I am not working up to the paradoxical conclusion that a man's spirituality varies inversely with his appreciation of beautiful surroundings. There is, indeed, the highest of precedents for the choice of mountains for a spiritual retreat, but these withdrawals serve as a preparation for the life among men. "He had compassion on the multitude."

It is foolish to invite the ridicule of the discerning by making claims for mountaineering which cannot be substantiated. Mountaineering is neither a substitute for religion nor a civic duty. It is a sport; for we climb, not to benefit the human race, but to amuse ourselves. In so far as mountaineering is something more than a sport we must base this claim on the fact that it is carried out in surroundings which suggest spiritual truths even to the unspiritual. Ruskin compared mountains to cathedrals, and the comparison is sound; for one does not worship cathedrals, though one may worship in the cathedrals of man or among the cathedrals of nature. ˎ

All evil, as a great mediæval thinker remarked, is the result of mistaking means for ends. Mountaineering is not an end in itself, but a means to an end. "For it is true," as the first mountaineer to ascend the throne of St. Peter (Pius XI) remarked:

> "For it is true that, of all innocent pleasures, none more than this one (excepting where unnecessary risks are taken) may be considered as being helpful mentally and physically, because, through the efforts required for climbing in the rarefied mountain air, energy is renewed; and owing to the difficulties overcome the climber thereby becomes better equipped and strengthened to resist the difficulties encountered in life, and by admiring the beauties and grandeur of the scenery as seen from the mighty peaks of the Alps his spirit is uplifted to the Creator of all."

The last few hundred feet of curving descent through a pattern of pine carried us from the colour and radiance of the high mountains into the kingdom of unchallenged winter. We had reached the sheltered and shadowed valley, where the firs sagged beneath their burden of snow, and where the river bed was a stranger to the benediction of the sun. We called a short halt beside an inn whose rafters stooped towards and almost met the snow. A group of pines on a western hill suddenly burst into flames as the sun set behind their snow-laden branches.

Easy wood-running and open glades led from Schwarzwald to Rosenlaui. The crystalline flaky snow rustled under our ski like autumn leaves. It is only in the most sheltered of valleys and in the neighbourhood of river banks that one finds this most perfect of all forms of powder snow.

The last hint of daylight had vanished from the west as we started slowly along the plain between Rosenlaui and the steep cliff over which the Reichenbach falls to Meiringen. The thin trickle of the river edged its dispirited way round ice-fretted boulders and beneath smothers of snow, and its icy breath reached us in a frosty trail of mist which stung like a whip. It was bitterly cold. The night had broken that bridge of human associations which man laboriously builds between himself and the mountains. All sense of companionship had disappeared. These shadowy masses fading by slow gradations into the sharper darkness of the star-pointed night had recovered their inhuman aloofness. They had forgotten the brief episode of contact with man, and were dreaming, not of that mere yesterday when mammoths lumbered across the rivers of ice which flow down the valley of the Aar, but of that remoter abyss in past time when the first island summits of the Alps appeared above the silent waters of the central seas.

The darkness and solitude and the lonely stars began to oppress us. *"Le silence éternel de ces expaces infinis m'effraie."* Then suddenly we turned a corner and the valley of Meiringen opened below us, and the inhabited hills sparkled with the cheerful constellations of human lights, evoking friendly pictures of snug interiors, and of the warm welcome which we knew would be awaiting us at the Bear at Meiringen. The Bear is one of those inns which still retain something of the atmosphere of romantic Switzerland. It is the sort of place in which Leslie Stephen or Byron would have felt at home.

The very phrase "cross-country ski-ing" implies travel. The perfect cross-country tour should not end under the same roof from which it started. Our mountain day had ended as all such days should end, not in a cocktail bar, but in a friendly kind of inn, where beer can be ordered *"vom Fass,"* and wine can be bought, not by the *bottle*, but by the *"Dezi."*

The books I enjoy writing are the books which I am going to write—next year. Few things are pleasanter than the vague ruminations which end when the book is begun, and few things are more tedious than translating those ruminations into words. No author learns with experience. I began this essay with high hopes, undeterred by previous failures. My memories of this memorable day were so vivid. . . . I knew exactly what I wanted to say before I began to say it. . . .

Si nemo me quaerat scio, si quaerate explicari vellim nescio.

The Piety of Cicely, Duchess of York:
A Study in Late Medieval Culture[1]

by C. A. J. ARMSTRONG

THE CONTRIBUTION of women to the contemplative piety of the later Middle Ages can scarcely be rated too high. When all is said, the figure of St. Catherine of Siena can be regarded with much justification as forming something of a water-shed in the history of mediaeval devoutness. The fifteenth century witnessed a general diffusion of a spirit characterized by an ardent humility, yet tender and intimate in its approach to the Godhead. Preoccupation with the human nature and sufferings of Our Lord did not fail to arouse pity for humanity itself, and introduced into the grandiose if more abstract visions of the earlier mystics an understanding for the pathos in human relations. The continuity of Christian piety was indeed perfectly preserved, but elements always present within it were now cherished with a sudden fondness. As ever in the history of types of thought, a new affection produced a special emphasis inside the traditional form, and thus arose a new phase which might be held to characterize an age.

Nor was it coincidence that a woman's figure, that of St. Catherine, has been chosen to mark the transition in the spirituality of the Middle Ages. It is not too fanciful to suppose that many of the traits so charming and so refreshing in the religious style of pre-Reformation times were first perceived and cultivated by the feminine genius. Throughout Europe the "Devotio Moderna" was greatly

[1] In her lifetime Cicely was styled or addressed Cecill, Cecille, Cecyll, the most usual form of her signature was Cecylee. Appendices to Historical Manuscripts Communion Reports 1-8 passim. In the face of such diversity the use of the form Cicely, common in the sixteenth century and after, seems justifiable.

encouraged and promoted by women, and England, if unacquainted with the more organized forms of this school as they flourished in the Netherlands, was perhaps the principal hearth of mysticism, and the especial home of that devotion to the Holy Name of Jesus so typical of the movement as a whole.[2]

Not least remarkable was the hold which pietism acquired upon the highest ranks of society.[3] When every allowance is made for the relative abundance of sources for the intellectual history of the upper as compared with other classes of society, the sensitiveness of the nobility toward these new influences emerges as a striking fact. Aristocratic ladies, who in England as on the continent were so powerfully attracted by religious contemplation, might seek indeed to find a refuge from the strokes of fortune. But their pursuit of holiness was too positive and too vigorous to be actuated solely by a desire to escape from worldly misfortunes. Equally misleading is the supposition that their spiritual trend was merely a reaction against extreme ceremonial and formalism in life. An emphasis altogether too great has been laid upon the alleged disharmony in the spirit of the waning middle ages. The picture of a society in ossified magnificence alternating with melancholy resignation between the feverish enjoyment of an outworn world and the lurid and terrifying contemplation of the next, ignores the very

[2] In the introduction to *Writings Ascribed to Richard Rolle*, ed. Hope Emily Allen, Modern Language Association of America, Monographs 1927, the exclusively English character of this cult is perhaps overemphasized, but unless the fourteenth-century mystics are to be ignored, it is impossible to admit that the cult of the Holy Name was brought from the continent to England in the fifteenth century as stated by W. Pronger. Thomas Gascoigne, English Historical Review, liii (1938), p. 626.

[3] Henry Beauchamp, earl, later created duke of Warwick, ob. 1446, said every day "unless he had great business" the entire psalter, which he knew by heart. The Rows Rol, ed. W. Pickering. London 1845, no. 54. His psalter which went to John Tiptoft earl of Worcester, who married his widow, was left by Tiptoft in Italy, and is now in the Dyson Perrins Library. G. F. Warner, Descriptive Catalogue of MSS. in library of C. Dyson Perrins, London, 1920, p. 64.

considerable degree of unity which existed in the mind
of that age. Contrast there may be, as in contemporary
polyphonic music, but no fundamental discord.

In the life of Cicely, Duchess of York, mother of Edward
IV and Richard III, it is possible to behold a tranquillity
of spirit, the existence of which has been insufficiently
recognized in most appreciations of the fifteenth century.
To draw a division between the saintly Lancastrians
and the worldly if politic Yorkists would be no less unreal
than to allow any preoccupation with Cicely, Duchess of
York, or Margaret of Burgundy to obscure the virtues of
Margaret Beaufort. The very nature of the Wars of the
Roses offers irrefutable if unfortunate evidence that the
nobility and the blood royal formed but a single whole,
and it would be idle to attempt a distinction of moral
categories within this extensive kinship of blood and
social interests. Cicely[4] the child of Ralph Neville, Earl
of Westmoreland, and wife of Richard, Duke of York,
was herself a grand-daughter of John of Gaunt, and before her death in 1495 her eldest grand-daughter, the
devout if somewhat colourless Elizabeth, had carried the
strongest title of the House of York to her husband Henry
Tudor.

To dwell upon the vicissitudes of Cicely's existence is
not only a superfluous but an altogether misleading introduction to her moral physiognomy. Neither the death in
battle of her husband, nor the fratricidal jealousy of her
sons, nor even the events of 1483, when the vilest slanders
accompanying a palace revolution doubled the bitterness
of civil war, could be considered an unusual sequence for
a daughter of the Nevilles or a mother of kings. Others,
such as Margaret of Anjou, had perhaps suffered more
acutely. The ladies of the great houses were not inferior
to the perils which their rank entailed. Their attitude was
too inflexible both to themselves and toward others for

[4] Born 3 May 1415, the 18th child of Ralph, and the 10th by his second
wife, Cicely married aged 9 before October 1424. Complete Peerage, ed.
G. E. C. (1898), vol. vii, p. 215.

it to be readily supposed that their state of mind was dis-united or morbid. They scarcely admit of distinction be-tween their individual and public existence, for, as mothers of families, and still more as heads of great house-holds their responsibilities, whether spiritual or worldly, were too constantly before their eyes.

Cicely, explaining to her household at supper her de-votional reading of the morning, her daughter Margaret of Burgundy accompanied by her ladies performing in stateliness the menial tasks of the corporal works of mercy,[5] and Margaret Beaufort preoccupied with the foundation of public lectureships and a college, offer a true picture of the late fifteenth century. Here is no dis-harmony in the soul, but a true humility accompanied by dignity, a responsibility toward others felt not only as a duty of high rank but as the product of intimate devoutness. Nothing irreconcilable exists between the ceremonial formalism of outward life and the inner aspirations toward mysticism; a disciplined sense of gravity informed each alike.

There is good reason to suppose that the royal title claimed by her husband was regarded with equal seri-ousness by Cicely herself. Was not her son Edmund born at Rouen, christened in the font where none had been baptised since the pagan Rollo, ancestor of William the Bastard, received Christianity from its waters?[6] Another son, George, the unhappy Clarence of subsequent years, was the first child of royal parentage to be given in bap-tism the name of England's patron. In later years the cult

[5] Miniature on f.1 of MS. 9296 Bibliothèque royale Brussels, of a treatise "Bien heureux seront les misericordieux" shows Margaret performing the seven corporal works: reproduced P. Durrien. La Miniature Flamande 1415-1530. Brussels 1921, pl. xlviii. The accounts of Margaret's domains at Malines and Binche preserved at the Archives Générales du Royaume, Brussels, substantially show that Margaret actually performed these char-ities, with such entries as "to be distributed secretly by the hands of the duchess to the poor" or "to be given to poor prisoners" and many others of the same sort.

[6] Wilhelmi Wyrcester Anekdota apud Liber Niger, ed. Hearne, Oxford, 1728, p. 525.

of St. George was much favoured by Edward IV, but the fact of this christening in the year 1449 sufficiently attests the honour which the House of York paid to St. George long before its accession to power.[7] The official style employed by the duchess in King Edward's reign "Cecilli the kyngs mooder and late wyf unto Richard rightfull kyng of England etc." was accepted by her in all its implications.[8]

How seriously the royal title was entertained, though it could only be accorded posthumously to Duke Richard, his reburial at Fotheringay in 1476 plainly showed.[9] At this ceremony, in which Cicely was the foremost participant, the king only excepted, and to the ordering of which she could not fail to contribute, the bones of Duke Richard were placed on a chariot which conveyed them from Wakefield to Fotheringay. At his feet stood the figure of an angel clad in white bearing a crown of gold to signify that of right he was a king. Above the funeral image of the Duke was stretched a black cloth of majesty with the figure of Our Lord sitting on the rainbow beaten in gold, but having at every corner a shield of France and England quarterly.

The picture of Christ seated in majesty upon the rainbow nimbus displaying the sacred Wounds of the Passion was an image familiar to Cicely and her contemporaries from the miniatures and woodcuts of their primers. Nor could the royal arms appear out of keeping, and least of

[7] Edward IV had especial recourse to the patronage of St. George when in exile 1470-71. Historie of the Arrival of Edward IV, ed. J. Bruce, Camden Society, 1838, p. 13. J. de Wavrin, Croniques, ed. W. Hardy, Rolls Series, vol. v, p. 665. Edward's own son George of Windsor died young. C. Scofield, Life and Reign of Edward IV, ii vols. London, 1923, vol. ii, pp. 210, 214, 249. Among her tapestries Cicely possessed one of St. George. Wills from Doctors' Commons, ed. J. G. Nichols and J. Bruce, Camden Society, 1863, p. 2.

[8] Historical Manuscripts Commission, Second Report (1871), Appendix, p. 94.

[9] Narrative of the ceremony, British Museum, Harleian MS. 48, ff. 78-91; extracts from which are printed in F. Sandford, Genealogical History of the Kings and Queens of England, London, 1707, pp. 391-2, but under the false date of 1466.

all to one whose husband had felt so far entitled to their use as to bring death on himself and civil war to the kingdom. The occasion was in itself an almost perfect manifestation of the single-mindedness of contemporary culture. Closely related artistic forms were employed to commemorate the fallen Duke and to honour the majesty of the Almighty.

This similarity did not spring from a confusion of things sacred and profane, nor even of iconographical symbols; rather was it the direct product of a mind intent upon the majesty of God. The piety of the House of York had no reluctance in placing the royal arms beside the most sacred emblems, any more than in striking the "Angel," its distinctive issue of coinage, with the sign of the Cross and the invocation "Per Crucem Tuam Salva Nos." This was no chance phenomenon; for, quite apart from the King's Touch, an inseparable attribute of the Crown which Edward IV was bound to maintain if only to disprove Lancastrian assertions on behalf of Henry VI in exile, the Yorkists were intensely pre-occupied with the sacred character of kingship.[10] The very ceremonial which their court did so much to elaborate and define was an outcome of this attitude of mind, and was designed to display the gradations of honour and duty inherent in office. Equally symptomatic of the underlying psychological unity of her generation was the carefully ordered ceremonial of spiritual and worldly duties followed as if in cadence by the Duchess Cicely and her household.

The record of the daily life of Cicely and her establishment is preserved in a document which belongs to a class

[10] C. Oman, Coinage of England, Oxford, 1931, pp. 219-21, pl. xxiii. It has been suggested that the Angel was coined largely as a touch-piece and for use as a talisman. H. Farquhar, Angels as healing pieces for the Kings Evil, British Numismatic Journal, vol. xii (1916), pp. 49-50, 69. M. Bloch, Les Rois Thaumaturges, Strasbourg, 1924, pp. 111-114. Defensio Iuris Domus Lancastrie, apud Fortescue's Works, ed. Clermont, Vol. I, pp. 70, 508.

generally known as the household ordinance.[11] Fortunately this particular example was not drawn up solely to register procedure and perquisites among the different officials. On the contrary, the document in its first half is wholly narrative, as if the aim of the anonymous author was to place on record a devout method of life, as a precedent for other noble ladies. Like much besides in the literature of the period this short account is formal in design and didactic in scope, but retains the vivacity and charm of a work undertaken in the service of an ideal. To what extent the author was dominated by the Christian ideal is apparent in his closing words:—"I trust to our Lordes mercy that this noble princess thus devideth the howers to his highe pleasure."

Judging from his knowledge of precise details, the writer was either an actual member of Cicely's household, or wrote on the instruction of such a person; in either case with the consent and, indeed, approval of the mistress herself. Despite its economy of detail this ordinance succeeds in outlining a distinct manner of life, and in presenting a type of individual sanctity which leaves a clear impression on the mind.

Rising at seven in the morning, Cicely prepared herself to recite with one of her chaplains, who awaited her pleasure, the matins of the day, to be followed by the matins from the Little Office of Our Lady.[12] When she was "fully

[11] A Collection of Ordinances and Regulations for the Government of the Royal Household, London Society of Antiquaries, 1790, pp. 37-9. Orders and Rules of the Princess Cecill. Probably composed between 1485 and her death in 1495; certainly after 1483 as Cicely is called "late mother unto King Edward," but scarcely earlier than August 1485 as she is not styled the king's mother as would be the case during Richard's reign. In the reign of Henry VII Cicely could style herself late mother to king Edward, as in her will, but no mention of Richard III was possible. Wills from Doctors' Commons, ed. J. G. Nichols and J. Bruce, Camden Society, 1863, p. 1.

[12] Some account of the division of the primer is to be found in the introduction to The Prymer or Lay Folks Prayer Book, ed. H. Littlehales, 2 pts. Early English Text Society, No. 71, 1895, 1897. The daily routine of Margaret Beaufort as described by St. John Fisher in his sermon on the month's mind of the Countess of Richmond conforms to the same type both outwardly and spiritually. English Works of John Fisher, ed. J. E. B. Mayor, Early English Text Society, extra series xxvii, 1876, pp. 294-5.

ready" she heard a Low Mass in her chamber, and then breakfasted. So far her devotions had been of a private character, but after breakfast she entered the chapel, where it might be supposed a part of her household was assembled, and here she assisted at the Office of the day and two Low Masses. As was then customary with princes she made her first public appearance when, leaving her chapel, she passed straightway to dinner. The meal was accompanied by the reading aloud of some pious work, such as Hilton's *Contemplative and Active Life*, Bonaventure's *Life of Christ*, the apocryphal *Infancy of the Saviour*, or the *Golden Legend*.[13] Frequently the subject would be taken from the visions of the great mystics for whom the Duchess had an obvious predilection, such as B. Matilda of Hackeborn, St. Catherine of Siena or St. Bridget of Sweden.

After dinner for the space of a full hour Cicely gave audience to all who had any business to set before her. This was the classic moment when suitors thronged the audience chamber of the great in eager pursuit of patronage; during her son's reign petitioners besought Cicely for a favourable word,[14] but in Tudor days there were other and more promising ante-rooms.

Having absolved her public duties the Duchess composed herself for rest, though it was her habit to sleep for no more than a quarter of an hour. Refreshed by this pause she turned on waking to prayer and contemplation; now at her private devotions she would follow in the path of the mystics whose work she dwelt upon so affectionately. In the secrecy of this inner life the Duchess of York was completely merged in the humble seeker of divine mercy,

[13] Owing to a mistaken punctuation (Collection of Ordinances . . . op. cit., p. 37.) the printed edition runs as follows:—"Bonaventure de infancia, Salvatoris legenda aurea." A work "de infancia" by Bonaventure is unknown, equally unfamiliar is the "Salvatoris legenda aurea." The proper reading should be "Bonaventure, de infancia Salvatoris, legenda aurea." The misplaced comma has made two where there should be three separate works: namely, a treatise designated as Bonaventure, the reputed author, the reasons for believing this to be the "Life of Christ" are discussed below, the "de infancia Salvatoris," and the "legenda aurea."

[14] J. Gairdner, Richard III (1898), p. 22 n. Stonor Letters. Camden Society, Third Series, Vol. XXX, p. 14.

just as the character of the mystic had co-existed all the while in the great lady who presided over the secular duties of the day. Thus she continued until the first peal rang for evensong, a note which in princely households sounded the end of the serious business for the day.[15]

At the first stroke of the bell Cicely would drink some wine or ale until her chaplain was ready to accompany her in reciting both evensongs, that of the day and of the Little Office. Finally, as the bells died away she entered the chapel to hear evensong chanted by the choir. When evensong was over she departed to supper, where the Duchess repeated to those around her the spiritual reading she had heard at dinner. With supper ended the time had come for the mistress of the household to spend the evening in familiarity with her ladies amidst happiness and mirth so long as the bounds of honesty were observed.

No ribald tapestries adorned the walls with scenes of courtly love manufactured for the Burgundian taste on the looms of Tournai. But a grave series set forth the Passion, the legends of St. John the Baptist, St. George, St. Mary Magdalen. Alone among them, the Wheel of Fortune stood out the solitary profane subject, but one which was so familiar to the age and not least to the mistress of the house, as to be endowed with a moral and almost sacred significance.[16] An hour before retiring Cicely refreshed herself with wine, doubtless from the little malmsey pot with the cover of silver and gilt which she afterwards bequeathed to Anne Pinchbeke. Thereupon she withdrew to prayer in her private apartments, where,

[15] Cf. the famous lines of Stephen Hawes, groom of chamber to Henry VII in the Passetyme of Pleasure, cap. xlii:

> "For though the day be never so long
> At last the belles ringeth to evensong."

Stephen Hawes, ed. W. E. Mead, Early English Text Society, no. 173, (1928), p. 208.

[16] Morelowski, Der Krakauer Schwaritter Wandteppich und Sein Verhältnis zu den französischen Teppichen des XV Jahrhunderts, Jahrbuch des Kunsthistorischen Institutes der K. u. K. Zentralkommission für Denkmälerpflege, 1912. Wills from Doctors' Commons, op. cit., p. 2.

taking leave of God for that night she was in bed once more by eight o'clock.

There is reason to believe that this was the actual cycle of daily life led by the widowed Duchess of York at Berkhamsted, her principal residence, or at Baynard's Castle within London, from which she beheld, with what emotions it may be conjectured, the accession of her sons Edward and Richard.[17] Her routine presented a rigid concentration on the Christian life.

But it might be asked, did the picture contain elements other than the conventional? As is well-known it was not uncommon in that day to hear more than one Low Mass of a morning;[18] the Office of the day, and to a greater extent the lesser Offices of Our Lady and of the Holy Cross, were said by many, as witness the great number of manuscript and printed primers. The chapel and its choir, which in the fifteenth century became more elaborate than ever, was an integral part of any noble household. All these things, it might be contested, Cicely observed out of dignity or respect for convention, just as she, like others of her rank, stayed at monastic houses for convenience or displayed friendship for the religious orders by taking out letters of confraternity.[19]

But on closer examination it grows increasingly hard

[17] In what degree Richard aspersed the honour of Cicely to further his own schemes of usurpation, and to what extent these aspersions were created by rumour, must remain a matter of doubt. Great Chronicle, ed. A. H. Thomas, London, 1938, p. 230. D. Mancinus, De Occupatione Regni Angli . . . ed. C. A. J. Armstrong, Oxford, 1936, pp. 12, 133. Polydor Vergil, Anglicae Historiae, ed. Thysius, Leiden, 1651, p. 692.

A dignified and even affectionate letter from Richard to his mother is printed by J. Gairdner, Richard the Third, (1898), pp. 189-90.

[18] Lady Margaret who rose at 5 o'clock heard 4 or 5 Masses before breakfast. English Works of John Fisher, op. cit., p. 294.

[19] Cicely stayed at St. Bennet at Holm in 1475. Paston Letters (library edition), ed. J. Gairdner, V. 236. Confraternity of the Benedictines granted to her in 1480. General and Provincial Chapters of Black Monks, ed. W. A. Pantin, vol. iii, (Camden Society 1937), p. 119. A benefaction by Cicely to the London Charterhouse posthumously recorded is mentioned by E. M. Thompson, Carthusian Order in England, London, 1930, p. 196. Her arms also appeared in a niche on the steeple of St. Bennet's, Pauls Wharf, engraved in Sandford, op. cit., p. 387.

to deny the inner spirituality and religious feeling which sustained the whole order of public and private observance centering around her person. If the spiritual exercises to which Cicely retired in the secrecy of her chamber must remain for ever unknown, the books which she cherished may reveal something. In her attachment to the peaceful consolations of devout literature the duchess was in keeping with a very prevalent spirit of the times; a spirit that is for ever preserved in the *Imitation of Christ.* "In een hoekje met een boekje" was a saying attributed to the Dutch founder of the Devotio Moderna, and it would seem to have distinct affinities with the meditation of Cicely and her contemporaries in England. Moreover, the works themselves to which she was so singularly attached that she listened to them, taught from them, and finally bequeathed them to her grandchildren, were of no miscellaneous kind. Indeed, they share in common such marked characteristics as to reveal a deep and personal love of mysticism.

In speaking of the "holy matter" read aloud at the Duchess's table the ordinance mentions in the first place *Hilton on Contemplative and Active Life and* then *Bonaventure.* Since no title was considered necessary to designate the work, it is natural to suppose that the best known of all those attributed to Bonaventure was intended. By far the most common and generally known was the *Life of Christ* which for long passed under his name, though it can no longer be regarded as the work of the Seraphic Doctor.[20] Not without reason did the ordinance cast together Hilton and Bonaventure, or pseudo-Bonaventure, as we should say. The author of the household relation observed details closely, for Cicely actually possessed the two treatises bound together in a single volume, which she bequeathed to her grand-daughter, Anne de la Pole, Prioress of Syon, as "a book of Bonaventure and Hilton in the same in English." This reference in her will would imply that the Bonaventure and Hilton were both alike in Eng-

[20] M. Deanesly, The Lollard Bible and other Medieval Biblical Versions, Cambridge, 1920, pp. 152 n. 2, 322-325.

lish. If so the former would almost certainly be *The Mirrour of the Blessed Lyf of Jesu Christ* by Nicholas Love,
prior of Mount Grace, a free translation of the accepted
Latin text of the pseudo-Bonaventure. It is probably true
to describe this book as more popular than any other in
the fifteenth century.

Nor was it quite fortuitous that Cicely should have these
two treatises united under one cover, nor that the two together should head the list of pious works read at her
table. Nicholas Love had translated the pseudo-Bonaventure with the double purpose of providing in the first
place a strictly orthodox work of edification, while at the
same time offering to the more spiritually adventurous an
introduction by which the mystical side of religion might
be approached. The charter house of Mount Grace was, as
the remnants of its library still attest, a fountain of mystical devotion, and until the Reformation this house of
the most secluded of religious remained a constant inspiration to the lay world. When Nicholas Love treats
of Mary and Martha, the customary commonplace to consider the merits of the two modes of life represented in
the story, he directly recommends the very treatise of
Hilton on the "medled lyf that is to saye sometyme actyf
sometyme contemplatyf as it longeth to dyverse persones
that in worldely astate haven grace of goostly love."[21]

Cicely had accepted and acted upon this advice, she who
availed herself so eagerly of every devotion and each pious
usage proffered by the Church had sought to approach the
mystical way by means of the most orthodox of manuals.
The Mirrour of the Blessed Lyf of Jesu Christ had been
submitted by its author to the approval of Archbishop
Arundel and recommended by him as appropriate reading
for the laity and as an antidote to insidious Lollardry.[22]
The book was soberly constructed with chapters appor-
tioned to the different days of the week, where narrative

[21] *The Mirrour of the Blessed Lyf of Jesu Christ*, ed. L. F. Powell, Oxford 1908, p. 165.
[22] Cf. Love's preface.

and meditation relieved one another, but its principal aim was to stir a deep affection for the person of the Saviour that culminated in the contemplation of the Passion. To Cicely and her contemporaries the Holy Name was the focus of a tender and overwhelming charity, and she reserved for the only one of her grandsons to enter the priesthood the legacy of a vestment of crimson satin for the Jesus Mass.[23]

The book of Hilton on "active and contemplative life" must have been of no small personal interest to the Duchess of York.[24] Addressed originally to a great lord living in the world it sought to prove how a life principally directed to prayer and meditation could be lived amidst the active duties of a secular existence. Far from disparaging the spiritual value in these latter, Hilton enjoined their punctual and conscientious fulfilment. A person placed in a position of authority who should ignore his duty to servants, tenants and fellow Christians to devote himself wholly to contemplation was likened to one who adorned the face of the Saviour always fair and left bare and unattended His suffering limbs.[25] But Hilton taught very clearly that worldly duties, however onerous, were spiritually of little or no worth if unaccompanied by that love for Our Lord to which the soul might best attain through humble yet assiduous prayer avoiding over-enthusiasm and the consequent dangers of disillusionment. His system, for all its ardour, and its demand for watching by night and

[23] Wills from Doctors' Commons, op. cit., p. 3. Humphrey was ordained an acolite by John Alcock, bishop of Ely, on 25 Sept. 1491 at Downham: he fervently begged to be ordained sub-deacon on the same day but this Alcock refused on the grounds that he was only 17 years old, and that two orders could not be conferred on the same day, though on this latter point authorities were not unanimous. William of Worcester Annals, apud Wars of the English in France, ed. J. Stevenson, Rolls Series, vol. ii, pt. 2 (1864), p. 792.

[24] Walter Hilton's Epistle on Mixed Life, critical edition in Richard Rolle of Hampole, ed. C. Horstman, ii vols., London, 1895, vol. i, pp. 264-292. An edition with modernized spelling in Minor Works of Walter Hilton, ed. D. Jones, London, 1929.

[25] This image comes originally from St. Augustine. D. Jones, op. cit., p. 29 note.

fasting by day, was reasonable and discreet, well calculated to appeal to the tranquil and orderly mind.

Of the other books recorded among Cicely's library two at least, the *De Infantia Salvatoris*[26] and the *Legenda Aurea* were predominantly narrative. The former was a short tract giving an apocryphal story of the infancy of Christ.[27] During Cicely's lifetime it was printed by Caxton, and though this edition only survives in one perfect example, a copy may well have belonged to her, who was unlikely to share the prejudices of the finer collectors against printed books. As a collection of short stories, miracles for the most part, it was well suited for public reading, and from the author's final words it may have been composed to some extent for this purpose:—
"Valeant diu in domino omnes legentes et audientes istum tractatum de infancia domini scriptum et completum quemadmodum a Judaeis persecutando didici et in ipsorum Judaeorum codicibus inveni."[28]

The *Legenda Aurea* is so familiar that it needs no comment. It contained those legends of the saints that for centuries had served to quicken the faith and refresh the imagination of Christians. Perhaps Cicely possessed both these works in Latin texts, though it should be noted that the *Legenda Aurea* continued to be known by this familiar name even when Englished.[29] However, the title *De Infantia Salvatoris* which is used by the household ordinance would suggest a Latin text, such as Caxton printed, and if she were to appreciate it Cicely must have understood something of Latin. Nevertheless it should not be assumed

[26] E. Gordon Duff, Fifteenth-Century English Books. Bibliographical Society, 1917, no. 222. Modern edition with introduction, W. Caxton's, Infantia Salvatoris, ed. F. Holthausen, Halle, 1891.

[27] R. Reinsch, Die Pseudo-Evangelien von Jesu und Maria's Kindheit in der romanischen und germanischen Literatur . . . aus Pariser und Londoner Handschriften. Halle, 1879, pp. 13-14, 124-138.

[28] Holthausen, op. cit., p. 22. The author of the De Infantia wilfully conceals his name out of modesty. "Nomen meum vobis non indicabo eo quod gloriam propriam non quero" ibidem.

[29] As in the English translations printed by Caxton and de Worde. Gordon Duff, op. cit., pp. 114-115.

that her knowledge of this language was in the least profound, even if it existed at all.[30]

It is, however, the three final items of reading, "St. Maude, St. Katherine of Senys, the Revelacions of St. Bridgett," that most attract attention when considered together. There is little reason to doubt that the "St. Maude" or "the boke of St. Matilde" as the Duchess refers to it in her will, is in fact the English translation of the *Liber Specialis Gratie* of B. Matilda of Hackeborn, known as the book of St. Maud or the book of Ghostly Grace.[31]

Matilda had lived as a Cistercian nun at Helfta in northern Germany in the thirteenth century. Her visions recorded in her lifetime, and with her consent, by two companions are among the most beautiful and delicate creations of German mysticism, and exerted an influence which ranged far beyond their time and country. B. Matilda was among the earliest mystics of the Sacred Heart; one of her first visions was to behold a pipe of gold springing from the heart of Our Lord. On another occasion she fell in a rapture of worship, and where she fell she found a cross from which proceeded a sharp dart that pierced her own heart.

The life of St. Catherine of Siena was most probably the English translation of her life written by her Dominican confessor, Raymond de Vineis. This text was sufficiently appreciated in England to be printed by Wynkyn de Worde about 1493 together with the life of St. Elizabeth of Hungary.[32] Admitting that the household ordinance dates from the last year of Cicely's life, this might be

[30] It seems safe to suppose that Cicely knew enough Latin to understand the liturgy and the rubric, according to St. John Fisher this was the case with Margaret Beaufort, who complained that she had never learnt Latin in her youth, though her tastes were probably more learned than those of Cicely. English Works of John Fisher, ed. J. E. B. Mayor, Early English Text Society, extra series, xxvii, 1876, p. 292.

[31] Liber Specialis Gratie printed in Revelationes Gertrudianae ac Mechtildianae, cura Solesmensium, ii vols., Paris 1877. MS. Bodlein 220 of the first half of the fifteenth century contains an English translation. The account of her life in the Allgemeine Deutsche Biographie provides a conspectus of her works and their diffusion.

[32] Gordon Duff, op. cit., no. 403.

a copy from de Worde's press, making another printed book in her possession.

But of the three mystical works the Revelations of St. Bridget was the one to affect England most deeply.[33] The visions of St. Bridget had certain affinities with those of B. Matilda, more especially in those passages where each alike described the state of former friends as they beheld their souls after death. But the literary remains of the Swedish princess, whose style had the vigour of a Hebrew prophet and the authority of a royal lady, were so much more powerful as to be of far greater interest in assessing Cicely's personal attitude to mysticism, and to a lesser degree that of the England of her day. The attraction of St. Bridget, exotic and almost terrifyingly austere, lay in the closeness of religious experience which her Revelations conveyed. This quality rather than any artifice in presentation produced the extraordinary realism of her visionary experiences. It can have been no quietist mysticism that could bear to contemplate the over-mastering grandeur of her embodiments of the sacred mysteries.

The little collection of books which Cicely is known to have kept supplies interesting evidence of the ties that united the monastic orders and the laity. It is easy to picture the fifteenth century as a period of increasing worldliness when the monasteries and the ideals they sheltered were receding from the notice of laymen. But again this view would exaggerate the disintegration of traditional unity: the ideal cohesion of society was still preserved, and owing to the remarkable expansion of devout literature in the later Middle Ages a larger public than ever before came to share in the spiritual treasure won in monastic solitude. St. Catherine of Siena, St. Bridget and B. Matilda of Hackeborn were essentially monastic saints, and their lives and visions had for the most part been recorded by those living under vows. Thus the literature

[33] The Revelations of St. Birgitta, ed. W. P. Cumming, Early English Text Society, no. 178, 1929. Survey of MSS. pp. xi-xxi the Revelations in England, pp. xxix-xxxix.

of mysticism conveyed monastic ideals to the faithful living in the world, with the result that the spiritual life of Christendom was still largely maintained by a holiness having its origins in monasticism.

In the fifteenth century those who were prevented by temperament or circumstances from entering religion yet strove to model their spiritual life on the virtues of the cloister. *The Abbey of the Holy Ghost* was written to teach those who were unable to leave the world how they might build an abbey in their soul and keep the rules of an order in their heart. A daughter of Cicely, Margaret of Burgundy, owned a copy of this particular work, and doubtless found in it that same consolation which her mother derived from her reading among the great mystics.[34] As the case of Cicely shows, monastic influences upon lay society, especially in its higher ranks, were pervasive if not easy to define. Remote yet almost close at hand, thanks to an abundant devotional literature, monasticism still defended in more ways than one the spiritual unity of society.

The cult of St. Bridget in England is an undeniable instance of monastic sanctity exerting a powerful appeal far beyond the narrow limits of a particular order. The clients of St. Bridget increased despite—perhaps because of—the fact that her cult was not rooted in any traditional or popular veneration of the English countryside. The devotion to her, in which notable Englishmen were among the first to participate, found a focus in the great double foundation at Syon for men and women living under the Augustinian rule reformed by St. Bridget. For the nuns of Syon, Thomas Gascoigne translated from the Latin a life of St. Bridget; and Syon in proximity to London and the royal residences had bestowed upon it the munificence of kings and noblemen.[35]

[34] *The Abbey of the Holy Ghost,* ed. G. Perry in Religious Pieces, Early English Text Society, 1867. L'Abbaye du Saint Esperit in Bodleian, MS. Douce 365 copied for Margaret at Ghent in 1475 by David Aubert.

[35] Cicely left to Syon "two of the best coopes of crymyson clothe of gold." (Wills from Doctors Commons, op. cit., p. 2). Her patronage was remem-

Unlike some famous monastic houses Syon did not possess within its walls the actual body of the order's founder, but it was in a true sense a great national shrine to St. Bridget. The cult of the Swedish saint was fostered not by numerous and popular centres, but by the whole power of monasticism concentrated with all its strength at a single spot.

It was owing to Cicely's love of her memory that the name of the Swedish princess was commemorated in that of an English royal child. When on the 11th November 1480 Cicely stood godmother at the christening of the tenth child and seventh daughter of King Edward IV, the infant grandchild of the Duchess received from her the name of Bridget.[36] Possibly Bridget had been vowed in her cradle to a religious life, or perhaps it was as a result of the misfortunes of her family and the change of dynasty that she entered the house of Dominican nuns at Dartford. This convent, where Elizabeth, a sister of St. John Fisher, also became a nun, enjoyed a great reputation for its strict observance of the Dominican rule. Dartford too, though less well known and documented than Syon, would seem to have been a centre of mysticism at this time.[37]

Cicely retained an affectionate interest in Bridget, who received the principal literary bequest under her will, the *Legenda Aurea* on vellum, the life of St. Catherine and the visions of B. Matilda. If it was natural to leave to her, a Dominican nun, the life of St. Catherine, it is witness to the insoluble link between the cult of St. Bridget

bered in the Syon obituary "the vii obit is in Ester . . . for alle frendis and benefactours and specialli for the duke Richard and Cecillie his spouse parenters unto kynge Edward (Aungier, History . . . of Syon, 1840, p. 527). Syon regarded Edward IV as its second founder after Henry V (ibidem). W. Pronger, Thomas Gascoigne, English Historical Review, LIII (1938), p. 624-25.

[36] A herald's account of the ceremony in British Museum, Add. MS. 6113 f. 59ᵛ printed by F. M. [adden], Gentleman's Magazine, 1831, pt. i, pp. 25 sqq.

[37] C. F. R. Palmer, History of Dartford Priory. Archaeological Journal xxxvi (1879), pp. 241-309 and A. G. Little, Victoria County History of Kent, vol. ii, pp. 181-9.

and Syon that the copy of St. Bridget's Revelations, Cicely left, not to her godchild Bridget, whose name would seem to give her the best title to it, but to another grandchild Anne de la Pole, Prioress of Syon.[38]

It was characteristic of a household whose whole routine rested upon the forms of religious observance, that the chapel should be sumptuously provided with an enormous number of precious vestments, ranging through every colour and material. The will of Cicely disposes of many complete sets of crimson cloth of gold and damask vestments accompanied by similar altar frontals and even, as in the case of those bequeathed to Fotheringay, of a canopy and supporters of like design.[39] The wealth of service books too is almost unending: missals, graduals, antiphonaries, processionals in profusion, besides gospels and epistolaries. To Fotheringay alone three missals, three graduals, three processionals, and to Stoke by Clare, the other great Yorkist foundation, four antiphonaries, four graduals and six processionals were bequeathed.

Numbers such as these, and many more service books are found among the minor bequests, denote a chapel where the office was performed on an exceptional scale judged even by the lavish standards of that age. But the liturgical books were not confined solely to the chapel, for in her closet where the Duchess heard her first Mass of the day, reposed a missal, a primer bound in blue velvet, and a psalter in white leather.

Cicely's whole heart was centred on worship both public and private, and her will reveals no great concern for the intellectual advancement of religion such as induced her daughter Margaret of Burgundy[40] or her cousin Margaret Beaufort to endow scholarships, lectureships and sermons. True it is, that among the beneficiaries of her

[38] Wills from Doctors Commons, op. cit., p. 3.
[39] Cicely's will is printed in extenso, ibidem, pp. 1-8.
[40] Margaret made her will at Malines October 21, 1503, only a small section is preserved in a copy made for the town of Malines, but it contains a bequest of 30 livres a year to keep a student of theology at Louvain, Lille, Archives du Nord, Chambres des Comptes. B. 458/17919.

will was St. Anthony's School, London, a foundation for which Henry VI must largely be given credit.[41] But Cicely left only an antiphonary with the rules of music at the end, clearly with the intention of assisting the song school attached to St. Anthony's for the training of future choristers in the praise of God and the melodious harmony of the chapel. The monastic houses to receive legacies were either those such as Fotheringay[42] and Stoke by Clare,[43] to both of which she was tied by long tradition of her family, and Syon which, as was seen, possessed a very special attraction, or else a foundation such as the Austin canons of Ashridge in relative proximity to her residence at Berkhamsted.

The mind of Cicely, inwardly devout, was not so much concerned to leave behind a monument of costly devotion or the memory of a patroness to erudition. The disposition of her goods took greater account of the traditional responsibility of a feudal lady for the members of her household. Her books of piety and mysticism she divided, as has been said, among her grandchildren for the most part. A psalter, in all probability the most sumptuous, went, together with a relic of St. Christopher, to her granddaughter Queen Elizabeth, and a portuous or breviary to Margaret Beaufort, also a king's mother. But the remainder of her collection with the exception of the tapestries, the proper hangings for rooms of state, was distributed among persons of much less standing. In this respect it is remarkable that her principal relic, the piece of the True Cross, set in a cross of silver gilt and beryl stones, famous for their curative virtue, went, not to one of her royal descendants but to a neighbour in Buckinghamshire, Sir

[41] Rose Graham, Order of St. Antoine de Viennois and its English Commandary St. Anthony in Threadneedle Street, Archaeological Journal, LXXXIV, 1930, pp. 341-407.

[42] Dugdale, Monasticon (1846), vol. vi, pp. 1411 sqq.; Tanner Notitia Monastica (1787), Northants xvi.

[43] Dugdale, Monasticon (1846), vol. vi, pp. 1415-23. Victoria County History of Suffolk, vol. ii, p. 147.

John Verney, attached like his father before him to the Yorkist cause.[44]

It is not surprising that Cicely should have possessed those aids to devotion, the rosary and the Agnus Dei, which with other pious usages propagated themselves with such rapidity at a time when the emotions were increasingly directed towards religion. The number of Agnus Dei is particularly striking; they include the great Agnus of gold with the figure of the Trinity, St. Erasmus and the Annunciation, an Agnus of Our Lady and St. Barbara, and ten others besides of the Trinity. So exceptionally large a collection was due probably to Master Richard Lessy, the steward of the Duchess and a Papal chamberlain,[45] who had brought them back from Rome. While the cult of the Agnus Dei[46] represents a definite stage in the formation of religious symbolism in the later middle ages, St. Erasmus would appear to have received a special honour in England,[47] and St. Barbara should be

[44] Nicholas Cusanus addressed his treatise De Beryllo to the Benedictine monks of Tegernsee, in which he distinguished between the superstitious use of the stone, and the legitimate exploitation of its supposed medical properties, which were not to be associated with religious rites. P. V. Redlich, Tegernsee und die Deutsche Geitesgeschichte im fünfzehnten Jahrhundert, Munich 1931, p. 95. Beryls frequently occur in English wills of the fifteenth century. Register of Henry Chichele, ed. E. F. Jacob, vol. ii (Oxford 1938), pp. 40, 119, 478. For Sir John Verney, vide the introduction Verney Papers, ed. J. Bruce, Camden Society, 1845.

[45] Richard Lessy described as a papal chamberlain in November 1483. Rymer, Foedera (1912), vol. xii, p. 206. Steward of the Duchess of York in 1495, Chronicles of London, ed. C. L. Kingsford, p. 204.

[46] History and bibliography of the Agnus Dei in article by E. Mangenot. Dictionnaire de Théologie Catholique, vol. I, (1923), cols. 605-613.

[47] References to the cult of St. Erasmus at this time are numerous though scattered: of the foundation by Queen Elizabeth Woodville of the St. Erasmus chapel at Westminster. D. MacGibbon, Elizabeth Woodville, London, 1938, p. 109. His statue was prominent among those on the walls of Henry the seventh's chapel. J. T. Micklethwaite, Notes on Imagery of Henry VII's chapel. Archaeologia xlvii (1881), p. 379. The life of St. Erasmus was printed by Notary in 1520, H. R. Plomer Wynkyn de Worde and his contemporaries, London, 1925, p. 175. St. Erasmus was among those saints habitually invoked by Englishmen, as would appear from the story of Henry Walter of Guildford who was wounded at sea c. 1484 and called upon St. Erasmus and Henry VI. Henrici vi . . . Miracula Postuma, ed. P. Grosjean. Brussels, 1935, pp. 98-101.

reckoned at this period among the most frequently portrayed of all the saints. Indeed, Memlinc actually painted St. Barbara under the features of Cicely's daughter Margaret Duchess of Burgundy.[48]

Besides a small rosary of amber Cicely owned one of the large and beautiful specimens which were beginning to appear in England.[49] This chaplet consisted of six sets of ten gold beads each, divided by six square enamel stones; both the large and small beads would be engraved with saints' figures. The rosary was completed by a cross of gold besides which hung a scallop shell of jet, this latter suggesting some pilgrim returned from St. James,[50] both were attached to the chaplet by a single chain of two large beads.

Among the various objects in the possession of Cicely one that calls for special mention is described in her will as "a cloth of St. John Baptist of sarcenett painted." This was probably a painted representation of St. John, most likely his martyrdom, upon which the eyes might rest while the mind was directed in prayer. In support of this interpretation it may be noted that Cicely had a particular regard for St. John, as witness the tapestry of his life which she left to the Duke of York, later King Henry VIII. Further, in making her will she commended her soul after Our Lady to the care of St. John Baptist, the traditional patron of the Yorkist foundation at Stoke by Clare.

[48] K. Künstle, Ikonographie der Christlichen Kunst, 2 vols., Freiburg i. B. 1926. vol. ii, p. 113. In the triptych of the Mystic Marriage of St. Catherine at the Sint Jansgasthuis, Bruges, Margaret perhaps appears as St. Barbara. M. O. Rubbrecht, L'Origine du type famillial de la Maison de Habsbourg, Brussels 1910, chap. 1.

[49] E. Maclagan & C. C. Oman, An English gold rosary of about 1500. Archaeologia, 1935, LXXXV, pp. 1-22. Englishmen were not indifferent to the great wave of devotion to the rosary sweeping the Rhineland. Sir Robert Plumpton a Yorkshire knight was enrolled in the confraternity of the Rosary of Our Lady of Cologne, Plumpton Correspondence, ed. T. Stapleton, Camden Society, 1839, p. 50.

[50] Perhaps from Anthony Woodville, Earl Rivers, whose visit to Compostella in 1473 is commemorated in his prologue to his translation of the "Dictes of the Philosophres." Prologues & Epilogues of William Caxton, ed. W. J. B. Crotch, Early English Text Society, no. 176, 1929, p. 112.

In this connection it should be remembered that King Henry VI was wont never to sit down to dinner without his almoner first placed before him a dish with the Five Wounds painted upon it which the king might contemplate devoutly.[51] The "cross cloth" which is mentioned in the will together with the cloth of St. John was probably some representation of the Instruments of the Passion which Cicely would gaze upon to incite the mind to the exercise of piety.

When the Duchess of York completed and signed her will at her castle of Berkhamsted on 31st May 1495 her strength was ebbing and her death expected at any moment.[52] But the mother of the House of York, as she commended her soul to God and to the protection of all the host of heaven, was still mindful of the loyal servants of her dynasty, not only in providing for them to the best of her ability, but in one case at least by a direct recommendation to the mercy of the reigning king. Richard Boyville, one of those who accompanied Margaret in 1468 to her wedding with Charles the Bold in Flanders and attended her twelve years later on her visit to England, could be sufficiently cared for by the legacy of a carriage, horses, various articles of clothing and jewellery for himself and his wife.[53] But Master Richard Lessy had involved himself in the treason which emanated from Flanders and proved fatal to Sir William Stanley and many others early in 1495.[54] To him was left a sum from certain Yorkshire revenues to assist in paying his fine to the Crown, with the trustful request that the king might graciously curtail the charge.

[51] J. Blakman, De Virtutibus et Miraculis Henrici VI, ed. M. R. James, Cambridge, 1919, p. 13.

[52] Grants of her lands in reversion were made early in 1495 as though in expectation of her early death. Calendar of Patent Rolls, 1494-1509, pp. 9-12.

[53] Lille, Archives du Nord, Compte de l'Argenterie, 1468, f. 159$^{\mathrm{r}\mathrm{o}}$. Calendar of Patent Rolls, 1477-1485, p. 217.

[54] Great Chronicle, ed. A. H. Thomas, London, 1938, p. 257. Chronicles of London, op. cit., p. 204.

On her death in June 1495[55] Cicely was laid in accordance with her wishes beside her husband Duke Richard in his tomb at Fotheringay College, where her arms, those of Neville, impaling England and France borne by Richard, decorated the windows of the choir. To the last a faithful daughter of the church, Cicely was buried with a papal indulgence tied about her neck with a silk ribbon. When her tomb was violated by the iconoclasts of the Reformation it was found fair and fresh in a fine Roman hand as if it had been written but the day before.[56]

[55] Chronicles of London, op. cit., 205.
[56] Sandford, op. cit., pp. 387-391.

The Meaning of Anthony Trollope

by CHRISTOPHER HOLLIS

THE HISTORY of Trollope's reputation has been most curious. Confidently acclaimed as the leading English novelist of his day some years before his death, in his last years he had already begun to decline in reputation. In his obituary notice the *Times* with the never-failing confidence of Printing House Square prophesied a rapid oblivion for his works. "It would be rash," said the pontiff, "to prophesy that his work will long be read; most of it lacks some of the qualifications which that stern official who draws up the passports for the Land of Matters Unforgot insists upon."

By the end of the century it seemed that the prophecy of the *Times* had proved itself correct. Herbert Paul, one of the most excellent critics of the day, wrote with complete confidence that Trollope was "not only dead but dead beyond all hopes of resurrection." A few years afterwards there came the first stirrings of a new spring. Leslie Stephen cautiously prophesied that, though to the writer no longer readable, yet Trollope might have a future. The high-brow poet and the lover of art would indeed no longer read him, thought Stephen, but he might be of interest to the social historian. Now today the tide is at its height. A librarian tells me that he lends out more of Trollope than of all other Victorian novelists put together. The Poet Laureate puts him into the small class of great English creators, and the world of the aesthete, which in his own day he had despised and which had despised him, now hails in him an artist, the superior of all his contemporaries.

The praise pours in from every quarter. He is the master of artists; he is the master of realists. The moralists hold up to us the wholesomeness of his teaching; the

aesthetes thank God that here was a man who was content
to tell a story and did not aspire to preach a sermon. The
lovers of the Autobiography hail a plain, blunt man who
called a trade a trade and was honest enough to confess that he plied it for money. Even the illiterate say
that he was, if not the most lovable of men, at least the
most lovable of writers (which is a very different story,
for writers are the least attractive of human beings). In
this cataract of praise, almost all of it deserved, if not quite
all of it self-consistent, they tend to overlook the one
deficiency, confessed to with characteristic honesty by
Trollope himself—that he did not know very much about
Anglican clergymen.

Trollope was in many ways the Dr. Johnson of the nineteenth century. A lady told him that he seemed to have
a very good appetite. "None at all," he replied, "but,
thank God, I am very greedy." It is genuine Johnson,
though crisp instead of rotund in phrasing. He resembled
the Doctor in many ways; and sometimes, where he differed from him, he differed from him in being the more
Johnsonian of the two. Thus Johnson clearly ought to
have drunk beer; Trollope did drink it. Johnson's admirers have sometimes even to this day to blush for his
rudeness; Trollope's admirers never have need to apolo-
gise. But at least in their John Bullishness the two were
much alike, and in nothing more alike than in their frank
refusal to pretend indifference to the monetary rewards of
literature.

> "Oh, Amos Cottle, for a moment think
> What meagre profits spread from pen and ink,"

ran Trollope's favourite quotation. All the world knows
that Dr. Johnson said that "no one but a blockhead ever
wrote except for money," and most of the world knows
the story of Trollope's engagingly clock-work and business-
like habits of work. But it has not, I think, been sufficiently
noticed that Trollope, like other people, was the child of
two parents, and of two parents, whose literary philoso-

phies, if one may call them so, were as poles apart from one another. Thomas Trollope spent his life in sordidly growing poverty, dismally compiling his absurd Ecclesiastical Encyclopaedia, which had little hope of ever being finished and no hope of ever obtaining a publisher, a royalty or a reader. Fanny Trollope, on the other hand, being in want of money at the age of fifty, sat down and wrote a book. Finding that it was both a pleasant and a moderately remunerative way of passing the time, she argued that what had been done once could be done again. Therefore she set to and wrote a hundred and fourteen more before dying in high spirits and comfortable circumstances at the age of eighty-three. Anthony had always a great, and on the whole justified, respect for her achievement.

Now Anthony inherited from both his parents. From his mother he inherited his sense of letters as a trade, of the necessity of striking a clear and business-like bargain for his work. Having written, he hawked to the best advantage, but it was far from the whole truth to say that he wrote merely for money. Dr. Johnson's *mot* is certainly a foolish falsehood; it neglects all those who have written from a sense of duty of one sort or another, and, though a high proportion of these may have been blockheads, it is surely a sweeping generalisation to say that they all have been so. But, beyond them, there are those who have suffered from the *cacoethes scribendi*, the nervous necessity which compels them to be for ever putting words down on paper.

The vast majority of the human race feels no great urge to write at all. Others write, when there is a motive for writing, whether the motive of the desire for money or that of having something to say. To both these classes the third class, that of those who must write, is quite unintelligible. Yet of its existence there can be no doubt. There are people who find themselves beginning to suffer from a sort of nervous derangement, if they cannot with fair regularity turn out their daily quota of words. It is the act of writing which their nature needs, and it needs it very much as the dipsomaniac needs a drink, or the inveterate smoker needs another cigarette. They must write, whether they write ill or well, whether they have at the moment anything to say or not. Such people often do not particularly like their own writing; they often try to break themselves of their habit and swear that this book is to be the last. But, like Omar Khayyam, they swore, but were they sober when they swore? Before they know where they are, they are always back again at the desk.

We all of us probably have acquaintances whose cupboards are filled with manuscript mounting manuscript, though they have long lost all hope of seeing the manuscripts in print. On the other hand there have been plenty of the sufferers from this disease, scattered through history, who have risen to high, if not to the highest, rank. A most obvious example in modern times is that of the Benson brothers. "I have nothing to write about," complained one Benson to another. "Then write a book about having nothing to write about," came the answer. And it was done, for what else are the Upton Letters but that? Petrarch was of this company, and Pope, and Southey. Such a man as Shakespeare was emphatically not of it, and had no difficulty, it seems, in drowning the book deeper than did plummet ever sound, when he had wrought with it sufficiently.

Yet this need to write has no particular connection either with literary excellence or the lack of it. It has one great advantage and one great disadvantage. On the one hand, a writer of any sort of competence is likely to progress to a certain capacity through mere abundance of practice. On the other hand, pruning is to him an agony. It is an interruption from getting on with further writing, and he finds it far easier to write four bad books than one good one.

Now there was never a more notable or more noble member of this strange class than Anthony Trollope. He wrote continually. He often wrote well, for he was a man of genius. But he as often wrote ill, for he had little power of self-criticism and indeed had a positive liking for always attempting new ventures to see whether he could achieve them rather than repeating that in which he knew himself competent. It was writing that he liked, not being read. Except for the money, he cared little whether he was published or not, and anyone who has ever read him in a first edition will know that he never bothered even to read his proofs properly. The stories are marred by endless mistakes concerning the Christian names and the relationships of his characters. His pride lay rather in the punctual performance of a covenanted task— whether of a self-appointed task to write so many words a day or of a contractual task to deliver a completed manuscript by a certain date. The story might, as chance dictated, be good or bad; what was unpardonable was that it should be late. "I finished on Thursday the novel I was writing," he tells his brother towards the end of his life, "and on Friday I began another. Nothing really frightens me but the idea of enforced idleness. As long as I can write books, even though they be not published, I think that I can be happy."

Now all this, it may be said, is most strange. And so indeed it is, for vanity is so nearly an universal failing that the man who lacks it, while he is the most blessed of beings, necessarily appears an eccentric. Yet eccentricity is not in itself more interesting than conventionality. We ask of a writer sincerity. But sincerity is not in itself enough. Sincerity is a moral virtue in a bore, but it is not a reason why we should read him. What is the quality in Trollope that has won for him his astonishing come-back? The question cannot be better answered than by an estimate of the debt which Mr. Belloc owes to Trollope.

The debt of Mr. Belloc to Anthony Trollope is immense and has been acknowledged with characteristic generosity by Mr. Maurice Baring, who has complained that he has never been able to get any of Trollope's books out of the London Library because they are always pre-empted

by Mr. Belloc. In Mr. Belloc's novels the insincerity of
the politicians is not demonstrated, nor even asserted; it
is simply taken for granted. Or, it may be, insincerity
is the wrong word. For insincerity implies a profession
which is false. In Mr. Belloc's novels there is no profession of a political faith. It is merely taken for granted
that politics is a trade and that the politician has no interest except in the emoluments that he can annex.

Now the inventor of that technique was Anthony Trollope. Trollope was ready enough to apply it to politics
when occasion served. His Giants and Titans are as nobly
nonsensical as any of the political parties of the Chester-
belloc. Yet it was of course the Anglican Church rather
than the politicians who received the full attention of
Trollope's satire. Before his day, as indeed since, there
had been pious writers and impious writers, pro-clerical
and anti-clerical, but there has never been another writer
so dominated by the bland assumption concerning clergymen, not so much that they were insincere as that they
were quite uninfluenced by their professed beliefs. Swift,
and others besides Swift, have used their satire to argue
that the party politics of religion were meaningless, but
Trollope's was in this a deeper satire. He is little concerned whether his clergymen are of the High or the Low
Church. He does not linger upon their beliefs, because
their beliefs are the least important thing about them.
What are important are their characters, and here Trollope
does not fall into the anti-clerical crudity of making them
all worse than other men. There are among Trollope's
clergymen good men and bad men, wise men and foolish.
But the importance about them is that they are not in the
least religious men. There is no motive from which they
act from which a man might not just as well have acted
had he never heard of the Christian religion. We are
given neither High Church nor Low Church propaganda,
for the characters are not shown as sufficiently interested
in the Christian religion to bother which school of theological thought is its correct interpreter. And, where there

are exceptions to this generalisation such as Mr. Crawley
and Mr. Fenwick, they are not made the more attractive
for being so.

Now all this would have been of little interest had
Trollope been an avowed enemy of religion, or on the
other hand had the Church of England of the mid-
nineteenth century been but "a mummer stuffed and dead."
It is of interest because neither of these things is true.
Trollope himself was an avowed Christian. When he was
the editor of the Fortnightly Review, he made it an explicit condition that no criticism of the Divinity of Christ
should appear in its pages. He was a decent man, writing,
if we are to believe his Autobiography, with a confessedly
didactic purpose. He will allow no suggestion that right
is not right and wrong wrong in the full traditional sense
—even if sometimes there is a good deal more wrong than
right in the scenes which he sees fit to depict—and, though
always ready to arouse sympathy with the sinner, he never
suggests a denial of the sin. If it would be too theological
a proposition for Trollope's taste to say that the wages
of sin was death, he was at least entirely certain that the
wages of folly was social embarrassment.

On the other hand, the Anglicanism of which he wrote,
was the Anglicanism of Pusey and Keble and Church—
the Anglicanism of an England in which Gladstone ruled.
It was an England in which it was no doubt possible to
find Archdeacon Grantleys, but the suggestion that it
was an England populated by Archdeacon Grantleys was
an absurdity. Trollope could only draw it so because, as
he frankly confessed, "I never met an Archdeacon." We
may approve or disapprove of the great Anglican divines
of the mid-nineteenth century, but we cannot seriously
suggest that they were not interested in theology. Trollope is a great realist in the sense that, granted that the
characters are as he depicts them, the development of the
plot contains no improbabilities. And his characters, we
will admit, are possible, but there is a great violence to
probability in suggesting that they are typical.

Trollope's own defence of himself was of course perfectly simple. He was a Christian but he was not a Churchman. He thought that Christ was God but did not think that He had founded a Church. The sacramental side of religion was without meaning to him. This is clearly not the place for a criticism of such a faith. It is for the moment rather more important to ask why the Anglican clergy of his day were not more anxious to refute it. Why did they not resent Trollope's portrait of themselves?

The Church of England in Trollope's time still possessed considerable external dignity. How enormous, for instance, has been the decline in the part played by clergymen in the lives of the Universities! What is a Canon of Christ Church today compared with what he was in 1870? But, apart from external dignity, it then produced, as indeed it does today, many lives of piety and learning and indeed of holiness. It was not yet the fashion to deny its teaching. None of Trollope's clergymen, for instance, would have dreamed of adding to his income by publicly attacking the doctrines of Christianity. Such a solecism would have seemed intolerably ill-bred, and the highest praise which he will give to his favourite among them, the Bishop of Elmham, was that he "was never known to declare" them.

But on the other hand under the assaults of Whiggery, of revolution and agnosticism, of aristocracy and democracy, Anglicanism had already lost its nerve. The Church allowed the tacit assumption that the problems of the world could be settled without any overt appeal to Christian principles to go unchallenged. They could be settled, of course, only because men had in them a very fair quantity of general decency, and it was the private opinion of pious Christians that this decency was the product of generations of Christianity, that, had there been no Christianity, people would have been far less decent. But that was a private opinion. It would have been bad manners to insist upon it too loudly or too frequently. The great essential fact which nobody could deny was the existence of decency. People were decent; and, since in addition to Christianity there was also progress, it was confidently assumed that with the passage of time they would grow more decent still.

It was this combination of a feeling of the security of society with an inferiority complex about their own position which was responsible for the clergy's absence of resentment at Trollope's portrait of them. It would have been bad sportsmanship, they felt, not to join in a laugh against themselves, and, as for the intricacies of theology, they had been taught by experience that that was shop and that laymen were easily bored by such topics. And anyway why did it matter since in any event things were destined to progress? It is this final complacent assumption which is always the mark that, as Bishop Blougram would put it, "signifies some faith's about to die." The England of Trollope was very soon to become the England of Jowett—an England in which the Christian doctrines were going to be explicitly attacked by persons receiving the emoluments of Christian ministers.

Trollope's own anti-clericalism was far from Voltairean. He did not dislike the Anglican clergy because they were priests. It never occurred to him for a single second that they were priests. He knew that the Catholic priest, Father Barham, in *The Way We Live Now* thought of himself as a priest and he disliked him heartily for doing so, but it never occurred to him that the Anglicans even thought of themselves as priests. Nor did he dislike them as tyrants over the mind. The possibility of such a tyranny was hardly present to him. There is no trace in all his works of anybody believing anything because a clergyman said it. His criticism of the clergy was entirely a social one. They were a guild, or more colloquially a "gang," and, as such, funny.

It is interesting to see Trollope's conception of a likeable clergyman. The popularity of the Barchester novels has caused readers to overlook the much more flattering portrait of the Bishop of Elmham. "He laboured at schools, and was zealous in improving the social comforts of the poor," runs his character, "but he was never known to declare to man or woman that the human soul must live or die for ever according to its faith. Perhaps there was no bishop in England more loved or more useful in his diocese than the Bishop of Elmham." "Then it occurred" to Roger Carbury "that he had known the Bishop of Elmham intimately for a dozen years and had never heard from the bishop's mouth—except when in the pulpit— a single word concerning religious teaching; whereas this man, who was a stranger to him, divided from him by the very fact of his creed, was always talking to him about his faith. Roger Carbury was not a man given to much deep thinking, but he felt that the bishop's manner was the pleasanter of the two."

Mr. Belloc has given the opinion that Lewis Carroll's art is essentially the art of a stable society and that with social disintegration such a work as Alice in Wonderland can hardly survive. Trollope's art was the art of a stable society—of a society in which authority could be mocked at with good-natured impunity, for the foundations were not in peril. It would all last his time anyway. But, saying that, we must draw a distinction. We are apt to divide the world into those who believe in imminent catastrophe and those who believe in indefinite progress towards rosy dawns. Trollope was of neither class. His opinion was that things would go on somehow, that they were remarkably good fun but that they were getting worse. They were getting worse because of progress.

In that remarkable and somewhat strangely overlooked novel, *The Way We Live Now,* written in 1873, Trollope preached this gospel. It was progress itself—what men called progress—which was the evil. It was good communications which were corrupting good manners. A world in which people were for ever rushing about, in which false pride was for ever tempting people to live beyond their means and therefore bringing them to the clutches of usury, in which industry was ousting agriculture and finance was ousting industry, where "the wrong Jews came ever more blandly to the right houses,"—this was to Trollope the world of the eighteen seventies. In opposition to what the social historians would tell us he found this debauched and disintegrating society in contrast to a stricter and more nearly golden age which he thought had preceded it.

It may be objected that, for all his praise of the stationary life, Trollope was himself an inveterate traveller. It may be objected that laments over the evils of the times are the stock-in-trade of most writers, and of mid-Victorian writers in particular. There is nothing that Trollope said that cannot be paralleled in Matthew Arnold, or Tennyson for all his optimism, or even in Carlyle whom Trollope detested. It may be objected, too, that Trollope came afterwards to say that *The Way We Live Now* was an exaggerated book, and indeed it is certainly true that the characters are, in their want of private affection, odious beyond the capacity of human nature.

Yet an allowance must be made for it that Trollope always deprecated his own work so as to make certain that none should ever consider him as a major prophet. The truth is that it is a remarkable, and indeed somewhat prophetic, novel. The Barchester novels are treasured for their Victorianism. In *The Way We Live Now* Trollope sketched out the shape of things to come. The vices are the vices generally associated with an Edwardian rather than a Victorian society, and indeed in the young men of the Beargarden we find a fatuity in vice that is even Georgian and post-war rather than Edwardian. In the parties of Lady Monogram those of Lady Metroland are found casting their prevenient shadow.

It was not so much that people like Lady Carbury, the lady writer who racketeers the press in order to get reviews, did not exist in Victorian England as that they do not elsewhere appear in Victorian novels. One has only to delve into the private letters of Dickens or the essays of Macaulay to find that the Victorians had little to learn from the moderns in these arts. But they did not wash their dirty linen in public. Victorian writers had a much higher sense than the moderns of the esoteric companionship of letters. They had none of the modern readiness to let the public in on the game. They exposed mercilessly all abuses save those upon which writers flourished.

Trollope, alone of the great Victorian writers, had none of this sense of membership of a mystic fraternity. On the contrary, his strongest moral feeling was that of a dislike of a caste, which, as he thought, tried to impose itself upon society. If he was not an anti-clerical, he was at any rate always a pro-laical. In so far as he disliked clergymen, it was because he thought of them as the defenders of an entrenched monopoly. For the same reason he disliked lawyers, money-lenders, politicians. He disliked the reforms in the Civil Service which would give birth, he thought, to a new caste, the bureaucrat, as ready as any other caste to give itself airs and exploit the public. And, disliking all other castes, he had no wish to exempt his own from the general censure. He disliked writers and took an especial pleasure in exposing the tricks of their trade.

Now it is not hard to think of arguments by which such an attitude can be attacked. He can perhaps be accused of fouling his own nest—and a nest which had served him for a long time as a very satisfactory and remunerative refuge. And the enemy might perhaps plead that he did not give evidence of that high singleness of moral purpose which could alone justify such ruthlessness. Be that as it may, one Anthony Trollope in a literary world, where the faults of almost all other writers were of exactly the opposite nature, was a good, healthy corrective. It was the argument of the young Morleyan radicals, with whom he quarrelled, that a world in which everything was settled by free speech would be an equal world, where none would have an unfair advantage over another. On the contrary, said Trollope, it would give a most unfair advantage to those who happened to be able to speak best—

an arbitrary class, who had no more inherent likelihood of being right than aristocrats, or landowners or the inheritors of mining royalties. It was an argument that would have been tiresome had it become overwhelmingly popular, but it was a wholesome corrective to society that there should be one man of genius to advance it in an age which had not yet learnt to distinguish between intellectualism and intelligence as clearly as our later tragedies have compelled us to do.

In party politics Trollope called himself a dissident liberal—principally because he disliked change and rightly thought that under Disraeli the Conservatives would make many more changes than the Liberals. He disliked that "happy mixture of radicalism and old-fogyism, of which we have lately heard from a political master, whose eloquence has been employed in teaching us that progress can only be expected from those whose declared purpose it is to stand still." He was in truth profoundly sceptical of all systems; his mind was dominated by the healthy conviction that men mattered a great deal more than measures. He disliked radicalism, for the very sensible reason that he disliked radicals. Not caring greatly what were the principles they professed, he asked himself whether these were men of a sort to know what happiness was or likely to give it to others, and he answered his question in the negative.

There is something profoundly satisfying when in a world of doctrinaires we come across one who judges a man as a man rather than as an exemplification of a formula. To do so is in itself neither Toryism nor Whiggery, neither radicalism, communism, nor fascism. We find this happy virtue in a radical like Burns, in a Tory like Johnson or in a very conservative sort of liberal like Trollope. We can find equally the absence of it in men of every creed.

Such was Trollope. Death came to him at last in the strangest of all manners—as strange and as typical of the life of this strange man as anything can be. He died, quite literally, of laughing at Anstey's *Vice Versa*.

If we consider him as an intellectual, we may judge that the cause was inadequate; if we consider him as the possessor of an immortal soul, we may judge it unworthy. The transmigrations of Mr. Bultitude are not substitutes in meditation for the Four Last Things. Yet it is well that we should have examples at the highest even of that which is inadequate. Here was a man to whom the high mystic moments and the great poetic inspirations meant nothing. Yet it is a great thing to love horse-back and the open air, generosity, hospitality, the life of the village, the companionship of neighbours, "slaughter and the love of friends." All these Trollope loved, and he hated whatever was at enmity with them. And it is not surprising that in these disintegrating times men are turning more and more for comfort to this great mocker of the follies. There are deeper truths that they will not learn from him. But it is at least a sign of health if they turn to one who never bowed his knee to the pomposities, the sophistries and the presumptions, still less to "the puerilities and the despairs."

Byzantium to Oxford

by GERVASE MATHEW, O.P.

A GROUP of Oxford manuscripts suggest an unexpected link between the twelfth-century Byzantine court in its effortless sophistication and the early years of the University with the quick clamour of its city schools. It might seem an improbable relationship. In the year 1200 even the fragments of the Byzantine Empire still retained something of the artificiality of an ancient and secure civilisation, patterned in thought and specialised in perception. At Oxford, the thirteenth century University with its crudeness, its freshness and its dawn-like assurance of the efficacy of its own values, might have seemed too remote for contact. Yet the manuscript evidence appears to imply a vital influence from medieval Constantinople on the thought forms in that small surging northern town.

A Corpus Plato[1] contains a translation of the *Phaedo* and the *Meno* composed for Robert of Cricklade Prior of St. Frideswides, by Henry Aristippos who had been employed in Constantinople at the court of Manuel I Comnenos. It marks the first coming of the Platonic *Dialogues* to the west through the chance contact of an Oxford patron. It was to be cited in the University by the Franciscan John of Wales. Richard of Bury knew it. With the Tudors the manuscript was to pass with so much else that was esoteric into the private library of Dr. Dee. Its more effective influence lay in Italy, for a copy gained from the Dominicans by Coluccio Salutati was to be among the sources of Florentine Platonism. In contrast, a Corpus Aristotle[2] represents the most dynamic of the influences on thirteenth-century Oxford. It is a twelfth-century Byzantine manuscript, glossed in late Comnenian

[1] Corpus Christi College MS. 243. ff. 115V-135V; ff. 184V-193V.
[2] Corpus Christi College MS. 108.

Minuscle and with Latin annotations in a thirteenth-century English hand. It is significant that it consists primarily of the *Animalia,* for it is tenable that the impact of the new Aristotelianism was due primarily to its conception of a material world order, subsistent not merely symbolic, intelligible in itself precisely because in itself real, a fit object for a human *scientia* precisely because in itself intelligible.

A similar interest in the ordered laws of phenomena marks the *Liber Thesauri Occulti* in Digby MS. 103. This contains citations from the *Animalia* but it seems primarily based upon a twelfth-century Byzantine treatise on dream interpretations. A note in a late twelfth-century hand states that it was compiled at Constantinople in 1165.[3] The same volume contains a Latin version of the *Oneirocriticon.*[4] The translator elaborately neo-Classic in Latinity is clearly not identical with the author of the *Liber Thesauri Occulti* but possesses the same range of interests and his work also can be dated with exactness. He held some Byzantine court appointment for he styles himself Interpreter of the letters of the Augustus and he notes that his preface is composed as he is following the unconquered Emperor Manuel through the confines of Bithynia and Lycaonia; since he also mentions the condemnation of the philosopher Demetrius of Lampe in 1166, this can only refer to the campaign before Myriokephalon, ten years later. The *De Virtute Aquilae* of a certain Willelmus Anglicus can also be connected with the court circle of Manuel I Comnenos through its obvious reliance on the Kirannides. It has been preserved both in a manuscript at Merton and in Bodley MS. E Museaeo 219.[5] It seems to be in part identical with a much longer treatise the *Liber Kirannis* in Ashmole MS. 1471.[6] This is an elaborated study of the effects and properties of herbs

[3] Digby MS. 103 f. 41.
[4] Digby MS. 103 ff. 59-127V.
[5] f. 138V seq.
[6] f. 143V seq.

and stones and stars and its preface closes with the note "Transfertur itaque liber iste Constantinopoli Manuele imperante."[7]

All four treatises are governed by that taste for the slightly occult and for the less obvious explanation of phenomena which marked the late Comnenian court. But it is not their explanations but the conviction that it is possible to explain that has significance. It is this that marks the rediscovery of Nature in the West. Beyond them lay that thirteenth-century English movement always aspiring if frequently fantastic which finds expression in the works of Roger Bacon. Behind them lay the setting of the Imperial palace and that serene Byzantine zest for a Nature, frozen and transmuted; the small rooms with their walls mosaicked with flowers, the floors strewn with rosemary and myrtle, the golden pineapples and the enamelled birds in the trees of gilded bronze.

In the twelfth-century Byzantine court there is no evidence of that overburdened consciousness of moral tension which had been an Augustinian legacy to the West. But an interest in the natural properties of jewels, of herbs or of the planets was combined with much lucid speculation upon Ethics conceived as the laws that govern human action and give purpose and therefore structure to a society or a state. There was nothing incompatible between such studies. Both presupposed a conception of the intelligibility of nature, a conviction of the causality of law and a world view of hierarchic order. Both reflect the underlying serenity of that self-concentrated Byzantine culture with its recognition of the dominance of the Idea and of the rule of cool and temperate mind.

Balliol MS. 116 represents this trend in speculation. This contains the commentaries on the *Nicomachean Ethics* composed by the twelfth-century Byzantine philosopher Eustratios of Nicaea and includes three books of commentary by an eleventh-century philosopher of the court circle, Michael of Ephesus. It has been established

[7] Ashmole MS. 1471. f. 144.

that it is a Latin version of a single Byzantine Manuscript brought to England in the thirteenth century and
translated there by members of the Grosseteste circle
about the year 1250. It has been suggested that it was
acquired for Bishop Grosseteste by Nicholas the Greek,
a scholar in his employ. Nine leaves at the end of a thirteenth-century manuscript at Merton were filled in with
rough notes, perhaps by Master Richard Burnell an early
Fellow of the College.

Professor Powicke has established that they emanate
from the Grosseteste circle[8] and presuppose work in the
bishop's household upon the Greek of Eustratios. They
begin with an explanation of his conception of the State
and a phrase from the first gloss may perhaps convey
some of the impact of the new concepts on an English
milieu; Policeia dicitur a polis que est civitas pro quo
nomine translatores ponunt hoc nomen urbanitas vel
civilitas. As late as 1412 Amplonius was to refer to the
"divine Eustacius" and to "that great philosopher the
Ephesian Michael." They would seem to have retained
authority in Oxford. Robert Kilwardby cites them and in
the reign of Edward III they lie as basic sources behind
the *Commentary on Ethics* by Walter Burley. Theirs had
been a curious transition. Their too-clear, too-analytic
thought had had its share in the intimacies of the bishop's
manor house at Buckden and in the simple direct delibera-
tions of the ecclesiastical advisers of De Montfort. But
the setting of each depersonalised analysis of human motive had been the decor of the Byzantine court; the blue
silk robes tight girdled, the scented tapering beards, the
harsh cosmetic, and the great officials holding in their
hands the red enamelled apples of their rank.

Primarily it had been stray contact that had linked
together such divergent cultures. Historical accident had
rendered possible a sporadic Byzantine influence in the
North. In the mid-twelfth-century a phase of acute cultural receptivity in Western Europe had coincided with

[8] Cf. F. M. Powicke, "Robert Grosseteste and the Nicomachean Ethics."

the new orientation of the Byzantine state under John II and Manuel I Comnenos. The elaborate system of alliance North and West, first perhaps clearly evolved under John II had reached its full development with his son. The reign of Manuel I from 1143 to 1180 at least provided all the necessary conditions for the exercise of a Byzantine cultural influence in a Latin milieu. The Danube route had at last been cleared by the campaigns against the Petchenegs, northward the empire bordered Hungary, westward the Norman kingdom of Sicily, partly Byzantine in its culture, so closely linked in policy with the eastern Mediterranean, formed a natural bridge to the Anglo-Norman world. Robert of Selby had been the Sicilian Chancellor, Simon of Apulia was the "amicus carus et familiaris" of Henry II, John of Salisbury had acquired in Norman Italy such Greek as he possessed. The *Physics*, the Fourth Book on Meteors, the *De Anima*, part of Euclid, part of Ptolemy and the *Mechanics* of Hero of Alexandria came northwestward from Byzantium by the Sicilian route.

By chance the Cartularies of St. Frideswide, the Icelandic Thomas Saga Erkibyskups and a preface by Henry Aristippos combine to explain the passage of the Platonic Dialogues to Oxford. The Cartularies show that Prior Robert of Cricklade was present at the papal court on the 26th of February in 1158;[9] he had gone from Oxford to Italy on business of his house, apparently connected with an Osney lawsuit. A letter from him preserved in the Thomas Saga refers to a journey along the coast road from Catania to Syracuse.[10] Aristippos mentions him as close to Syracuse and about to return to England.[11] Aristippos had only lately returned from Constantinople, he had acquired a manuscript from the Imperial library and possessed a Byzantine approach both to fit subjects for study and to his patron; he offered Robert of Cricklade

[9] Cartulary of St. Frideswide 1.27. no. 23.
[10] Thomas Saga Erkibyskups cap. CXI.
[11] Corpus Christi College MS. 243 f. 115V.

treatises on optics and mechanics as well as the *Phaedo* and styled himself his whetstone not his blade.

It is rare to find such unbroken links of evidence for the passage of any text. But the presence of Byzantine manuscripts in medieval England seems primarily the sequel of unplanned, sporadic and essentially personal contacts. Already by 1176, Digby MS. 103 would seem to suggest a more direct relation with the Comnenian court. In the thirteenth-century the Archdeacon of Leicester John of Basingstoke claimed to have learnt more at Athens than at Paris and William of Faversham was a bishop in the Peloponnese, at least one manuscript can be shown to have come directly to the West from the small Greek court at Nicea between 1222 and 1254.[12] But a statement by Roger Bacon would imply that the normal manuscript route to England was still held to pass through what had once been Norman Italy.[13] Yet the significance of the passage of a manuscript from Byzantium to Oxford does not lie in the material details of its coming. It is only when it is considered as a passage from one culture to another utterly divergent that it can convey something of that receptivity that marked the formative phase in medieval English thought.

The twelfth-century Byzantines were still the conscious inheritors of an Hellenic tradition, frozen and formalised. It was a heritage which inevitably coloured their conception of any possible relation to Barbarians. The *Alexiad* thus describes a conflict with the Normans "but the Caesar's bow was indeed the very bow of Apollo and he did not after the manner of the Homeric Greeks draw the string but like a second Herakles" and again "the Queen still stayed in the palace for she was anxious about the fair haired Menelaus as the poet says." This was a convention that provided a sufficiently decorous setting for the pursuit of polite philosophy and good letters; "I perused the works of Aristotle and the dialogues of

[12] Vat. MS. gr. 60.
[13] Roger Bacon, "Compendium Studii Philosophiae" cap VI.

Plato carefully and enriched my mind by the quaternion of learning."[14] For the medieval Byzantine this approach to "the portals of Aristotelian philosophy and symbols of Platonic teaching"[15] was governed by a very accurate estimate of Attic style and combined with an appreciation of natural beauty when sanctioned by epithet and sufficiently ordered; "the gracious gold flowered crocus, the anemone; the narcissus gleaming whiter than the snow."[16] Both led to the creation of types of philosopher which had no counterpart in the medieval West.

A description by Michael Psellos in his *Chronographia* perhaps conveys the ideal of his milieu. Constantine Leichudes, he notes, acted always philosopherwise, "he was a man of noble birth, possessed of great eloquence, ready and prepared for every shade of meaning, and moreover accurately versed in affairs of state. . . . He had moreover something harmonious and distinctive about him especially when he was proclaiming the Imperial Decrees as from on high."[17] A rather different impression of a late twelfth-century philosophic underworld is suggested by the satires of Theodore Prodromos; "when he was studying he did not know the entrance to the Baths but now he takes the Baths three times each week. Once he possessed fleas as great as almonds and now gold pieces with Manuel's effigy upon them."[18] Neither the Ideal nor the Real was paralleled among the Oxford scholastics. The contrast lay not only in the change of personalities and in the absence of tradition but in a divergent approach to knowledge.

There is much definite if often unreliable evidence for some familiarity with Greek in thirteenth-century England but with the possible exception of the case of John of Basingstoke it was probably superficial enough. Even Robert Grosseteste would seem to have been de-

[14] Anna Comnena. Preface to the Alexiad.
[15] Michael Psellos Chronographia lll. 3.
[16] Johns Geometres, On the Spring (P.G. 106. col. 984. cf. col. 857).
[17] Chronographia VI. 178.
[18] Prodromic to Manuel Comnenos (ed. Hesseling and Pernot p. 73).

pendent for the niceties of translation on the Greek
scholars in his employment. It is difficult to conceive of any
English scholastic who could find his pleasure in the
Phaedo or who would associate philosophy and good letters, nor were there any of the associations with an im-
memorial yet remembered past. "Plato," "Aristoteles,"
"Eustacius" came to them as auctoritates outside time
sequence, immediate and actual; it was the purpose of
philosophers to satisfy the desire to know. The career of a
teacher in an English "studium," already professionalised,
ecclesiastical in its rewards, provided the stiff framework
of their studies.

Adam of Buckfield is possibly the most significant of
thirteenth-century Oxford philosophers. He was the first
in England to comment upon the *Metaphysics*. He had acquired the new conception of the range of learning and
lectured not only *De Anima* but *De Plantis*. It is only very
recently that he has been rediscovered but all the details
known of his life suggest a certain monotony in its setting;
the Oxford riots of 1238 in which he was involved, his
presentation to the living of Rumgeton three years later,
his rectorship of the church at Iver, the canonry, official
business with the nuns at Marlow, the law suit for his
rights to common pasture. The years of his teaching and
speculation were passed among the crooked alley ways
of a pre-collegiate Oxford, the low booths, the narrow
wooden houses and the rain. It had been a life with
limited if clear horizons. Only once is it known to have
been linked with action; 1238, the riot by the river and the
murder of the Legate's cook at Osney. Temporal achievement would come slowly; the years of study and of dis-
putation against the background of some crowded garret,
the mastership, the lease of a lecture-room above an alley,
some revenue from a chance benefice and then perhaps
at last the signs and privilege of established status, the
house of substance with stone undercroft, the long dark
woollen surcoats and fur tippets, security and adequate
respect. But he had been trained to memorise and to argue,

and seeking learning had found certitude. In thirteenth-century Oxford the study of philosophy was primarily dynamised by a desire to know; avid, essentially individual, freely satisfied.

The court philosophers in Byzantium, secular by association, depersonalised in their approach to study, were primarily intent on the perpetuation of a heritage. For them a treatise in philosophy was linked with good letters rather than theology. A consciousness of past thought, conceived as corporate rather than as individual, some scepticism, and a certain irony, led easily to a serene but light acceptance of conclusions that were apparently divergent. A panegyric on Eustathios of Thessalonica, composed shortly before the year 1200, notes that he had been peripatetic both in the groves of Academy and in the Porch, a Byzantine mind, darting and uncertain was repelled by crude form and statement; the eternity of a transcendent truth seemed best expressed by remote formulae, imperfectly revealing. A phrase of Michael Psellos is suggestive; "when you have stolen from intelligence the incorporeal quality in things and have realised the light within the body of the sun then you will turn with keenest vision to the incorporeal itself." The laws of thought were static like the laws of rhetoric. Byzantine speculation like Byzantine Art remained evocative not representational.

The Cloud of Unknowing could not have been written save in a medieval English milieu. Yet it is directly dependent on the commentaries by Vercellensis on Pseudo-Dionysius still preserved in manuscript at Merton. Behind it lies a pure Byzantine concept "the ray of the Divine Darkness."[19] So behind many of the certitudes of medieval Oxford lay a Byzantine heritage, texts and the commentaries upon texts and a vision of an intelligible world order. For Oxford came to being through a characteristic common to all thirteenth-century western culture; the power to receive and then transform.

[19] Merton College MS. 69.

The Library at Naworth

by DAVID MATHEW

Lord William Howard was now old, and a hard life had
increased through the years that self-sufficiency which had
always marked him. He had been born to the share of a
great heritage, and a keen appreciation of the qualities of
generous blood had only been emphasized by the misfortunes of his house. His father and his grandfather had been
sacrificed by the English sovereigns, victims of their own
unskilfulness in the face of the Renaissance monarchy.
His mother had died at his birth and his father on the
scaffold some nine years later. It is not surprising that
there was a vein of hardness in Lord William Howard and
that his antiquarian tastes served as a foil to a character
which was at once courteous, watchful and ungentle. To
an extent very rare in his own day he maintained a reso-
lute privateness of life carried through on a scale of some
magnificence and marked by a curiously complete detachment.

Towards his successive sovereigns Lord William's attitude was very clear and cold. Yet he was rightly trusted
and he had an unbiassed loyalty on which the Stuart Kings
could place a calm reliance. Hot views were most distaste-
ful to him, whether they were those of Sir Walter Raleigh
or of Father Parsons. The dignity of his order and the
qualities of a *grand seigneur* meant very much to him.
He was a collector rather than a patron; very conscious of
his obligations. The role of a great landowner came to
him easily and there is some reason to suppose that he
had a justified and hard confidence in the political future
of the landed families. It is less easy to determine whether
he was convinced that Catholicism would be maintained in
his own country.

He was by choice a Catholic, and there was added to

his conviction an interest in religious things which deepened with the years. He was attached in a measured fashion to the Benedictines; attracted by the mystical writers; independent; a trace self-conscious. It is obvious that he viewed the Anglican church order without prejudice or the least trace of hostility. As a young man he had endeavoured to make good his right of presentation to Greystock parsonage. He supported the oath of allegiance in King James' reign, and he provided the bread and wine for the communion service at Cumwhitton Church. The impression is conveyed that he saw the Established Church move forward as an appanage of that new State which was to him both irresistible and welcome.

He cherished his Catholic faith in privacy, and in the accounts of the great household[1] which he ruled in his later years there are hardly any entries which refer to the proscribed worship with any certainty. There are purchases of candles and silver bells and a curious entry of xxvijs.jd received in exchange for an old chalice. A considerable sum was paid for garnishing a picture in crystal of St. Ignatius. But it is clear that Lord William and his steward both intended that it should not be possible to distinguish the devotional from the artistic uses. The outline of his slight public service alike reflects the same fixed caution and security. Cornelius Jansen has left an interesting portrait of Lord William Howard in which the long and bearded face, with the high forehead and the nose with its coarse modelling, is rendered remarkable by the dark eyes at once commanding and very watchful.

His only published work was his translation of Florence of Worcester and he was jealous of his Latinity. There was in fact one aspect from which he could be regarded as over-educated in the sense of Castiglione's *Il Cortegiano*. His phrasing in English was very forceful and marked by an almost Predestinarian bias. It did not appear to him that there was need to expect that God

[1] *The Household Books of the Lord William Howard of Naworth Castle*, ed. Rev. George Ornsby, Surtees Society 1878.

should show much mercy. For twenty years he had had
to struggle against first the Dacres and then the Lowthers
who tried in vain to bar his way to his wife's inheritance as
co-heiress of the great Border family of the Lords Dacres
of the North. In this connection a sentence from his narrative of this conflict, which is written in the third person,
will throw light upon Lord William's views. "The former
firebrand Gerard Lowther," he wrote,[2] "did again stir
up the coales, for now to his former ambitious and
covetous humour he had also united and added infinite
malice, being taught by his Master Machevyll to stryke
home, and synk deep enough under the water, the Earl
of Arundel and Lord William Howard, whom before he
had wounded and made bleed but not mortally." His
conceptions were large and touched by an Elizabethan
rhetoric.

Towards the end of the same narrative there are two
further passages which reveal his standpoint still more
clearly. "I cannot in better sort conclude this discourse,"
he wrote,[3] "than shew, by aunccient evidences and authen-
ticke recordes, how the sayd possessions have descended in
elder ages, and how often they have heartofore, by heires
generall, been transferred into several surnames; the
which, noe question, was then the handy-worke of God,
and He being whear He was, it is past the power of any
Lowther or human creature, to alter His desynes or to
oppose against His determination." "And therefore,"
he concluded,[4] "LET GOD MAKE HEIRES, for *in
vanum laborant* that endevour the contrary, and it is
directly *contra consilium Domini*, as allsoe, noe question, great presumption in the frayle creature to oppose
against, and to crosse the designment of the omnipotent
Creator." These sentences will serve to indicate the stiff
almost Castilian sense of pure descent which is set
against the Augustinian background of Lord William's

---

[2] *Lord Dacre's Possessions*, a MS composed by Lord William Howard,
Household Accounts, p. 372.

[3] *Ibid*, p. 391.

[4] *Ibid*, p. 393.

thought. He and his wife Elizabeth Dacres lived at Naworth on their wide estates from the time of King James' accession until they died in 1639 and 1640.

A study of the Household Books gives some impression of the life led at Naworth Castle on the Scottish Border in the stronghold of the Dacres which looked across the Irthing to the Waste of Bewcastle. It was an isolated way of living with a rather primitive and cumbered dignity, and it is always surprising that such a library, the fruit of twenty years of antiquarian and religious reading, should have been brought up in the carts which carried the pictures and the household stuffs from Newburn to Naworth across the fells. In return for further books, which were sent from London, Lord William would send to the antiquaries in the South such stones with Roman inscriptions as he could find. "Till haie tyme was past," he wrote[5] on one occasion in this connection to Sir Robert Cotton, "I could get no draughts to undertake to carrie them."

The patriarchal element had a binding force in the routine at Naworth, and it is interesting to observe the way in which the lord's personal interests in genealogy and antiquities and herbals are reflected in the list of casual sums disbursed[6] at the castle door.

"To widdow Hetherton for finding honey vi[d]
To W. Bowman's son for finding an earthen pot v s.
To ij boyes for getting yvie for the deer iv[d]
To Mr. Lowden's man bringing saxifrage vj[d]
To Jo. Lambert bringing cherries xij[d]
For drawing a pedigre, to Mr. Pryce i s.
To iij musicians at the gate xij[d]."

Journeys to London took place from time to time and in his later years Lord William had a set of lodgings in

[5] Letter from Lord William Howard to Sir Robert Cotton, dated from Naworth Castle 13 August 1608, printed in Household Accounts, appendix, p. 412.
[6] Nearly all the following items appear in October accounts under the heading "Rewards, and given to the Pore," Household Accounts, pp. 88-89.

Arundel House. His principal servants were put up[7] at the *Angel* behind St. Clement Dane's, and he used the stables of this inn during his visits to the capital. But he would very soon be back in the North again. There is record of a single journey to the Spa in the Low Countries made for the sake of the waters in 1623.

The state of his health seems to have occasioned several of the London visits, for there are notes of consultations with Catholic physicians of this period, Dr. Moore and Mr. Hickes, the latter an apothecary whose nostrums were at that time greatly valued. Compared to the small sums spent on books and the very slight expenditure on boat hire[8] from Arundel House steps, the payments to the doctors seem considerable. Among the charges met were £10 to Dr. Moore, a bill of four guineas from Mr. Hickes, and one of ten shillings from Mr. Clarke, the tooth drawer. Lord William's life was not without a certain valetudinarian background.

In the fine weather he would sometimes ride down to Lady Wyntour's house at Lydney, staying on the way at Shiffnal Manor with his sister-in-law Lady Arundel for whom he entertained a deep respect. Journeys into Lancashire were more frequent, and there is evidence that he would occasionally in the house of some Catholic gentleman obtain a book which he could not have purchased in the open market. Thus a copy of the office *de Beata* had belonged[9] to Mr. Thomas Talbot of Lancaster before Lord William acquired it in his Naworth period. It was possibly his association with these Lancashire recusants

[7] Under the heading "Riding Charges and Errands" for November 1633 there are interesting details of the various charges at the *Angel* and of the sums given to ostlers and chamberlains, *ibid*, p. 333.

[8] A pair of oars bringing Lord William from the Temple Stairs to the Old Swan or from Arundel House to the Old Swan cost xij[d] which was likewise the cost of a pair of oars from Arundel House to Westminster. The charge for two pairs of oars from Arundel House to Westminster was xviij[d], *ibid*, pp. 262-3, 333.

[9] This copy of the *Horae in laudem Beatissimae Virginis Mariae, ad usum Romanum* published at Paris in 1531 has the following entry written on the flyleaf. "Liber Thomas Talbotti, Lancastr., qui obiit 10 die Julii, 1598. Willm Howard, Naward."

that led him to make a journey to St. Winifred's shrine at
Holywell in 1629 in company with his friends Sir Cuthbert
Clifton of Lytham and Mr. Preston of the Manor Furness.

At Naworth a certain formal hospitality was practised
and visits were exchanged with the Bishop of Carlisle at
Rose Castle. The coach, which appears frequently in these
accounts, with its curtains and leather hangings, was sent
on occasion as far as Appleby to meet distinguished travellers. It is also clear that, as he grew old, Lord William's
interest in mechanical contrivances developed. There were
constant repairs to the clock which he had installed in a
wainscot case and he busied himself with an astrolabe and
dials and compasses. It will be seen that his literary interests were likewise marked by this same concern for the
description of physical phenomena. He can be imagined
bending over his instruments or examining the well-
tricked arms in his heraldic manuscripts. His green spectacles would be exchanged for the multiplying glasses
with which he was used to scan each detail. Beside him
would stand his diet drink of oat malt and on his head his
satin cap to save him from the draughts of winter.

Lord William's numerous sons remain somewhat indis-
tinct in these household records, and his wife's personality
emerges less clearly than his own. She was obviously very
fond of cards and spent a considerable sum on this diversion. This is perhaps sufficient detail to introduce a
consideration of the library itself.

The information about the books and manuscripts then
at Naworth can be checked from three sources. In the
first place there is the *Catalogus Librorum Manuscrip-*
torum Honoratissimi D. Caroli Howard, Comitis Carlioli,
in Bibliotheca apud Castrum suum de Naworth in
Comitatu Cumbriae; quos collegit Abavus ejus Domini
Wilhelmus Howard. In a certain number of cases the
printed books contain Lord William's signature or his
motto *volo non valeo.* The rare occasions on which a date
is entered in the volume would seem to indicate the times
of purchase. It seems to be only certain of the books which

he bought when he was forming his collection as a young man in the years before the Armada that are thus dated. In other instances the purchase of the books is mentioned in the household accounts, although unfortunately their titles are seldom given.

All the printed books in this catalogue can be checked by their date of publication. In one or two cases, and notably in that of Sir Nathaniel Brent's translation of Soano's History of the Council of Trent, there is some doubt as to whether the volume actually arrived before the founder of the library had died. This book, which was published in the year of his death, was probably at any rate on order. The greater part of the library was in Latin, with many English books and a good deal in French. There were occasional volumes in Greek. Lord William's notes in a copy of Casa-Galateo's *Trattato de Costumi* suggest that he prided himself upon a knowledge of Italian. Although he survived so long, he had been born three years before the Earl of Essex and thus belonged to that Elizabethan generation which regarded some playing with Italian as the necessary and supreme accomplishment.

More interesting than the *Trattato de Costumi* and the modish volumes of the *Cinquecento* is the series of volumes which dealt from different angles with the English Catholic tradition. He had, of course, the *Chronicles*, Berners' *Froissart*, and *Polychronicon*, the History of Sir John Madeville, Harding's *Chronicle* and the *Chronicle of Fabian*. But the special nature of his interest is shown by the religious writings. There is John Gwinneth's *Declaration of an heretique* and with it two other tracts by Thomas Berthelet, both dating from Queen Mary's reign, *A manifest Detection of the notable falsehood of John Frithe's book* and *A playne Demonstration of John Frithe's lack of witte and learninge.* He had a fifteenth century metrical life in English of St. Cuthbert, a life of Thomas à Becket and the Wynkyn de Worde edition of the *Orcharde of Sion*, "in the which is conteyned the revela-

cyon of Seynt Katheryne of Sene, with ghostly frujtes and
precjous plantes for the helthe of mannes soul."

These were supported by manuscripts of the lives of
English saints, John Lidgate's *Vita S. Edmundi Regis &
Martyris*, and accounts of St. Guthlac of Ely, St. Botolph
and St. Anselm. There were also codices of the works of
St. Aldhelm and of the Venerable Bede.

The religious works in Latin which were of English
provenance are very numerous. Two of these are Marian
editions, the *Exetasis Testimoniorum quae Martinus
Bucer ex S. Patribus non sancte edidit* of Stephen Gardi-
ner, Bishop of Winchester and the *De Veritate Corporis
et Sanguinis Domini* of Cuthbert Tunstall, Bishop of
Durham. The library possessed a manuscript volume containing several treatises of Richard Rolle of Hampole including the *De Amore Dei et contemptu mundi*. There
was Thomas Netter of Walden's book against the heresy
of Wycliffe and one of the controversial works of Thomas
Stapleton. In the case of this last book, which was published at Antwerp in 1592, there is a note in the accounts
stating that it was bought by Lord William Howard on 6
August 1623 at Dunkirk for two shillings, while he was
waiting in that port for a ship for Newcastle on his return
journey from the Spa.

In this connection it is worth noting that in many cases
Lord William appears to have bought modern books on
publication. An unusually large number of the works in
his library were published at Cologne, Louvain and Antwerp; but it seems probable that the actual arrangements
for their purchase were made through London booksellers.
At the same time this would raise an interesting problem,
since the volumes dealt for the most part with Catholic
theology and controversy. Technically they were liable to
seizure since they were Popish books imported from the
dominions of the Archdukes and of the Spiritual Electors.

By contrast almost the only Anglican book in the whole
library was William Page's *A further Justification of Bowing at the name of Jesus*, which had been published at

Oxford in 1631 and had come into his possession in his last years. There was also a copy of the Jacobean controversial work *Tortura Torti*. Two volumes advocating the principles of the Reformation contained warning notes. On the flyleaf of a copy of Calvin's *Institutio* there is written in Lord William's handwriting the text, *"Qui sibi videtur stare, videat ne cadat,"* while the cover of *Antisanderus* has the words *"Parce nobis Domine"* cut right across it. Such a sentiment would have been echoed in any Catholic house in regard to that attack on Dr. Sanders, the defender of the Papacy.

On the other hand, one entry in a Catholic sense has a special interest. It is not easy to determine which of the printed books and manuscripts at Naworth had belonged to the house in the days of the Lords Dacres, although the Register of Lanercost had descended from that time. But there was in the library an Antwerp edition of an *Hymnorum cum notis opusculum ad usum Sarum* printed just before the religious changes in 1528. The back of the title page has an inscription stating that on 3 September 1553 Mass was again said at St. Cuthbert's Church in the city of Carlisle.

The general spiritual and mystical writers are well represented. There was a Cologne edition of Rupert of Deutz's *de Divinis Officiis*, a *Martyrologium Romanum* printed at Antwerp which appears to have been purchased after Lord William came to Naworth, and Richard of St. Victor's *in Trinitate*. There were of course the eight volumes of Mosander's edition of Surius' *Vitae Sanctorum*. In addition to a work in praise of Sanctae Brigidae Thaumaturgae the library contained copies of St. Bonaventure *de Vita S. Francisci* and of the *Consuetudines* of Dom Guigo, prior of the Grande Chartreuse. Some of the books were modern editions of spiritual classics as in the case of Ludolph of Saxony's *Vita Jesu Christi*, which was purchased in the Antwerp variant of 1612. Towards the Carthusians, as to the Benedictines, Lord William showed himself most generous. According to a manuscript formerly at Corby he left one quarter of a sum of £200, set aside for Masses, to the Carthusians "particularly desiring that these might have a share in what he intended for such uses."[10] It is possible that he may have visited the English charterhouse at Nieuport on his journey to the Low Countries, but the dispersal of the archives of that monastery in 1782 makes it difficult to determine whether Lord William Howard was among the rare patrons of Sheen Anglorum.

Naturally the works of the sixteenth-century defenders of Catholicism were not neglected[11] in the formation of Naworth library. Ribadeneira's *Les Fleurs des Vies Saincts*, Martin Becanus' *Manuale Controversiarum*, Canisius *in Evangelicas Lectiones* and Suarez' *Opuscula Theologica* give an indication of the titles. There were books by Possevino and Hosius and Gregory of Valencia, and several works of Bellarmine and a Latin edition of the letters of St. Francis Xavier.

In the more general section St. Augustine was represented by an imperfect copy of the *De Civitate Dei*. There is no reference to the Confessions. The situation with regard to St. Thomas was rather curious. There was a fifteenth-century edition of a *Textus Sententiarum*, a copy of the *Summa contra Gentiles* printed at Lyons in 1586 in which was inscribed the name "Charles Howard, Naward," and a copy of the *prima pars* of the *Summa Theologica*. In the library there was also a copy of the *tertia pars* in a late sixteenth century Venetian edition. This had the words "Sr. Willm Howarde of Thornthwaite" on the fly leaf. The two inscribed volumes clearly belonged to Lord Howard's younger sons and this raises the question as to

[10] This paper is quoted in the introduction to the *Household Books of Lord William Howard of Naworth*, p. xl and was at Corby in 1878. It is naturally not explicitly stated that the pious uses in question were in fact Mass stipends.

[11] Lord William's interest in the field of spiritual writing was maintained and one of the last of his purchases was the *Lilia Cistercii* of Chrysostom Henriquez. He also possessed an abridged French version of pieces from the *Thesaurarium* of Luis of Granada.

whether they may have been put through a prescribed course of reading with the chaplain.

It seems certain that Fr. Augustine Hungate O.S.B.[12] must have had a definite influence on the formation of at any rate a portion of the library. From 1633 entries of sums given to him "by my Lord's command" appear in the Accounts, and he was obviously on a most intimate footing with the family. He came of the old Yorkshire stock of the Hungates of Saxton, and his sister Mary was married to Lord William's son Sir William Howard.

One section of the library, the school books, must have lain very definitely within the chaplain's province. Among the sums expended in March 1621 there figured[13] "A grammer xij^d, Terence xij^d, and Vives vj^d, for Mr. Thomas." The last entry presumably refers to the *Epistola de ratione studii puerilis, cum rudimentis Grammatices,* composed in 1523. The education of children in the North still went on in the Tudor fashion. Among the school books was a Cicero and a Horace, and in 1619 a Latin primer was procured for Lord William's daughter Mary, who later married Sir John Wyntour. There is not enough evidence to determine whether this book was a manual of devotion[14] or whether her father bestowed special pains upon the education of his favourite daughter.

The whole question of the price paid for books is full of interest. Eighteen pence would be given for binding a volume and two shillings and six pence for such work in parchment. The sums laid out were strictly moderate. A bill of £2:4, sent in by Mr. Lownes the London book-

[12] The various entries relating to the chaplain are invariably headed "Mr. Hungate" and the editor of the Household Accounts could not determine whether the priest in question was Dom Augustine Hungate or his brother Robert. It was, however, Fr. Augustine who retired in his old age to the house of Vicountess Fairfax, who figures in the Accounts as Lord William's grand daughter Alathea. He seems to have been the priest who was so closely linked with the Howards throughout his long career.

[13] *Household Books,* p. 179 under the heading "Utensils or Necessaries."

[14] This entry comes under the heading of Payments for Nessessareis and Extraordinaries sence the viij October, 1619 and the price paid for the volume was six shillings and six pence. This figure rather suggests a present than a school book.

seller, would appear to be among the larger items, but the prices were seldom recorded except in the case of the current heraldic and antiquarian works like Camden's *Remains* (half-a-crown). Very occasionally a book of doctrinal character is included in the orders sent to London through the steward. A couple of shillings was paid for one of Bishop Fisher's treatises.

Almanacs, costing a few pence each, were sent for regularly and the numbers of *Mercurius Gallo-Belgicus*, published half-yearly, would enable the family at Naworth to keep up with a somewhat inefficient presentation of fairly recent world events. This periodical was well supplied with maps in which Lord William clearly took a curious pleasure. In this same field the Book of the Duchy of Cornwall and the Doomsday Book "with picktures" must have made a real appeal. It is necessary to stress in regard to any library of this period the element of serious perusal. Past all those volumes which were kept for show or courtesy there lay that range of study in which a man of generous blood would find support. In this as in so many cases it was surely the great heraldic manuscripts which gave the mind its characteristic and most solid nutriment.

To explain this more clearly a single instance can be taken from among those *schemata* which the owner of Naworth Castle had ordered to be prepared for his own use. In one MS the arms which depicted the quarterings of his own house were found blazoned in the margin in their crude right colours, while down the centre of the parchment ran the brief sustaining narrative. There Lord William could study carefully the lineage of the Dacre ancestors. "Thomas VI," he would read,[15] "married Elizabeth Graystocke, reigned xxx years. Further at God's pleasure."

By unsuspected ways the religious conception was always

[15] This is taken from a record at Naworth Castle made by Lord William Howard of the lineage of the Dacres, as given in an armorial window at Kirkoswald.

entering. There lay the Dacres in the tombs at Lanercost
and a new line had entered into their inheritance. But
Lord William held to his conception of a Divine protection guarding over the destinies of the established order.
Justice and right descent; LET GOD MAKE HEIRES.
Among the doctrines one was by now of almost universal
acceptation that of the unrestricted nature of the Rights
of Property. It was hedged about by dignity, and lucid
and incontestable. There is a certain uniformity about
the history of those families who passed through the Civil
Wars as Cavaliers but holding great possessions. Already
at Naworth there could be discerned a central calm and
a possessive quality, assured and most enduring. Such a
family was carried forward to its own destiny. As in the
cases of the Paulets and the Lumleys their adherence to
Catholicism would drop away before the pressure of a caste
opinion. Very smoothly these families would come into
their place, and the Carlisle Howards entered the haven
of the Whigs.

Under another aspect the library at Naworth would
foreshadow that of the country houses of the future with
their reasoned and ample furnishing. There stood the
editions of the *Statutes at Large,* those tall and calf-
bound volumes which, behind the glass of the locked
book cases, would form a background for the gentlemen of
England in their chosen leisure. Already that character
of magnificence which was to mark the English library
could be discerned. Beyond the *Statutes* there stretched
forward a line of dignified and handsome folios the Annals of Baronius, and Gratian, Hakluyt's edition of the
Navigacions, the Universal Histories and the Lexicog-
raphers. The *Acts of Parliament,* and books of these two
last categories, ministered to a clear distinctive need as
the dust settled on the fine thick calf. They were among
the earlier experiments in the arranged background.

This idea was only just emerging. In the North pictures
were still conceived as casual decoration, like fitted panels
which could as well be used for any other ornament.

Among the payments made at Naworth is one which throws a clear light upon this way of life. "June 10. To Mr. Heskett for mending my Lord's closett, guilding a bedstead, drawing Mrs. Elizabeth and Mrs. Marye's pictures, and Mr. Thomas', x^{li}." In keeping with this entry is a note under November 1633 which mentions the large sum of £44:8 given "for one sute of Lanskipp hangings, containinge 148 ells, at 6s an ell."[16] This was an approach very remote from that of the Mortlake tapestries and Buckingham and his expert advisers. Landscape work ordered in this fashion resembled the Elizabethan tapestry which was primarily a seemly and uninteresting covering for the rough wall spaces. In some respects these accounts of Naworth resemble those of Wardour some thirty years before. The fashions of the earlier reign still lingered in these northern parts which were so far removed from the capital and its new influence.

It was not the detail of the house furnishing but Lord William's personal effects which suggested a more modern spirit, the quadrant and dial, "the needle for one Austrolobb," the drills and pliers. And on another side he had those antiquarian interests in Roman inscriptions and in the markings on the Cross of Bewcastle which were to characterise the Stuart century. With this there went a general concern for natural history. Thus the Cornish diamonds which Thomas Roscarrock, Lord William's old friend and quasi-pensioner, had brought to Naworth were the quiet precursors of those curious objects of nature which the Restoration world and the eighteenth century would soon collect. In time they would be set out and classified in the specimen cases between the pilasters in the nobleman's seats under the Hanoverians.

Though there was much at Naworth to suggest the general lines of reading in the Stuart period there was little which reflects the constitutional troubles of the time or the approaching conflict. Among the manuscripts there

[16] Extraordinary Paiment, Household Accounts, p. 182.

was a single folio volume comprising Arguments for Ship money; *Pro & Con*. A copy of Jean Bodin's *Methodus* is an example of a kind of writing which was likewise ill-represented. In really modern controversy there was a book by Marco Antonio de Dominis, printed by the Jesuit press at Dillingen and written after his return from England. But it was the calmer writing which was more characteristic of this library, the quiet description of events recorded within the framework of established values; the volumes of the *Concilia Generalia*; the genealogies of sixty-seven noble houses by Estienne de Cypre; the *Annales Sultanorum Othmanidarum*. A complement to this world view was a work much favoured throughout this century Philemon Holland's translation of Suetonius. Perhaps the keynote of the patron of letters in Lord William's youth had been the desire to be versatile. At Naworth in his later years we can see this versatility reduced to serried order.

In the summer of 1639 Lady William Howard died. The eldest son was dead since many years and the way of life at Naworth did not survive Lord William's time. His grandson and heir, Sir William Howard, was already a widower and only survived till 1644. The first Earl of Carlisle was brought up with a very different set of values to those of his great-grandfather. In the summer of 1640 Lord William's health was clearly failing. In the accounts there is a payment to Lord Fairfax's man for bringing conserve of primrose for my Lord and for coals which were carried up to the Carlisle Tower. He was past dragon water and mythridate and Dr. Steven's potion and clove water. In the early autumn there was a payment of 12^d to the brewer for bags for putting in herbs for my Lord's beer. The disbursal of £15 paid at Michaelmas for the printing of "St. Marie of Egipt her life in Vearse" attests Lord William's interest as a patron. On 7 October there occurs a final entry "for a coffine for my Lord."

André Chénier

by J. B. MORTON

IN THE early months of the year 1794 there lived in a
little house in the rue de Satory at Versailles, No:69, a
young poet. Though he was already in his thirty-second
year, only his friends and a few who had literary judgment spoke of him as a man whose verse might one day
be famous. At the moment, the name André Chénier was
better known as that of a pamphleteer, a journalist and an
orator. Of him Lacretelle had said that he alone might
have rivalled Vergniaud in a contest of eloquence. Nevertheless, it was as the last of the great classical poets that he
was to be remembered; the inheritor of Malherbe's legacy
to French poetry. By the time his scattered poems had been
collected and published, twenty-five years after his death,
there had begun the reaction of the romantic school against
the restraint and sense of proportion of the Classic. But it
was a romantic, Chateaubriand, who first drew attention
to the high quality of Chénier's poetry.

The romantic poets of the nineteenth century often
claimed Chénier as their precursor. But there was nothing
in common between Chénier's insistence on order and
form, and the disorder of the romantics; between his self-
control and their sentimentality. There was nothing in his
work to prepare the mind for René and Manfred, Corinne
and Werther. Moreover, we have it in his own words that
his ambition was *"créer avec les anciens."* He knew the
Greek and Latin poets by heart, and in his best poems
the reader constantly pauses to listen to a distant echo of
Tibullus or Propertius or Theocritus. To the men of
the time, whose writing and conversation were so full
of the classics, the ancient world was something which
they had found between the covers of books, but to Chénier
it was a reality. Son of a Greek mother, he had, in his

blood, as it were, a memory of ordered beauty; born in Constantinople, he had received in infancy something upon which his imagination fed for the rest of his life. And when he, like the other young men, saw Liberty in a vision, she was a familiar goddess from the glades of Parnassus. It is the fact that the antique world was so real to him, and its literature so much a part of his daily habit of thought, which distinguished him, even when he was imitating the classics, from other writers who were attracted by the poetry of Greece and Rome.

The sense of proportion, which is form, inherited from his mother, inspired not only his poetry but his polemics. The same sure instinct which made him distrust exaggeration and uncontrolled emotion in a poem, gave him a strong distaste for all that was loud and wild in the Revolution. What he saw in the streets or in the Assembly—but particularly at the Jacobins—was loosely organised ferocity. And the burden of all his warnings, in his speeches, his verse and his articles, was the peril of mere destructiveness which must lead to chaos. He would have responded to Saint-Just's "Formons la Cité." But, unlike Saint-Just, unlike so many of the men who began as monarchists, he would never admit that the City could not be established by persuasion. And by the time the mob had become an army, he had despaired of the Revolution.

André Chénier was born on October 30th, 1762, in the suburb of Galata. His father, Louis Chénier, representative of a business house in Marseilles, was also French Consul. His mother, Elizabeth Santi-Lomaca, was a Greek of good family. When André was three years old his father was appointed Consul-General in Morocco, and it was arranged that the mother should take her four boys and her daughter to France to be educated. The youngest of the children was the careerist Marie-Joseph who became a Jacobin, and wrote the Magnificent *Chant du Départ*, for which Méhul composed the music. In Paris the mother and her children settled in the Marais quarter, and it was not long before Mme. Chénier had gathered about her a salon of poets and artists and scholars.

Mme. Vigée-Lebrun and David were frequent visitors. Here he met such men as the poet Florian, the author of *"Plaisir d'Amour"*; Guys, the writer and antiquarian; Alfieri, the Italian dramatist; Cazes, who illustrated the Iliad for Mme. Chénier; the great chemist and physicist Lavoisier; Suvé, who painted his portrait in prison; and the loathsome Lebrun, whom they called Pindar, and whose artificial elegies had considerable influence on the young Chénier. Lebrun was a great admirer of Tibullus, and was one of the leaders of a literary circle whose members attended lectures on the classical poets, translated their works, and painstakingly imitated them. He was the best of a group of poets whose insincerity is their most striking characteristic. The very names of most of them are forgotten. One, Parny, will probably be remembered only because Chateaubriand knew his work by heart.

In this atmosphere of cultured ease young Chénier grew up. At the College of Navarre he made friends with those whose tastes were similar to his own—particularly with the Trudaine brothers. When he left school, family influence secured for him a gentleman-cadetship in an infantry regiment, and in Strasbourg he carried out his duties without enthusiasm, being completely unfitted, physically and by temperament, for such a career. The drilling and the marching exhausted him, and finally affected his health, so that after a few months he abandoned all hope of ever becoming a soldier, and returned to Paris. Here he spent a year studying and amusing himself —for he was a gay companion and attractive to women. In 1783, when he was twenty-one, he travelled in Italy and Switzerland with the Trudaine brothers, partly for his health, and partly to see the world of which he had read so much. Greece was to end the holiday, but he never reached it. He returned, ill, from Naples and once more settled down in Paris, to read and write poems.

For the next three years he lived with his father, now retired, and his mother in the rue Cléry, passing his leisure agreeably enough in discussion and in numerous love affairs. He went through all the ardours and despairs of young men in love, being unusual, in such a time and place, that he took the most ephemeral passion seriously—which did not interfere with his prodigious appetite for good food. It was also the period of the best of his elegies, and a student with leisure might well amuse himself in trying to identify the various ladies who are celebrated in his verse during these years. There is no sign in these elegies of the journalist or the orator to come. He appears as one who enjoyed to the full the normal life of a young Parisian gentleman with time on his hands. He liked solitude, but not for too long. And the kind of life he led as a youth may be found in the pages of Rétif de la Bretonne. Mme. Hocquart described him as ugly but full of charm, and he certainly appears to have had no difficulty in conducting trivial love-affairs.

But his parents thought it time that he should discipline himself with some regular work, and the obvious thing to do was to place him in the diplomatic service. He had shown no eagerness for such a career nor any aptitude for it, but his father and mother did not like the idea of a young man leading what seemed to them to be a useless life. So a secretaryship was found for him at the Embassy in London, and in December, 1787, he crossed to Dover in weather so bad that the poem in which he describes his sufferings seems worthy of a graver peril than sea-sickness.

London, by its very strangeness, interested him, and for a while he was happy—but not for long. Not only did he regret his old life in Paris, but once more he realized that he could not subdue himself to discipline. A regular task, set by a task-master, appalled him, and he began to suffer again those moods of despair which he so often took care to commit to verse or prose, with the date and the place in which they were written attached to them.

There are evidences that the young Englishmen of his own rank and age managed to indicate to him that no amount of wit or gaiety could compensate for his poverty. So he passed lonely days, despatching copies of his poems to his brother in Paris, and getting through his official work in boredom and annoyance.

When the Revolution broke out in Paris he responded to it as though he had been waiting all his life for it. His work in London was no longer taken seriously, and he spent more and more of his time in Paris, in a circle of friends which included Pastoret, de Pange, Barthélemy and the Trudaine brothers. His whole family supported the Revolution, the mother with moderation, the father with enthusiasm, but never beyond the constitutional frontier, Marie-Joseph more violently. André himself was a moderate, an idealist, who, at the very outset, saw the dangers ahead. He mistrusted the effect upon the people of a sudden, strong draught of liberty. *"Dirigez sa bouillante enfance,"* he cries in the poem he wrote for David on the occasion of his picture of the Oath of the Tennis Court.

He had not long to wait to see his fears realized, and the rest of his short life is a progress of disillusionment, which, before it reached despair, flared up in a flame of scorn and indignation. For a while he watched events, and then, after the Feast of Pikes in July, 1790, he published his "Avis au Peuple Français" calling upon the nation to pause and collect its thoughts before degrading the ideal which had been the inspiration of the Revolution. He reminded his readers, in a passage that Montesquieu would have admired and Burke (whom Chénier despised) applauded, that liberty does not mean anarchy; that there must be a law; and that the mere madness of a mob may leave in ruins all that wiser men have tried to build. In a hundred articles and speeches and booklets he developed this idea during the coming months, modelling his political theory upon the Declaration of the Rights of Man. With the greatest courage he antagonized the

leaders of the extremists, uttering his thoughts without
fear of the consequences. He had no ambition to be himself a leader, but the integrity of his character forced him
to speak the truth as he saw it. In his anger he attributed
the lowest motives not to this individual or to that, but to
all save the moderates.

He believed sincerely in the principles of the Revolution
but he hated disorder and violence, and had no knowledge
of the people. He was a Constitutional Monarchist, and
his ideas were the ideas of the well-to-do young men who
were his intimate friends. Like them, he would have been
content with the abolition of irksome privilege and the
curtailing of the power of the King—with half a Revolution. He could not share in that larger vision of the men
who dreamed of remaking Europe. The amazing thing is
that he who detested the hurly burly of conflict and the
noise of the mob, should have consented to abandon the
life he loved—good food and the company of ladies of
leisure and the conversation of his equals—for the labours
and irritations of political controversy. Yet, even this work
was performed in pleasant enough surroundings. For, in
his unceasing campaign against the Jacobins, he made use
of the *Journal de Paris,* which was directed by a friend,
Suard. Others of his friends were among the contributors
to the paper; Roucher, an indifferent poet, Lacretelle,
and de Pange, the wealthy and extremely courageous disciple of Condorcet.

Among his rhetoric is an attack on the Jacobins, which
will give an idea of how he used this instrument. . . .

"The Constitution was based upon this eternal truth;
that the people is sovereign. But this Constitution has
merely persuaded the tribunes of the Club that they are
the people. . . . a few hundred idlers massing in a
garden or at a public spectacle, a party or two of bandits,
pillaging shops—these (with what effrontery) are called
the people. The most insolent despots of history never
received from their most sycophantic courtiers a viler

or more tiresome flattery than that with which, every day the writers and orators of these Jacobin societies (the scourge of France) intoxicate two or three thousand usurpers of the sovereignty of the Nation."

Several newspapers reprinted this article, and the enraged Jacobins raised the cry of fratricide, reminding Chénier that his own brother was a member of the Club. But he made them even angrier by retorting that his patriotism did not rise to the heights of denouncing his own brother, a habit he left to the Jacobins. They then chose Marie-Joseph Chénier to be their champion, and the younger brother, who had a hunger for notoriety and was without depth, though possessed of considerable talent, had no objection to using this chance. But clearly his heart was not really in the business. He knew his brother too well, and he must have foreseen the danger in which André stood already, having antagonised so many powerful men. It would have done Marie-Joseph honour if he had refused to write a reply. As it was he wrote it without vigour, and so wounded his brother without doing any good service to the Club. André continued the correspondence the next day, treating his brother with dignified contempt, repeating, for the thousandth time, his doctrine, and emphasizing, in the plainest terms, his loathing of the Jacobins. A week elapsed before Marie-Joseph wrote the final article in this unusual debate, and one historian has detected, rightly I think, the hand of Robespierre.

As time passed and Chénier saw all that he had believed in and defended, fade like a dream, his prose hardened. He felt himself at bay, and he became more defiant. In reading him, we are uplifted not only by his courage, but by the purity of his faith in that moderate Revolution of which he never lost sight. And then, after June 20th 1792, he almost permitted himself to hope. The behaviour of the King on that day made a profound impression on him, and he exaggerated to himself the possible effect of the addresses from the departments, deploring the insult offered to the monarchy. In what he wrote of the day of June 20th, he castigated Pétion, who had talked of the "pride and dignity of free men," in connection with the incursion of the mob.

"But that day, notable for many reasons, will awaken something more than unhappy memories. That day has shown to the people of France the highest of her public functionaries, charged with the execution of her laws, filling worthily, and at the risk of his life, the position to which he has been called. Every Frenchman who has retained some idea of justice, equity, humanity; every Frenchman who honours and wishes to obey that Constitution so often invoked by good citizens and bad citizens alike; every Frenchman who grieves to see it outraged daily by those who profess reverence for it, and misunderstood by those whose task it is to administer it or to see that others administer it; every Frenchman who contemplates with horror an attack on the sanctity of monarchy, and with grief the frequent justification in the Assembly of such attacks; in effect, every Frenchman who wishes to be free, and who knows how to be free, cannot but feel a patriotic satisfaction at the firm and manly conduct of the King on this occasion. . . ."

When Lafayette returned from the Army and went to the Jacobins to condemn the insurrectionaries of June 20th Chénier supported him enthusiastically with his pen. But the King did nothing to help Lafayette and the protest was without effect. The pitifully absurd incident of the *Baiser de Lamourette* was equally barren of result.

So his hope did not live long, and his final and complete disillusionment was a more tragic thing than that of Mme. Roland, or of any other of the idealists. When he was forced to admit to himself that the current of events was too strong for him, when he perceived the curse that has worked in man since the Fall, and knew that the noblest ideal, when put into practice by men, must be corrupted and debased, then he abandoned the struggle, and surrendered to bitterness. His misery was the stronger in that his faith had been so vigorous. August 10th came, and the day of dreamers was then done.

Chénier left Paris, and moved unhappily from town to town, resolved to take no further part in public affairs. Sick in mind and body, he was unable to separate the machinery of revolution from the idea that drove the leaders, whom he confused with the dregs of the mob, and whose motives seemed to him to be of the most contemptible; and when, at the close of the year 1792, he began to write again, no fire burned in him. He denied, coldly and reasonably, the right of the Convention to judge Louis, and argued that any such attempt would make the Constitution a laughingstock. He drew up with great care the line of argument which he thought the defence of the King should take, and in this was probably helped by Malesherbes, whose uncle had been his chief at the Embassy in London, and whom he had met frequently in the houses of his friends. In his apologia, he admits the weakness of the King, but claims that weakness is no crime. For him the capital point in the whole story of the fall of the monarchy is the flight to Varennes. From that moment the nation could not trust its King.

But such faults, committed a thousand times, do not entitle a body that has usurped the sovereignty of the people to pass judgement on a monarch. There must be an appeal to the people. The sections and the popular assemblies must have the case put before them dispassionately. And as he visualizes this appeal to the people, his old faith in human nature returns for a moment, and he apostrophizes the citizens of Paris, and warns them against the propaganda of their leaders.

"Hitherto, to you who are men, to you who are called upon to judge, they have spoken but of hatred. He who writes this speaks to you of humanity. They have talked of vengeance; he who writes this talks of justice. They have reminded you of your power; he reminds you of your conscience."

And he claims that he is a better republican than any of them. He even writes a speech for the defence, which he puts into the King's mouth. But it was all of no avail, and when the vote was taken in the Convention, among those who voted for the death penalty was his brother Marie-Joseph Chénier. There is in an article which he wrote at this time, an interesting sentence: "Louis XVI whom I very willingly call Louis the last . . ." And he said that a second Revolution was being planned. Although he was now ready to be a Republican, he could not reconcile himself to the use of force to establish the principles of the Revolution.

After January 21st he retired to the little house in Versailles and attempted to heal his spirit in a place where he could forget the noise of the tempest in which he had lived for so long. Near by, at Louveciennes, he had friends, Mme. Pourrat and her two daughters, and in their house he found friendship and sympathy—and an old love. For there he met again the gracious, melancholy lady who is the "Fanny" of his poems—Mme. Laurent Lecoulteux. Many a time he walked to see her, along the old road from Versailles which Sisley and Manet and Pissarro have made famous. In human affection he found consolation for all that he had endured, and a lassitude settled over him, as though he had said to himself, "I am powerless to influence events. Why, therefore, should I spend my already impaired strength in a hopeless contest?" But his character was not of that stamp.

When Charlotte Corday was executed he broke his silence with a poem worthy of that young visionary, a poem that rings and reverberates with his old anger. No poet could have more fittingly celebrated her deed. Had he met her he would have understood that naive view of the Revolution which was hers, and together they would have talked of the perfect republic which each believed possi-

ble. Into these verses which he wrote for her, he poured
the distillation of long thoughts upon his bed at night,
and eased his mind in invective. The poem is a cry of
defiance; it is Charlotte Corday's monument, and may be
said to be the only sequel, apart from the temporary deifi-
cation of Marat, to her act of sacrifice. While André was
celebrating the heroism of Charlotte Corday, that brother
who was destined to be his antagonist all through his life
was demanding the throwing out of Mirabeau's ashes from
the Pantheon, to make room for Marat's.

He returned to Paris in the autumn, to the house of
his parents in the rue Cléry, but by the beginning of 1794
was once more at Versailles. During the Terror he remained there; sometimes he walked to Marly to see the
Trudaine brothers, and sometimes he loitered in the park,
among the busts and statues and pavilions which reminded
him of a more peaceful world. But how unsuccessful was
his attempt to find tranquillity we may judge from the
poem "Versailles," with the last verse that tells of the
ghosts of dead men haunting the fields and woods where
he walks. As the spring drew on, the people of the place
became accustomed to the sight of the swarthy young man
with the enormous head, and the small blue eyes. Nobody
from Paris came to trouble his peace, until, one day, a
messenger arrived with the news that his friend Pastoret
was about to be arrested.

Chénier set out at once for the house where his friend
lived, and entered it under cover of darkness. There he
found two women, the wife and mother-in-law of the
doomed man, who had himself disappeared. Chénier com-
forted the women and offered them the hospitality of his
house at Versailles, where they would be safe, and whither
he had intended to take Pastoret. But as they spoke together there came a blow upon the door, and while the
three of them stood still, they heard a voice demanding
admittance in the name of the Nation. When the door was
opened they saw that the house was surrounded. Three or
four members of the local revolutionary committee came

in. They had no warrant for Chénier's arrest, they did not know who he was, but he was submitted to a cross-examination which proves nothing but the illiteracy and imbecility of his questioners. They were incapable of understanding the answers to their own ridiculous questions, and the disdain with which the poet endured their blundering repetitions made them more antagonistic and more suspicious. His refusal to sign the procès-verbal clinched the matter. They marched him off to the prison of St. Lazare without more ado. It was March 11th.

In this prison he wrote those magnificent denunciatory poems in which anger and scorn are mingled; or, in other moods, verses full of tenderness, or of bitterness at the approach of certain death. Outside, Marie-Joseph and his father and mother were doing what they could to postpone the execution, or even to liberate him. Marie-Joseph hoped that André might be forgotten, like so many others, and so might save his head, but even so he made some amends for his previous treatment of his brother, and considering his position as an extremist, he certainly took risks. The father was even more active, and succeeded in extorting a promise from Barère that his son should be released in three days' time. The poor old man believed Barère! Meanwhile the conspiracy against Robespierre was growing, and that also may have given hope to the parents. André himself had apparently abandoned hope and resigned himself to death. Meanwhile he had found the inspiration for the most widely known of all his poems, which was to catch the eye of Chateaubriand when the poet was dead.

Chénier had seen, among his fellow-prisoners, one who became for him a symbol of innocence condemned to death, and summed up for him all the blundering cruelty of the Revolution. Outside the prison spring had come, and it seemed to him that something of spring's influence blew through the stenching courts and corridors where she had passed. He remembered that he was young, and, watching her, he made her immortal in his verse. He called his poem "La Jeune Captive" and in it he imagined her making her complaint that death should have chosen her. She pleads that she is on the threshold of life, has but sat down to the banquet and raised the cup to her lips, and bids death visit those who have lost their illusions and are weary of living. And the poet, he says, takes up his lyre to accompany her plaint, in the hope that in days to come some student may think it worth while to ask who she is.

Three days before the fall of Robespierre Chénier was transferred to the Conciergerie, and the next day, July 25th, he appeared before the Revolutionary Tribunal. Certain charges against his brother Sauveur were incorporated in the accusations against him, so that he found himself implicated in the treason of Dumouriez. But, in any case, the result was a foregone conclusion, and in the evening of that day he was executed with twenty-four others including Roucher, another poet. On the morning of this day he had written the last of his verse, a set of iambics, in which he describes how he is waiting for his name to be called, and how the long, dark corridors will hear that name when the soldiers come to take him away to his death.

Six months after his death the verses about the Young Captive were published in the "Décade Philosophique," but it was not until 1802, when Chateaubriand published his "Génie du Christianisme" that people began to suspect that Chénier's execution had been one of the stupidest crimes of the Revolution. Chateaubriand quoted him, compared him with Theocritus, and recalled to the public the poet's defence of Louis XVI, and the manner of his death. From that moment interest was aroused, and curiosity. Who was the Young Captive? For, apart from the beauty of the poem, men and women were drawn to read and re-read it by the mystery which surrounded it. When the first—and far from complete—collected edition appeared in 1819 Chénier's fame was secure and the story of the Young Captive became one of the romantic love-stories of history. In 1832 de Vigny was writing of her "Seventeen-year-old innocence," and although people said that she was a lady of such-and-such a family, her identity remained unpublished. As late as 1857 Sainte-Beuve got the right name, but the wrong lady. Nobody examined "L'Encyclopedie de l'an VII," in which an archaeologist named Millin had long ago solved the problem.

The innocent young girl had been imprisoned ten days before Chénier. Married at the age of fifteen, in 1784, to Fleury, she had been the mistress of Lauzun and of Lord Malmesbury, and had attached herself in prison to Montrond, whom she was to marry before seeking the protection of Garat, and then of Bruno de Boisgelin. She was that Aimée de Coigny who formed one of the circle of intriguing women of whom Talleyrand made such good use, and her chief characteristic, apart from her appetite for lovers, was a lack of principle as remarkable as her beauty, her charm and her intelligence. She was the mouthpiece of each lover in turn.

When Chénier saw her she was in her twenty-fifth year. Montrond had been imprisoned on the same day as herself, and she lost no time in falling in love with this handsome swashbuckler of twenty-four, who was as promiscuous in his love affairs as she could wish. The pair of them determined to gain their liberty, and fortune threw in their path one of those police-spies who acted the part of prisoners. This man, Jaubert, a Belgian actor, not content with the degradation of such a task, amused himself by betraying not only the prisoners but also his masters. His trick was to note down on his list of "conspirators" any rich man or woman. Then, for a consideration, he would cross off the name. While Chénier was watching the Young Captive and writing his verses, Montrond was negotiating with Jaubert, and finally his name and that of Aimée were deleted, and the police-spy pocketed a hundred louis. They were not released from prison until

two months after Thermidor, but they knew that their
lives were safe, and they looked forward with confidence
to their future. As for the melancholy man who had given
her a copy of verses, Aimée de Coigny possibly did not
bother to read them. At any rate she gave the poem to
Millin the archaeologist, who was a fellow-prisoner. And
it did not occur to her to interest herself in the author,
or to suggest to Montrond that they might try to save him.

So Chénier died, and the Duchesse de Fleury, Aimée de
Coigny, divorced her husband, which caused a scandal
even at that time, and married Montrond. She lived to act
as a go-between for Boisgelin, in his intrigue with Talleyrand, and to write those vivacious memoirs which are not
least valuable for their picture of Talleyrand himself in
his library in the rue St. Florentin, using his army of the
Faubourg St. Germain to destroy Napoleon. But her rest-
less temperament never found what it sought, and as lover
succeeded lover each diminishing happiness passed the
more quickly. After the Restoration she found herself
treated as the adventuress she was. Boisgelin left her, and
she was no longer of an age for fresh experiments. Her
health broke down, and by 1818 she could no longer
move about with ease. Lonely, suffering, disillusioned she
lived on until 1820. In that year, at the age of fifty-one,
she died. Her fellow-prisoner Montrond, lived to be
Talleyrand's last companion, and to spend the autumn
of 1837 at Valencay with him—the old statesman's farewell
to his country estate. And on that May morning when
Talleyrand lay dying in Paris, Montrond was among those
who waited in the antechamber for news.

Mme. Vigée-Lebrun, watching Aimée de Coigny one
day, read all the trouble and sorrow that such beauty
allied to such moral instability might bring upon her, and
prophesied for her an unquiet life. Her forebodings came
to pass, and the Young Captive had no time to notice that
she had once inspired the chivalrous devotion of a great
poet.

Ces chants, de ma prison témoins harmonieux,
Feront à quelque amant des loisirs studieux
Chercher quelle fut cette belle:
La grace décorait son front et ses discours,
Et comme elle, craindront de voir finir leurs jours
Ceux qui les passeront près d'elle.

The Pre-Conquest Saints of Canterbury

by W. A. PANTIN

THE CHURCH is not an abstract system, it is something always bound up with persons and places; and this is particularly well shown in the connexion which exists between certain places and certain Saints, what might be called the topography of the Saints. How do certain saints come to be connected with this or that place, and what have been the effects of that connexion?

If we try to answer that question, we can learn a good deal about the history of our civilization. From the earliest times every place, from Rome with its Apostles and countless martyrs down to the obscurest shrine, would naturally attach great importance to its own Saints and feel that it had a special claim upon their protection, a special hold upon them. This seems to be the idea, for instance, that underlies the remarkable phrase used in medieval Latin of the relics of the Saints: *pignora sanctorum*. The Saints have left their bodies with us, in this or that place, like something pledged or pawned, which they are therefore bound to watch over, until the last day when they come back to reclaim those pledges.

Something of the same idea is expressed by Prudentius in his fine poem on the eighteen martyrs of Saragossa: he pictures Christ coming at the Last Judgement, and all the cities coming before Him, each carrying the relics of its Saints, and happy the one who can show a large number—it reads almost like a variant of the parable of the talents:

> Plena magnorum domus angelorum
> Non timet mundi fragilis ruinam,
> Tot sinu gestans simul offerenda
> > Munera Christo.
> Orbe de magno caput excitata

> Obviam Christo properanter ibit
> Civitas quaeque preciosa portans
> Dona canistris.

Prudentius, almost like a guide book, runs through the cities of his corner of the Empire: there is Carthage with the bones of Cyprian, there is Cordova, Tarragona, Gerona *artubus sanctis locuples Gerona*, Calahorra, Barcelona, Narbonne, Arles, Merida, Complutum, Tangiers, Marseilles. The long line of suppliant cities carrying their offerings reminds one of a Byzantine mosaic frieze, or the picture of the provinces of the Empire doing homage to Otto III in the Reichenau Gospels.

This strong sense of the connexion between the Saints and their resting-places is particularly well expressed in the late Anglo-Saxon treatise entitled "Hae sunt notationes de sanctis qui in Anglica patria requiescunt."[1] This is a topographical guide to the resting places of the Saints throughout England; in fact it was probably intended as a guide-book for pilgrims. After beginning with the proto-martyr St. Alban, it goes very roughly in geographical order from north to south; from St. Columba at Dunkeld and St. Cuthbert newly arrived at Durham, it works down through Mercia and East Anglia to Kent and Wessex, giving the Saints who lie at each place. It was written in Anglo-Saxon, probably in Wessex, somewhere about the year 1000, and afterwards translated into Latin, and it came to be tacked on to an earlier treatise about the Saints of the royal house of Kent. It is one of the most attractive documents of the early Middle Ages; it is a perfect epitome of the local piety of the English people at a most interesting point of their history—just after the age of St. Dunstan and before the upheaval of the Norman Conquest.

In different regions, certain types of local Saints seem to predominate, according to historical circumstances. What

---

[1] Edited by Felix Liebermann as *Die Heiligen Englands*, Hanover 1889.

were the characteristics of England in this respect?[2] I think we can best approach this question by a contrast with France and the more central provinces of the Roman world generally, where the Church took root permanently during the periods of persecution. There naturally the martyrs take the first place; after all, the cult of the Saints is based upon the cult of the martyrs, as the very name of the martyrology reminds us. We may expect then to find the Saints of a French cathedral church headed by a martyred apostle and bishop, like St. Denys at Paris, St. Martial at Limoges, St. Benignus at Dijon, St. Saturnin at Toulouse, St. Sabinian and Potentian at Sens. The *gloria martyrum* comes first, then the *gloria confessorum*; that is the normal process, though sometimes a later confessor bishop like St. Martin or St. Germanus will overshadow the earlier martyrs.

Now in England this process is reversed or at any rate confused. When we speak of the "English Martyrs," we mean men of the sixteenth and seventeenth centuries. This is not entirely due to a historical short-sightedness, which only sees the foreground; it is partly because medieval English martyrs like St. Edmund or St. Alfege or St. Thomas are comparatively rare, though very distinguished; indeed their rarity helps to make them distinguished. The great bulk of medieval English Saints, the typical local Saints, are confessors. All this reflects and illustrates very nicely the history of the conversion and the growth of the Church in England. We must, it is true, put on one side, as exceptional, the earliest group of martyrs under the Romans, like St. Alban, and St. Aaron and Julius at Caerleon; that looks like the beginning of the same process that we have just seen on the continent, but it turned out to be a "false start"; at any rate, whatever happened under the Romans has left little mark on the calendar. And it may be noted that the most important

[2] The best general discussion of the early English Saints, done by a master hand, is Edmund Bishop's article on *English Hagiology*, in the Dublin Review, 1885, pp. 123-154. It is a great pity that this was not reprinted in his *Liturgica Historica*.

and far-reaching product of Roman Christianity in Britain was a confessor, St. Patrick.

The conversion of the Anglo-Saxons was a contrast to the conversion of the Roman Empire, for it was in its early stages remarkably bloodless; when trouble came, it was from pagan reaction in the North or pagan invasions. That is why the great founders and builders of the Anglo-Saxon Church were confessors, men like Augustine, Theodore, Dunstan, the Saints of Canterbury in fact, who do in this way represent the quintessence of medieval English sanctity. There were martyrs, but they were mostly of a different type, either, on the one hand, those produced for export, so to speak, like the English apostles of Germany and Scandinavia, or else belonging to that remarkable type, the martyr kings, who are so characteristic of early English hagiology.[3]

There are a surprising number of these martyr kings: SS. Oswald and Edwin of Northumbria, victims of Penda the pagan king of Mercia; St. Edmund of East Anglia, of course, the victim of the Danish invaders; and a large number, it must be admitted, who were the victims of the treachery or rivalry of their fellow Christians: SS. Oswin and Alkmund of Northumbria, SS. Kenelm and Wistan of Mercia, St. Ethelbert of East Anglia, St. Edward in Wessex, the princes Ethelbert and Ethelred in Kent. Perhaps in some of these cults we can see the same admiring pity or sense of pathos for a tragic end, which later led to the attempted canonization of Simon de Montfort, Henry VI, and even of Edward II and Thomas of Lancaster.

In England, as elsewhere, churches sometimes depend upon the presence of a single Saint, sometimes upon a whole collection of Saints. The late Anglo-Saxon catalogue of local Saints, the *Notationes de sanctis*, already referred to, shows a good many places with a single Saint. Some of the most important churches owed their importance to a single Saint, like St. Alban and St. Edmund at Bury and St. Edward at Westminster. The num-

---

[3] cf. Edmund Bishop, *op. cit.*, pp. 128, 139-40.

ber of local Saints connected with a particular church was not necessarily in proportion to that church's antiquity or importance. The great sees of Lichfield (the would-be metropolis of Mercia) and Dorchester-Lincoln have fewer Saints than one might expect. York had its first six archbishops from St. Paulinus; Hexham with St. Wilfrid's *confessio* crypt, and its rows of Saint bishops painted on the choir screen, is singularly impressive. Winchester had a group of Saint bishops rather later, from St. Swithun to St. Ethelwald and St. Alfege, in the ninth and tenth centuries. As we shall see, Canterbury far outstripped all other English Churches in the number of its Saints; next to it perhaps would come Glastonbury, with a remarkable series from St. Patrick onwards, reinforced by a number of great Northumbrian Saints, translated thither after the Danish invasion, apparently by King Edmund.

It may be noted that the tenth century saw quite a migration of relics from the North to the South of England; this was due mainly to the disappearance of Northumbrian monasticism in the Danish invasions, partly also to the monastic revival in the South. Besides what happened at Glastonbury, St. Odo, as we shall see, translated St. Wilfrid down to Canterbury, and St. Ethelwald translated many Saints, including St. Benedict Biscop from Wearmouth, to his foundation of Thorney in Cambridgeshire. Thorney, in fact, shows very well how a comparatively small and not very ancient or important monastery could more or less accidentally acquire an imposing collection of Saints. St. Ethelwald imported so many Saints' bodies that, as William of Malmesbury says, "almost every corner of the church is full of them," though he refuses to give their names, because they are so barbarous that they would only expose the Saints to ridicule.[4]

When we turn from a general consideration of the English churches and their Saints to examine Canterbury

---

[4] William of Malmesbury, *Gesta Pontificum*, ed. N. E. S. A. Hamilton (Rolls Series), p. 327.

in particular, it becomes clear that Canterbury stands out head and shoulders above the rest, and is in a class by itself; indeed it has few rivals outside Rome. There are several reasons for this preeminence; the very special connexion and analogies with Rome and the continent; the extraordinary number and importance of its Saints, steadily accumulating for five or six centuries after the Conversion; and the important effects, literary and historical, which this weight of accumulated cults had. And at almost every step the history of the Canterbury Saints touches on or lights up some piece of English history.

In the first place, it is important to understand that Canterbury, being a direct colony of the Roman church, is in a remarkable way a conscious imitation of Rome, a "new Rome" of the North. The Roman missionaries, St. Augustine and his companions, seem to have done their best to reproduce what they were familiar with at Rome, here at Canterbury, in the arrangement and dedication of the churches, and so forth. This imitation of Rome at Canterbury has several times been pointed out, by such different writers as the twelfth-century monk Eadmer,[5] Dean Stanley[6] and Duchesne.[7] "Canterbury était une petite Rome."

At Rome the Pope's cathedral church inside the walls is the basilica of St. Saviour, commonly called St. John Lateran; at Canterbury, too, the cathedral inside the Roman walls is the basilica of St. Saviour, commonly called Christ Church. At Rome, outside the walls, are the tombs and basilicas of the two Apostles, St. Peter's at the Vatican, and St. Paul's; at Canterbury, outside the walls is the monastery of St. Peter and St. Paul, later known as St. Augustine's. At Rome, and therefore at Canterbury, burial within the walls is forbidden; the first archbishops of Canterbury are buried outside the walls, in the monastery of St. Peter and St. Paul, which thus,

[5] *Edmeri Cantuariensis Cantoris nova opuscula,* ed. Dom André Wilmart, Revue des Sciences religieuses, 1935, p. 356.
[6] *Historical Memorials of Canterbury;* "the Landing of St. Augustine."
[7] Duchesne, *Autonomies ecclésiastiques,* p. 4 ff.

like its Roman prototypes, comes to have the tombs of its own Apostles, Augustine and the rest. In the same monastery and its cemetery are buried also abbots and members of the Kentish Royal family. Ethelbert is the Kentish Constantine, retiring gracefully from the royal city to make room for the church. At Canterbury, the Roman models are necessarily simplified and telescoped into one; the single monastery of St. Peter and Paul, with its cemetery, beside the Roman road to Sandwich, has to stand for both the Roman basilicas of the two Apostles, and for all the cemeteries that line the roads outside Rome.

The church of St. Pancras at Canterbury, built and consecrated by St. Augustine, is also an obvious Roman memory; and perhaps even the cathedral church of St. Andrew at Rochester is a memory of the missionaries' own monastery of St. Andrew's on the Caelian Hill. Rochester, too, in its close dependence upon Canterbury, may have some possible analogy with the suburban sees like Ostia and Albano that depend upon the Roman church. Perhaps Pope Urban II had some of these analogies with Rome in mind, when he described St. Anselm, in a famous phrase, as *alterius orbis Apostolicus et Patriarcha*.[8] In one respect the imitation of Rome left its mark on the whole country; the simple, fundamental dedications of the great Roman basilicas, St. Saviour, St. Mary, St. Peter and Paul, had almost a monopoly among the Anglo-Saxons, so that almost all the cathedrals and older monasteries were confined to one or other of these dedications.

Besides being a little Rome, Canterbury also, more perhaps than any other English see, had resemblances to the cathedral sees of neighbouring Gaul, though this was not a case of direct imitation, but rather was produced by similar circumstances. At Canterbury we have from the first a comparatively small diocese (and this distinguishes it from, say, York or Winchester) with its cathedral set within the walls of a Romano-British tribal capital, just like the cathedrals that one finds in Gallo-Roman

---

[8] Eadmer, *Historia Novorum*, ed. M. Rule (Rolls Series), p. 390.

tribal capitals all over France: Amiens, Chartres, Sens, Bourges, places that often have only the name of the tribe to use. This distinguishes Canterbury from the great rural, uncentralized dioceses of the rest of England. When Lanfranc after the Conquest ordered the removal of bishops' sees from country villages to *Civitates*, what he meant by a *Civitas* was obviously a place with Roman walls, like Chester or Lincoln or Chichester, and in this he may have had his own city of Canterbury in mind, as well as the almost universal practice of the continent.

Again, the position of the great abbey of St. Augustine just outside the city walls is curiously like those great abbeys that one so often finds outside the cathedral cities of France, like St. Denis at Paris, Marmoutier at Tours, Notre Dame de la Couture at Lemans, St. Martin at Autun, and so forth. Sometimes these great abbeys, especially if built over the tomb of a Saint, are so important that they can pull the population away from the cathedral city, and form a second and rival town round themselves: this is what happened at St. Front at Perigueux, and at St. Martial at Limoges. Nothing of this sort happened at Canterbury; but we can see how it could come about, if we imagine the Roman town of Verulam surviving side by side with the abbey and town that grew up round the tomb of St. Alban; and to a certain extent we have an actual example in London and Westminster.

Another thing that distinguished Canterbury was, as we have said, the steadily accumulating series of its Saints. This series falls quite naturally into two divisions, both as regards time and place: first, the series of Saints belonging to the Abbey of St. Peter and Paul (St. Augustine's), being mainly the early archbishops buried there down to Archbishop Cuthbert (740-760); secondly, the series connected with the cathedral of Christ Church, being also mainly the archbishops buried there since Cuthbert.

About the early history and appearance of St. Augustine's abbey church we fortunately know a good deal, thanks partly to excavations, partly to the writings of the

monk Goscelin, who described the rebuilding of the
church and the translation of the Saints in 1091.[9] Perhaps the first thing to notice is that before the Norman
rebuilding there was not one church, but several, lying
close together; the abbey church of St. Peter and Paul
itself; the church of Our Lady lying immediately to the
east of it; a small gate-tower, with an altar of Our Lady,
lying to the west; and at a greater distance to the east,
the church of St. Pancras. This multiplication of churches
within a single enclosure is interesting; one finds it elsewhere, for instance at Glastonbury, Monkwearmouth,
Hexham, and (later) Bury St. Edmunds, and also further
afield, as at St. Andrew's on the Caelian Hill and old St.
Peter's itself, at Rome, at St. Riquier, and in Ireland at
the monasteries of Clonmacnois and Glendalough. To
some extent no doubt it served the purpose of the numerous side altars of later times, but it must have made proces-
sions or visits from one altar to another into something
of a pilgrimage.

The original abbey church of St. Peter and Paul was
begun by St. Augustine in 598 and consecrated by his successor St. Laurence in 613. As a building, it belongs to
a group of seventh-century churches, what may be called
the Kentish or Augustinian basilicas, the other examples
being St. Mary's and St. Pancras nearby at Canterbury, the
original St. Andrew's at Rochester, and the churches at
Reculver and Lyminge in Kent, and at Bradwell-on-Sea
in Essex. These churches form a very vivid memorial and
symbol of the age when the English Church was being

[9] Goscelin's "History of the Translation of St. Augustine" is printed in
the *Acta Sanctorum*, May, vol. VI, p. 411 ff., and also (with some omissions)
in Migne, *Patrologia Latina,* vol. 155, col. 15 ff. For an explanation of
Goscelin's account, and descriptions of the excavations on the site, see W. St.
John Hope, *Recent discoveries in the Abbey Church of St. Austin at Canterbury* (Archaeologia Cantiana, XXXII, 1 ff.); R. U. Potts, *The tombs of the
Kings and Archbishops in St. Austin's Abbey* (Archaeologia Cantiana,
XXXVIII, 97); for the plan of St. Augustine's and the other basilicas of
the same type, see *Archaeologia,* LXXVII, p. 201; *Archaeological Journal,*
LVIII (1902), p. 402; A. W. Clapham, *English Romanesque Architecture
before the Conquest,* pp. 17 ff., 52.

founded; like the Roman villas before them, they show
the building methods and general arrangements of Rome
and the continent eagerly introduced, but with certain
necessary adaptations and simplifications and economies
in the plan. They are by no means literal copies of Roman
basilicas; they have no aisles opening into the nave through
rows of columns (there were few temples here to pillage
for ready-made columns); instead there is a fairly small
aisleless nave, and opening out of the nave by a narrow
archway on each side is a *porticus* or side chapel, which
can house an altar and burial places. The apse chancel
opens into the nave by three arches supported by columns,
not by the great triumphal arch of the Roman basilicas.

It is to this type that the abbey church belongs. The
nave was only 39 feet long by 27 feet wide. The high
altar was dedicated to St. Peter and Paul, the northern
porticus or side chapel to St. Gregory, the southern *porticus* to St. Martin. These two *porticus* are the most interesting parts of the church; their dedications are very
significant and appropriate; St. Gregory for obvious reasons presides over the tombs of the Roman missionaries,
St. Martin, the great patron of Gaul, over the Frankish
Bertha and her husband and chaplain.

St. Gregory's *porticus* contained the tombs of the earliest
archbishops, St. Augustine and his immediate successors,
most of them fellow monks and missionaries from Rome.
At St. Gregory's altar, Bede tells us, there was a special
Mass celebrated every Saturday. The two eldest sons of
St. Gregory, so to speak, lay on either side of his altar:
St. Augustine (d. 604) on the south, and his successor St.
Laurence (d. 619) on the north.

West of St. Laurence, continuing along the north wall
of the chapel, was St. Mellitus (d. 624), the third archbishop, who had previously been first bishop of London;
west of him, in the northwest corner of the chapel, was
Justus, the fourth archbishop (d. 627), previously the first
bishop of Rochester; south of him, in the middle of the
west end of the chapel, was St. Honorius, the fifth arch-

bishop (d. 653), who had sent St. Felix to convert East Anglia—it will be seen that these early rulers of Canterbury were also pioneers conquering the hinterland; and in the south west corner lay St. Deusdedit (d. 664), the first native English archbishop. These first six archbishops filled the little chapel of St. Gregory.

The monk Goscelin in a striking passage compares St. Gregory to a Roman patrician presiding over a family party: "The most blessed father of all these, Pope Gregory, having his altar in the middle like a patrician's chair, and protecting the same porticus dedicated to God, embraces with an everlasting love what are not so much the graves of those who are buried together, as the couches of those who feast together, *non tam funera consepultorum quam triclinia conviventium. Ecce ego et pueri mei quos dedit mihi Dominus.*"

The next archbishop, St. Theodore (d. 690), was of course one of the greatest of the Canterbury Saints; himself sent from Rome, and the second founder of the English Church, he was very much in the tradition, *Romanae praecellentiae subsecutor egregius,* as Goscelin calls him, and by rights he belonged to the Gregorian family in the north *porticus.* But since there was no more room inside the *porticus,* he was buried in the nave, as near as possible, right up against the south wall of the *porticus,* with only the wall between him and St. Augustine. His English successors, Brithwald (d. 731), formerly abbot of Reculver, and Tatwin (d. 735), were probably also buried in the nave near him to the west; Nothelm (d. 740), who had been to Rome, and was a friend of St. Bede and St. Boniface, was apparently buried in the *porticus* under St. Gregory's altar. He was the last archbishop to be buried at St. Augustine's, except for Jaenbert (d. 792), who was however buried not in the church but in the chapter house. After Nothelm, as we shall see, the archbishops were buried at Christ Church.

In St. Martin's *porticus* on the south side of the nave lay St. Ethelbert, the King, St. Bertha his wife, and St.

Liuthard, the Frankish bishop, her chaplain. This *porticus* did not develop further as a royal burial place, for its place was taken, as we shall see, by St. Mary's.

A few yards to the east of the main church of St. Peter and St. Paul stood the church of St. Mary, built by King Eadbald, son of Ethelbert, about 618, in reparation for his sins, and consecrated by Mellitus. We know little about its form, except that it was surrounded by *porticus*, so that it probably conformed to the "Kentish" type of basilica already described. It served as a burial place for members of the Kentish royal family, a "Pantheon of the Kings," for over a century, and its position in the heart of St. Augustine's symbolises very well the close connexion of the monarchy and the church.

It also contained, what is more to our purpose, some of the early abbots: St. Adrian (d. 708), the learned companion of St. Theodore, who made St. Augustine's famous as a school; his disciple and successor, St. Albinus (d. 732) and an Abbot John (d. 618). This church was, to take up again the comparison with Rome, the St. Mary Major of Canterbury. It was held in very special veneration by the local countrymen. Goscelin tells us that the English called it the *vestiarium* of Our Lady, and that on the feast of the Nativity of Our Lady, by ancient custom the people of the countryside, not only from Kent, but from London, Essex and Sussex, would flock to this church.

Its sanctity was not to be violated with impunity. When Abbot Wulfric (1047-59), with the best intentions, pulled down the west end of St. Mary's and the east end of St. Peter and Paul in order to build his new great rotunda to join the two churches, his death soon afterwards was interpreted as a punishment sent by Our Lady. Other miracles were reported in connexion with the church. One of the most attractive stories about St. Dunstan, a glimpse of the real man in between the cares of office, shows him slipping out by night to visit the "holy places" of Canterbury, *ut cervus ad fontes aquarum,* as Goscelin says; he goes to pray at the church of St. Peter and Paul, at the tombs of his predecessors, *pastorum ecclesiae limina,* and passing from one church to the other, he finds St. Mary's church on one occasion filled with great light and a choir singing the anthem *Gaudent in caelis animae sanctorum,* and another time he sees in the same church Our Lady with a choir of virgin Saints, singing the hymn of Sedulius *Cantemus socii Domino cantemus honorem.*[10]

Goscelin reports the same thing as happening several times in his own time, both in the old church, and in the new crypt that was built on its site: thus Abbot Scotland hears a choir as of men and boys *gratissimam consonantiam diapason reddentium.* Another monk sees Our Lady with a choir of virgins. A third hears the Introit *Salve sancta parens* sung; yet the place is shut and empty. St. Dunstan evidently had a particular interest in St. Augustine's. Goscelin records his saying that the place was so full of the Saints that you could hardly take a step in the church or cemetery without treading upon one of them; he re-consecrated the abbey church in honour of SS. Peter and Paul and St. Augustine, in 978, probably after enlarging it.

Most of the St. Augustine's Saints were, so to speak, indigenous; but there was one very important newcomer from outside, St. Mildred, who was translated here from Minster in Thanet in 1030, after the destruction of that monastery by the Danes. The story of St. Mildred is a very characteristic slice of early Kentish history: King Egbert murders his young cousins, the princes Ethelred and Ethelbert; their sister, St. Ermenburga, known as *Domna Eva,* evidently a strong-minded lady who would stand no nonsense, comes to the King to demand her brothers' *wergild* in the form of enough land in Thanet to found a nunnery, and sends her daughter Mildred across to France to be trained in the monastic life; Mildred returns, laden with relics, to receive the nunnery of Minster

[10] *Memorials of St. Dunstan,* ed. Stubbs (Rolls Series), p. 48, 118, 208.

to govern, together with the seventy virgins whom the King and her mother have collected to be trained by her: they take the veil from St. Theodore; this is the beginning of monastic life for women in Kent.

St. Mildred died in 725. When her body was brought to St. Augustine's in 1030, it was placed in a tomb before the high altar, with an altar at its head, at which the *Missa matutinalis* was celebrated. With her relics, all her land in the Isle of Thanet came to St. Augustine's. It should be added that St. Gregory's Priory at Canterbury made a rival claim to have the relics of St. Mildred.[11]

About 1050 Abbot Wulfric made his unfortunate attempt to connect the two churches of St. Peter and Paul and St. Mary with a great octagonal rotunda, probably intended to house the bodies of the Saints; this curious building may have been inspired by a similar rotunda at the church of St. Benignus at Dijon, which Wulfric may have seen on his way to visit the Pope at Reims in 1047. Wulfric's demolitions involved the removal of the bodies of St. Adrian (from St. Mary's) and St. Mildred (from before the high altar of SS. Peter and Paul) to the northern extension of the *Porticus* of St. Gregory.

The coming of the Normans inevitably meant rebuilding on a grand scale and therefore a general translation of all the Saints, who were mostly still lying in their original tombs. Abbot Scotland (1070-87), with Wulfric's fate before him, hesitated; but with the advice and sanction of Pope Alexander II, he began the rebuilding, which was completed by his successor Wido in 1091. Today we can still see the enormous sleeper walls of the Norman nave, riding ruthlessly over the tiny foundations of the original church and the empty tombs of the Saints. From one point of view, the contrast is a symbol of Norman arrogance and contempt for the Anglo-Saxon past; yet, in another way, it shows them captivated by that

[11] For St. Mildred, see Liebermann, *Die Heiligen Englands*, p. 4-6; Thorne's Chronicle in Twysden, *Hist. Angl. Scriptores Decem*, col. 1783, 1906 ff.

past, trying to build a worthier home for the Saints. The translated bodies were placed in shrines round the choir of the new church, and the whole process of translation was described with great enthusiasm by Goscelin, an eye-witness.

The Saints of the Cathedral of Christ Church, in comparison with those of St. Augustine's, are more numerous but also more miscellaneous and present a wider contrast in importance.[12] They fall in fact into several classes:

(1) First, there are some Saints of the very first rank, with a liturgical cult: SS. Dunstan, Alfege, and later SS. Anselm and Thomas, who are more important than any of the St. Augustine's series except SS. Augustine and Theodore; and to these should be added St. Odo and perhaps Aelfric. (2) Then there is a *turba magna* of lesser names, comprising almost all the archbishops from Cuthbert (d. 760) to Aethelnoth (d. 1038) of varying historical importance; these are really men "of holy memory" rather than "Saints," in the strict modern sense; they do not seem to have had a liturgical cult, still less, of course, was there any question of formal canonisation; but their relics were translated and preserved with some veneration in the cathedral as rebuilt after the Conquest, being placed for instance over side altars; and in the fourteenth century, as Edmund Bishop has pointed out, there seems to have arisen a popular cult of them, "popular at least among some members of the Christ Church community," so that they find their way into a calendar, and there are some lists of them, and a prayer.[13] To these may be added two

---

[12] For the local cults and calendar of Christ Church, see Gasquet and Bishop, *On the Bosworth psalter*, pp. 27 ff, 57 ff, 123 ff; *English Benedictine Calendars after A.D. 1100*, ed. F. Wormald (Henry Bradshaw Society), p. 63 ff; J. Wickham Legg and W. St. John Hope, *Inventories of Christ Church Canterbury*, pp. 29 ff; R. Willis, *Architectural History of Canterbury Cathedral*, chapters I-III passim, and the useful table of burial places and plan, p. 133 ff.

[13] Gasquet and Bishop, *op. cit.*, p. 123-5, where a prayer to these Saints is given. Eadmer wrote the life of one of these lesser Saints, St. Bregwin, *Anglia Sacra*, II, 184.

others whose bodies were kept with these "Saints": archbishop Lanfranc, whose obit appears in calendars as "Transitus Lanfranci," and Queen Ediva (d. 961), a noted benefactor, whose "table" or picture with descriptive verses still survives in the Cathedral.[14] (3) Thirdly, there were a number of relics brought in from outside, such as St. Blaise, St. Wilfrid of Ripon, and so forth.

As to the cathedral church itself in Anglo-Saxon times, we can get a much less clear picture of it than we can of St. Augustine's; here there are no foundations remaining, we only have the well known description by Eadmer[15] of the old church as it stood at the time of the Conquest, when it had already been partly rebuilt by Archbishop Odo (942-58). According to Eadmer, it was to some extent an imitation of St. Peter's of Rome; it had a nave and aisles; at the east end was an apse with a sanctuary raised upon a crypt, after the manner of a Roman *confessio*; in the apse stood the high altar, with another altar, the altar of Christ, in front of it; in front of this again, at the foot of the steps, was a third altar, the matutinal altar; at the west end was apparently another apse, containing the archiepiscopal chair, with the altar of Our Lady in front of it; two towers projected from the sides of the nave, the northern with an altar of St. Martin, the southern with an altar of St. Gregory—the same significant dedications that we have seen at St. Augustine's; the memory of these survived in the altars of St. Gregory and St. Martin in the eastern transept of the existing cathedral.

The starting point for our purpose comes with archbishop Cuthbert (740-760). He determined to break with the old rule of extra-mural burial at St. Augustine's, and obtained a privilege from the Pope, sanctioning the burial of subsequent archbishops in the cathedral. For this purpose he built a church dedicated to St. John the Baptist,

[14] *Archaeologia Cantiana*, XXXVI, 1.
[15] See Willis, *Architectural History*, Chapters I-II, where Eadmer and other authorities are collected; cf Dom Wilmart, *op. cit.*, pp. 365-6.

adjoining the cathedral to the east, to serve partly as a baptistery, partly as a place for ecclesiastical trials, partly as a burial-place for the archbishops; it was probably circular or octagonal in form, like other baptisteries and tombhouses of the period. In spite of the natural resistance of the monks of St. Augustine's, his plan was carried out; he and his successors, with the exception of Jaenbert (792), were buried at Christ Church, either in the cathedral itself or in the church of St. John.

There is not much to note for the next century, though the archbishops accumulate; but with Plegmund (890-914) we come to a more interesting period which goes on till the conquest. Plegmund is important in himself, he was the friend of Alfred, and he is also notable for our purpose as starting the process of importing Saints from outside; on his second visit to Rome in 908, he "bought the blessed martyr Blasius with a great sum of gold and silver," and brought him back to Canterbury. Even more important is St. Odo (942-958), "Odo the Good," as Dunstan called him; perhaps of Danish birth, he became the friend and counsellor of English Kings, and stood with Athelstan at the battle of Brunanburh; he was the uncle of St. Oswald and the patron of the St. Dunstan, and was one of the men who prepared the way for the great monastic revival of the tenth century; he was the patron of scholars like Abbo of Fleury and Fridegode. It was he who rebuilt the cathedral, and brought to it new relics, the body of St. Wilfrid from York which he placed in the high altar, and St. Audoen (or Ouen) from Rouen.[16] Fridegode's verse life of St. Wilfrid, made to celebrate this translation, marks the first revival of English hagiology since Bede, according to Edmund Bishop.[17] Odo's tomb "in the form of a pyramid" was on the south side of the altar of Christ in the cathedral; St. Dunstan never passed the tomb without kneeling.[18]

[16] For St. Audoen's translation, see Dom Wilmart, *op. cit.*, pp. 362 ff.
[17] *Dublin Review,* 1885, p. 150.
[18] *Memorials of St. Dunstan,* p. 109.

There is no need to enlarge upon the greatness of St. Dunstan himself (960-88), as the re-founder of English monasticism, as a reformer and statesman, as one of the men who made the new England of the tenth century; he is one of the greatest of all English saints. He, too, brought new relics into the cathedral, those of St. Siburgis. He himself before his death chose his burial place, in the middle of the choir of singers, immediately in front of the steps leading up to the altar, "leaving a mournful and loveable memorial," says Eadmer, "whether to those singing in the choir, or to those ascending the steps to the altar."

The last of these great pre-conquest archbishops was St. Alfege (1005-12), a notable product of the monastic revival, and the first martyr of the church of Canterbury; when he was translated from the see of Winchester to Canterbury, he brought with him the head of St. Swithun, which he placed in the altar of Christ in the front of the sanctuary. St. Alfege was martyred at Greenwich and his body was first taken to London; the story of his translation to Canterbury in 1023 is instructive. It is the Danish king Cnut who puts himself at the service of the martyr, as he did in translating that earlier victim of the Danes, St. Edmund; he is warned that he will have no peace unless he promises to bring back the relics to Canterbury *servato more antiquorum*—here we see the weight of tradition, Alfege must lie with his predecessors; the King in person brings the body out of London, crossing the Thames in his viking ship, *aureis rostrata draconibus,* his Housecarles keep the indignant Londoners at bay.[19]

There were other relics brought to the church, I do not know when: the head of St. Fursey, an Irish apostle of East Anglia (650), placed in the crypt beneath the high altar, the head of St. Austroberta, placed in the altar of Our Lady; the body of St. Wulgan; and the body of St. Salvius, bishop of Angoulême, which according to one account was given to the church by William the Con-

19 Wharton, *Anglia Sacra*, II, 143-7.

queror in 1085, but on the other hand seems to have had a cult here before that time.[20]

The Anglo-Saxon cathedral was burnt down in 1067. A new cathedral was built by Lanfranc a few years later, and during the century that followed Lanfranc's church was more than once modified by successive rebuildings and extensions of its eastern limb.[21] All this building activity had its effect upon the cult of the local Saints, and vice versa. First, as at St. Augustine's, so here the total rebuilding under Lanfranc necessarily meant the digging up and translation of the bodies of the Saints, including the rank and file of the archbishops buried in the tomb-house or baptistery of the old church. What had been tombs in the old church became shrines or relic chests in the new church; and this gave the Saints a new prominence. Lanfranc's church had a long nave, two storied transepts, and a very short choir; the space for the shrines was limited, and most of them were stored, so to speak, in the upper part of the north transept (over what was later the Martyrdom).[22]

In the early twelfth century, the choir was rebuilt on a much larger scale, with a pair of eastern transepts and chapels round the apse; this was the "glorious choir" of Prior Conrad, and it was consecrated in 1130; it made the cathedral one of the larger churches of northern Europe, comparable in size and plan to the great abbey church of Cluny. The new choir had many more side chapels, and therefore more space for the fitting display of the shrines; this may have been one of the motives for the extension. When the choir was rebuilt again after the disastrous fire of 1174, it was again extended eastwards, and this was explicitly for the purpose of housing the shrine of St. Thomas and his Corona. The translation of St. Thomas to this new shrine took place in 1220.

We can now see how the bodies of the Saints were dis-

[20] Gasquet and Bishop, *op. cit.*, pp. 36, 57-8.
[21] Willis, *Architectural History*, Chapters III-V.
[22] Willis, *op. cit.*, p. 16.

posed about the church, from the thirteenth century onwards, when these eastward extensions had been completed.[23] In the choir itself, the high altar was flanked
by the shrine of St. Dunstan on the south and St. Alfege
on the north; a beam over or behind the high altar carried
a number of relic chests, which included the relics of St.
Blaise and St. Salvius; and on the north side stood the
great almery or relic cupboard. Beyond the high altar, at
the top of a flight of steps, stood St. Thomas' shrine; beyond that again, in the eastern extremity of the church,
was the shrine of the "corona" of St. Thomas, flanked by
St. Wilfrid on the north and St. Odo on the south. In
the south east apsidal chapel of SS. Peter and Paul was
St. Anselm.

The two eastern transepts that flanked the choir, with
their small apsidal chapels, housed a large number of lesser
relics. In the south eastern transept, the altar of St.
Gregory had Bregwin on the south side, Plegmund on the
north; the altar of St. John had Aelfric on the north side,
Aethelgar on the south. In the north eastern transept,
over the altar of St. Martin, on a beam, stood the shrine
of St. Swithun, on the north side of the altar stood the
shrine of Living, with Queen Ediva below, and on the
south side Wulfred, with Lanfranc below; the names of
Ediva and Lanfranc can still be seen roughly scratched
on the wall over where their bodies lay. Over the altar of
St. Stephen stood the shrine of St. Wulgan, with Aethelard
to the north and Cuthbert to the south. In the main
western transepts there were at first more relics: at the
altar of St. Michael in the south transept, St. Siburgis and
Feleogild, and at the altar of St. Benedict in the north (or
Martyrdom) transept, lay Wulfhelm, Ceolnoth, Aethelm
and Aethelnoth; but when the western transepts were rebuilt by Prior Chillenden (1390-1411), these relics were
removed to the eastern part of the church, and placed
on beams over the altars of the south eastern transept and
over the entrance to the Corona.

[23] Willis, *op. cit.*, p. 133; Wickham Legg and St. John Hope, p. 32-40.

What were the historical and literary effects of the cult of these Canterbury Saints after the Conquest? In the first place, the Saints of Canterbury played an important part in the history of what really happened to England and the English people at the Norman Conquest. They are a symbol that is not at all irrelevant to the present day; from a materialist point of view, their cult was something intangible and inconsiderable, a theme for hagiographers, a liturgical curiosity, yet it proved so strong that the greatest political calamities and oppressions could not extinguish it; on the contrary, it captured the foreigner and the invader.

The Norman Conquest had for a time a disastrous effect upon old English religious traditions and cults, as it had upon certain forms of literature and art. This was due at worst to sheer arrogance and contempt for the Anglo-Saxon past—we hear of respectable Norman abbots contemptuously throwing away the bones of their predecessors, calling them boors and simpletons[24]—at best it was due to the desire of ecclesiastical martinets to have everything tidy and "correct," to abolish anything unfamiliar— as in the temporary suppression of the feast of the Conception. Edmund Bishop has shown how the Canterbury calendar was purged of its local feasts under Lanfranc; the metropolitan church even suffered the indignity of having the calendar of Winchester, the civil capital of the kingdom, imposed upon it: a curious display of political power.[25]

Gradually, however, in the course of the late eleventh and twelfth century, "Englishry" reasserts itself, the Old English cults find their way back. The beginning of this process can be seen in the well-known story of how St. Anselm persuaded Lanfranc to recognize St. Alfege as a true martyr. Among the English members of the community of Christ Church Canterbury, reviving devotion

[24] *Gesta Abbatum Sancti Albani*, I, 62; Will. Malmesb., *Gesta Pontificum*, 421.
[25] Gasquet and Bishop, *op. cit.*, pp. 27 ff.

to the local Saints showed itself, very happily, in literary form; Osbern the Precentor of Canterbury (d. c. 1100), at the command of Lanfranc, wrote up the life and translation of St. Alfege, and the life of St. Dunstan; Eadmer (d. 1140), the friend and disciple of St. Anselm, wrote lives of SS. Dunstan, Wilfrid, Odo, and Anselm, and other hagiographical works.[26] These men were sometimes very near to what they were writing about; Osbern tells us that at the translation of St. Alfege it was two monks who opened the martyr's tomb; one of these, named Alfward the Long, had been a disciple of St. Dunstan, *cui datum est magno quondam adhaesisse Dunstano*; the other, named Godric, a disciple of St. Alfege, lived to tell Osbern the story of the translation. Osbern and Eadmer had seen the cult of the local Saints eclipsed and then revived.

With Eadmer in particular, this cult is bound up with the patriotic feelings of Englishmen under the Norman yoke. "Eia inquam vos Angli" . . . he breaks out, in a sermon on St. Gregory; in more than one place he clearly expects his hearers or readers to have not only a veneration but a quite personal affection for the Saints of their own race and their own place.[27] When he is describing how Queen Emma and Cnut gave a relic of St. Bartholomew to Christ Church, he adds proudly and wistfully: "for in those days there this was the custom of the English, that they prized the patronage of the Saints above all the things of the world"[28]—it is the English version of *tales ambio defensores.* He sees in the revival of the feast of

[26] For Osbern and Eadmer, see *Dictionary of National Biography*; T. Wright, *Biographia Britannica Literaria (Anglo-Norman period)*, pp. 26, 80; Tanner, *Bibliotheca*, pp. 563, 243; and their works printed in *Anglia Sacra*, II, pp. 78-226 *passim.*

[27] Dom Wilmart, *op. cit.*, pp. 213, 190-1, 210 (ll.131-6).

[28] Eadmer, *Historia novorum*, 109. This attitude of the Anglo-Saxons towards the Saints and their relics may have contributed towards the peculiar strength and reliability of the oath of a "lawful man," upon which so much of English law was based, until the disintegration of the later middle ages (cf. the laws of Cnut, II, 36; and J. E. A. Jolliffe, *Constitutional History of Medieval England*, pp. 8, 410 ff); it also gives special point to the story of Harold's perjury and its punishment.

the Conception a "revindication of ancient English piety, an assertion against new Norman lordliness and learning of a despised and downtrodden Englishry," as Edmund Bishop has put it.[29] When he is bitterly rebuking the monks of Glastonbury for their claim to have St. Dunstan's body, he says that he is ashamed that such lies, and such ridiculous and clumsy lies at that, should be put forward by Englishmen; if they must fabricate lies, could they not have got help from one of those clever foreigners who are so much better at that sort of thing?[30]

It was only natural for Englishmen to feel strongly about their English Saints; what is much more remarkable, and really most moving, is to find, as we do find, the Saints of St. Augustine's being written up by foreigners. Goscelin, who wrote the history of the translation, as we have seen, was one of the numerous foreign clerks, Lorrainers, Flemings and Normans, who came over in the early eleventh century; he was a Fleming, a monk of St. Bertin, who came over in 1058, and eventually settled at St. Augustine's. He was a most prolific writer and devoted his whole life to English hagiography, writing the lives of the St. Augustine's Saints, the early archbishops from Augustine to Theodore, SS. Adrian, Mildred, Letard, and the history of their translation so often quoted above; and he also visited and wrote up the Saints of many other places in England. We can see how sincerely he entered into the feelings of the English towards their own Saints, by a phrase like this: "let Augustine be sought, in the place of his burial, by his own England, *a sua Anglia requiratur*"; or in the words which he puts into Abbot Scotland's mouth: "*quam veneranda aula universae genti Anglorum, quam beata patria sanctorum radiis illustrata patronorum!*" He was also a skilled musician. William of Malmesbury puts him next to Bede as an English hagiographer: *Felix lingua quae tot sanctis servierit, felix pec-*

tus quod tot vocales melodias emiserit.[31] Then about a generation later, a Poitevin, Reginald, came and settled as a monk at St. Augustine's, about 1092, and he too celebrated the Saints of St. Augustine's, this time in Latin verses.[32]

The successive lives of St. Dunstan show very well how a great Canterbury Saint could appeal to writers of different origins and types: first the anonymous writer (c. 1000), a "Saxon," perhaps a continental "Saxon"; then Adelard, monk of St. Peter's, Ghent (c. 1011), dedicating his work to St. Alfege; then Osbern and Eadmer, the local hagiographers; then in the early twelfth century William of Malmesbury, with a Glastonbury interest.

The rebuildings and the consequent translations at Canterbury must have kept attention fixed on the local Saints, particularly at Christ Church, where the relics had to be moved more than once. At one time the relics, as we have seen, were kept in wooden chests in an upper part of the cathedral church, probably the upper floor of the north transept; and Eadmer gives us a vivid picture of the sacristan lying up their at night before the shrine of St. Wilfrid; he wakes to find the church filled with light and angelic persons singing the office, and those who read the lessons or chant the responsories climb the winding stair to ask a blessing before the Saint's body.[33]

Another anecdote of Eadmer's shows us a foreign admirer of these Christ Church Saints, a German monk named Lambert, from Saxony, who had been brought over with King Henry I's second queen in 1121, and was living with the Christ Church monks. He began to frequent the place where the relics of the archbishops were kept, to pray there, to say Mass there, and to make himself at home there (*familiariter conversari*); he would ask the monks questions about the archbishops' relics, who this

[31] For Goscelin, see Tanner, *Bibliotheca*, p. 334; Dom André Wilmart, *La legende de Ste Edith en prose et vers par le moine Goscelin*, in *Analecta Bollandiana*, LVI.

[32] *Neues Archiv*, XIII, 519 ff.

[33] Willis, p. 16-7.

or that one had been, and what might be the name of the
one who rested in this or that coffin. When he was told
about St. Bregwin (who had been a fellow-countryman
of his by origin), he tried hard to persuade the archbishop,
the monks, and the King himself, to let him have the
Saint's body to take back to Germany, but without success.[34]

The twelfth century brought two new Saints of the
greatest importance, St. Anselm and St. Thomas, and the
fame and miracles of St. Thomas drew pilgrims from
everywhere. A process of centralization can be seen at work,
in pilgrimages as in everything else; a few great pilgrimages of international reputation seem to take the place of
the innumerable local cults that we see in the *Notationes de sanctis*. But it must not be thought that St.
Thomas drove out the older cults at Canterbury. Each
time a monk of Christ Church entered the choir for matins
or left it after compline, he had to make a visit to the
shrines of St. Dunstan and St. Alfege that stood on
each side of the high altar.[35] The devotion to these Saints
takes a very quaint form in one Canterbury charter, which
gives as its list of witnesses: "Our Lord Jesus Christ and
St. Mary ever Virgin and St. Thomas the Martyr and St.
Dunstan and St. Aelfege and all the Saints of our church,
and Robert the porter and Martin the Seneschal and
Gilbert of the Hall . . . and many others."[36] I have already mentioned the popular cult of the lesser Canterbury
Saints at Christ Church in the fourteenth century.

Finally we can see the cult of the local Saints on the
eve of the Dissolution in two Christ Church manuscripts,
typical monkish collectanea of the period; one of these,
MS 298 of Corpus Christi College, Cambridge, contains
a life of St. Thomas in English verse written by Laurence
Wade, a monk, in 1497, and early sixteenth century notes

[34] *Anglia Sacra*, II, 188-9.
[35] *Instructio Noviciorum secundum consuetudinem ecclesie Cantuariensis*,
Corpus Christi College Cambridge, MS 441, pp. 359 ff, esp. p. 376, 383.
[36] Cited by V. H. Galbraith, *The literacy of the medieval English Kings*,
p. 24.

about the relics of SS. Wilfrid, Swithun, Dunstan, Alfege
and Audoen; and the list of Christ Church monks that follows in the same MS shows us monks, between 1493 and
1527, adopting names like Anselm, Bekett, Elphee, Wilfrid,
Audoen, Austen, Gregory, as surnames, instead of the
names of their native villages as had been usual.[37] The
other manuscript, Lambeth MS 159, was written by Richard
Stone, a monk, in 1507, and passed through the hands
of several other monks, and from the note of an obit in
1546, it looks as though the last monk owner kept it after
the Dissolution. It contains a large and important collection of Saints' lives, SS. Dunstan, Odo, Bregwin, Alfege,
Blaise, Salvius, Audoen, Anselm, Augustine, Ethelbert;
there are included four miracles of St. Blaise performed
at Canterbury, one dated at 1451. In 1508 the controversy
with Glastonbury over the claim to have the body of St.
Dunstan was reopened, and archbishop Warham made a
solemn examination of the Canterbury shrine of the
Saint.[38]

What I have just been describing shows chiefly how the
local Saints coloured the lives of those who lived on the
spot, the monks of Christ Church and St. Augustine's.
More important historically but more difficult to gauge,
is the effect upon the successive archbishops themselves.
Wherever they turned, there were the "mournful and
lovable memorials" of the Saints, the "pyramid" by the
altar, the shrines and chests upon their beams and over
the altars; most of the Saints in this accumulating series
were their own predecessors; one day for better or worse
they themselves would have to be fitted into the series.
The effect on any sensitive or conscientious occupant of
the see must have been quite overwhelming. We have already seen how St. Dunstan felt towards the tombs and
"holy places" of Canterbury, and how St. Anselm vindi-

[37] *Chronicle of John Stone,* ed. W. G. Searle (*Cambridge Antiq. Soc.*),
p. 193 ff.
[38] *Memorials of St. Dunstan,* p. 426 ff.

cated St. Alfege; if the prayer to St. Dunstan formerly
attributed to St. Anselm is not really his work, it is no
doubt the work of one of his Canterbury disciples.[39]

Then as to St. Thomas: much has been written about
his life and character, and particularly about his "conversion" from chancellor to archbishop. I think he must
have been profoundly influenced by the memory of his
predecessors—obviously by St. Anselm, but also by the
others all round him. When he said his first Mass in the
Trinity chapel, he had in front of him the shrines of two
militant churchmen, St. Odo and St. Wilfrid, while
Lanfranc lay on his left hand, and Theobald on his right.
Every time he approached the high altar, he had to pass
between the shrines of St. Dunstan and St. Alfege. We
are told that as he waited during the chants of high Mass,
he used to read the prayers of his predecessor St. Anselm.
His friend John of Salisbury speaks of the archbishop returning in 1170 to Canterbury, "the city of the Saints."[40]
In his last sermon, on Christmas day, St. Thomas spoke
of the "holy fathers of the church of Canterbury," the
confessors and the one martyr, St. Alfege, adding that
they might soon have another martyr;[41] one can see that
he was not going out of his way to boast, but that, with
the sight of the shrines all round him, the idea was almost
forced upon him. Finally, when he died, the local Saints
seem to crowd in on his martyrdom; where he stood, in
the north transept, he had behind him in the chapel of St.
Benedict the tombs of Ceolnoth, Athelm (St. Dunstan's
uncle), Wulfhelm and Aethelnoth; in the chapel above
his head, the relics of St. Blaise,—the same upper chapel
where a ghostly singer had once asked a blessing of St.
Wilfrid's relics. Almost his last words were to commend

[39] Osbern, writing to urge St. Anselm to come to Canterbury, appeals to
the history of archbishops SS. Lawrence and Dunstan (St. Anselm, *epp.*
III, 2).

[40] *Materials for the history of Thomas Becket,* ed. J. C. Robertson (Rolls
Series), VII, 395.

[41] *Ibid.,* III, 130.

himself and his cause to God, St. Denis, *St. Alfege and the patron Saints of the church*.[42]

I have dwelt at some length on the early Saints of Canterbury and their cult, and I have stopped short of dealing with the cult of St. Anselm and St. Thomas themselves, because the latter are so familiar to every educated Englishman, that they need no comment here; whereas it is only too easy to lose sight of the earlier Saints, and to imagine that Canterbury, as a holy place, began with the martyrdom of St. Thomas. There could not be a greater mistake. Not only are the early Saints extremely important in themselves, but we cannot even understand the later Saints if we fail to realize that they came at the end of a great series that had been accumulating over half a thousand years. The history of these early Canterbury Saints brings out very clearly the importance of that most formative period of English history, the Anglo-Saxon period, that lies between the Conversion of the English and the Norman Conquest, and the strength and continuity of the culture and traditions that were formed then, which could not be destroyed by political upheavals like the Danish and Norman invasions; we have seen how the newcomers themselves were captivated. It was this indestructible continuity that impressed the monk Goscelin, when he contemplated the tomb of St. Augustine, remaining intact like the ark of Noah, amid *tot tempestatibus bellorum, tanto diluvio paganorum, exterminio populorum, subversione urbium et ecclesiarum*. And finally it may be said that at the present moment in history there is every reason why we should remember and look to these Saints, the founders and protectors of our civilization:

> Plena magnorum domus angelorum
> Non timet mundi fragilis ruinam.

[42] *Ibid.*, III, 141, 498-9, II, 320.

The Myth of Arthur

by DAVID JONES

In olde dayës of the King Arthoúr
Of which the Britons speake great honoúr
All was this land full fill'd of faërie
The elf-queen with her jolly company
Danced full oft in many a green mead
This is the old opinion as I read:
I speak of many hundred years ago.
Chaucer's Wife of Bath's tale

"THE STORIES of Arthur are the acts of Albion." So William Blake, in the Eighteenth Century, expresses in nine words a great part of a tradition around which so much has been written, and with so many differing emphases. It can be taken as the text to much that I would try to say in this essay, but not to the whole, for even his brief intuitive statement leaves a lot unimplied. But in that statement the Genius of Blake permitted him to register a 'bull' or certainly an 'inner' as she so frequently did, whatever the target should happen to be. We may begin by quoting one or two significant references from these "acts of Albion."

"In those days Arthur fought against them (i.e. Saxons) with the Kings of the Britons, but he, himself was *dux bellorum*." So Nennius, early in the Ninth Century, in explicit documentary form, gives us the rank, name, and number of a concrete historical military person of the later part of the Fifth Century.

"*Patricius Arthurus, Britannie, Gallie, Germanie, Dacie, Imperator.*" Thus Caxton in his preface to Malory describes the inscription on the supposed seal of King Arthur, existing for the credulity of the Fifteenth Century.

"Yet some men say in many parts of England that King Arthur is not dead, but had by the will of our Lord Jesu into another place; and men say that he shall come again and he shall win the holy cross. I will not say it shall be so, but rather I will say here in this world he changed his life. But many men say that there is written upon his tomb this verse: *Hic Jacet Arthurus Rex, quondam Rex que futurus."* So Malory in the last Book of the *Morte Darthur* begins to bid farewell to the hero of his Romance

> A grave for March, a grave for Gwythur
> A grave for Gwgawn of the ruddy sword
> Not wise (the thought) a grave for Arthur

This, according to the late Professor John Rhŷs is the translation of a Twelfth Century Welsh fragment (From the *Stanzas of the Graves*) referring to the chieftain, the *gwledig,* of native tradition. *Dux bellorum* says the historian, Emperor of the West says the bogus relic, the King once and the King who shall be says the Christian romance writer, the mysterious chief, for whose funeral-mound only a fool would search, says the bardic tradition.

All this and a good deal more is implicit in the name of Arthur. "Strange are the metamorphoses"—to restore again the plural number to the Victorian parlour-conundrum. How Nennius' sub-Roman war-duke, the cavalry commander of the 5th Century—(the organiser and leader of a mobile field-force, typical of the reorganised Imperial armies of that age) should have emerged as the pivotal figure of the most important cycle of romantic literature in Europe—that is of everlasting interest.

How came this upper-class Romano-Briton (at least, his name, *Artorius,* makes this status most likely) to be the focal point of medieval romance in Britain, France, Germany, Italy, Spain, all the West? And still more significant, how came he to be identified with the cult-heroes of a mythology, already venerable and decaying when he himself was living? How came this probably methodical, prosaic, civilised soldier of the *status quo,* with a grasp of the new continental cavalry tactic, who, no doubt with

Churchillian "blood and sweat and tears" pulled together, for half a life-time a situation very much out of hand in this island, to be the star figure in a vast body of literature spreading over many countries and centuries? This question must intrigue anyone capable of being intrigued at all. It is as though the organiser of the Home Guard became, in a thousand years' time, identified with Britannia and Poseidon, and further became the focal point of a romance-cycle, or as though General Wavell were to become confused with both Horus and Scipio Africanus, and Cyrus the Younger too, by a desert-association, then for there to gather round his name a film-romance sequence in the biggest Anglo-American racket of A.D. 2741; for it is an equivalent space of years that separates Arthur the man, from Arthur the hero of a full-fledged romance development.

The theories are numerous and hotly disputed. There are the "Celticists" of more than one school, and their opponents of many schools. French and German, English and Welsh scholars have all made their contributions and elucidations. Whatever the deposits and however unexpected the influences—whatever, for instance, be the importance of the Dodona myth, and of other classical ingredients, or of the Breton as opposed to the Welsh substrata—all have passed through, one way or another, one, a Celtic, two, a French chivalric sieve (either and), before they reach us to-day.

There is a native, one can perhaps say "English" tradition; it is poetic and literary and has a genuine sequence. Wace—Layamon—Geoffrey, echoes in Chaucer, Malory of course, Drayton, Camden, Spenser, and almost Milton, who drew back from writing his *Arthuriad* and chose the more lugubrious theme of the fall of Satan. It is interesting to surmise what he would have made of the Arthurian material; he certainly would have given it enormous prestige in the minds of Englishmen, but if all his tremendous poetic gifts did not redeem his dramatised theology when Satan was his hero, it seems likely that his natural an-

tipathy to the medieval synthesis would have been a disadvantage had he chosen Arthur. But his weight and
power would have influenced all subsequent approaches
to this material, and given it a new twist, and the associations and connotations which surround it for us today
would have been proportionately different.

For instance, it is unlikely that we should have the
Idylls of the King to contend with, had the formidable
figure of Milton stood over the Victorian bard. The statement with which this essay begins shows us to what degree Blake was susceptible to this British Myth. There is
no need to mention Morris and all the Pre-Raphaelites.
Just recently, and with a fresh interest and wider imagination and understanding Mr. Charles Williams, in *Taliessin through Logres* taps the same springs. In this poem,
I think for the first time, different elements of the legend
are employed together; Lancelot is, as it were, introduced
to Taliessin. The material is used freely and to Mr. Williams' own poetic purpose, so that he makes, for the first
time for a very long while, some contribution to the tradition, and restores something of its wider implications
in a very personal manner.

I suppose that for most English-speaking people Arthur
is still best known through Tennyson. One does not find
that Malory is very generally read—nor for that matter,
is Tennyson, but I mean that if one said the word
"Arthur" in a drawing-room and then asked what it in-
stantly evoked in the minds of those present, most would
reply "Tennyson," or the "Idylls of the King"—rather
than "Malory" and certainly rather than "Nennius" or
"late-Roman horse-troops" or "Celtic war-god" or "agriculture deity."

Whilst one comes across individuals for whom Malory
is an essential part of their luggage, it cannot be said that
the arthur saga has any great place in the consciousness
of the mass of our countrymen. A civil servant here, a
colonel, a typist, an artist there, will, however, be found

to light up when anything germane to this myth is mentioned.

If people with Welsh affinities are drawn toward this thing it is not because the Welsh topography is particularly rich in Arthurian associations; for that matter, Cornwall and parts of England proper, and the lowlands of Scotland are perhaps richer. Neither is it because there is a full popular, continuous, folk-tradition in Wales that might be regarded as, so to say, the "Q text" of the romances—this is not so, and such as there is, seems, according to the authorities, to be of indifferent authenticity and of "late" development.

What makes the Arthurian thing important to the Welsh is that there is no other tradition at all equally the common property of all the inhabitants of Britain (at all events of those south of the Antonine Wall), and the Welsh however "separatist" by historical, racial, and geographical accidents, are devoted to the unity of this island. There is, I think, some indication that though he were a Saxon, a Norman, an Angevin, an "Englishman," the man who wore "the crown in London" was regarded as the representative of the "monarchy of Britain," truly a usurper, truly a Hywel or a Rhodri ought to be wearing that crown, but still the King in London may well have been regarded with some awe, for he sat in the seat of the great ones of a largely imaginary past, or at least of a past in which the great names were metamorphosed and glorified.

These corruptible had put on, in a way, incorruption, Llyr, Coel, Lludd, Patern, Ætern, Beli, Bendigeidvran, Mascen Wledig, Arthur Wledig, Cadwaladr Vendigeid. Echoes of the Celtic migration-waves and of the more recent Belgic infiltrations, merge with Roman administrators and sub-Roman battle-chiefs. Later on, after the English pressure had divided the Welsh of Wales from those of Strathclyde and Cornwall, insignificant "heads of kindred" or leaders of war-bands, operating in areas as circumscribed as Arvon, Arguistli, Elmail (districts of Snowdonia, Plinlimon, west Radnorshire) came perhaps to be identified with heroes of previous and more generous dominion.

The oral style easily telescopes history and geography, and the bards may have deliberately done so, in singing the tune in praise of the prince who paid the piper. In his introduction to the *Lays of Ancient Rome* Macaulay suggests that the early Latin ballad-singers employed the terms and copied the formulae descriptive of the feats of Hector and Achilles; similarly, the domestic bards would describe the doings of the princes of Powys or even of the lord of a *cantref* as though their swords had been decisive in the fate of Europe.

By the same spirit the monastic compiler of the *Brut y Tywysogion* (The Chronicle of the Princes) could write, under the date 1201, of the too early death of a local chieftain: "About the feast of Peter and Paul, Meredudd son of Rhys, an extremely courteous young man, the terror of his enemies, the love of his friends, being like a lightening of fire between two armed hosts, the hope of the men of South Wales, the dread of England, the honour of cities, the ornament of the World, was slain."

This was the mood and this the mode, unrealistic, exaggerated, deserving the Scroogian retort "don't be flowery, Jacob," but determined by the spirit. "Our conversation is in heaven" urges Paul on Christians in the tenements of Roman Philippi—"Our conversation is with Arthur" urges the Bard of the Household on his patron, the lord of a sheep-run hill and half a valley, seated by the central hearth-stone, where the life of the household smoulders, between the central supports,—the song of the lost living-space of empire adding zest to the more immediate project turning in his mind, of how best to forestall his detested kinsman over the hill, in the matter of grazing rights and the cutting of timber.

Mr. Robert Graves tells a story of disgruntled Welsh soldiers of 1914-18, saying, through their appointed spokesman, something of this sort: "We do not like our Sergeant-Major, he do curse and he do swear, and he is moreover

a man of lowly origin" (I quote from memory). In the
Twelfth Century, Giraldus says "The Welsh esteem noble
birth and generous descent above all things . . . even
the common people preserve their genealogies." Neither
in the twelfth nor the twentieth centuries, is this, in
essence, "snob"—it is rather a pathetic consciousness of
past greatness in present meanness, and to that past greatness the name of Arthur is integral—even if, in actual
fact, his name plays a less important part in the most
authentic and earliest sources, than is sometimes supposed,
and even if, later, it is easily transpositioned with that
of Owen Lawgoch and Owain Glyn Dŵr. The sleeping
hero under the mound that drunken peasants stumble
upon at night over the mountain, and the many and varied
versions of this theme are continuous and valid, under
whatever name.

Indeed, just as in some districts later heroes have taken
the place of Arthur as the sleeping-hero-who-will-come-
again, so his tradition echoes a still earlier one. Rhŷs in
his chapter on cave legends in *Celtic Folklore, Welsh and
Manx*, quotes from a passage in Plutarch's *De Defectu
Oraculorum*, with reference to the British Islands, "Moreover, there is, they said, an island in which Cronus is imprisoned, with Briarius keeping guard over him as he
sleeps; for as they put it, sleep is the bond of Cronus.
They add that around him are many divinities, his hench-
men and attendants."

The tradition of the returning saviour in Welsh folk-
lore seems at least as positive as that of the return of Our
Lord in the Christian scheme. The hope of "the bright-
ness of his coming" was potent enough to affect actual,
hard, sordid, political, practical affairs. The Owen Lawgoch mentioned above is the Yvain de Galles of Froissart's
Chronicle; he had great reputation as a soldier of fortune
and fought for the French King on land and sea against
the English in the Hundred Years' War. Presumably his
long absence from his native land and travellers' tales of
his exploits gained him a place in this honourable se-

quence. He was assassinated by a paid English agent. His bones lie in a church of Saint-Léger, in France, but he nevertheless sleeps in a cave in South Wales, in his majestic role of successor to the great Arthur and to the greater and more elemental Cronus.[1]

That Owain Glyn Dŵr should have been assimilated into this succession of returning saviours, is easy enough to understand; the wonder is, as Rhŷs suggests, that there was much room for the other Owen (their dates over-lap). He suggests that the Welsh found it wiser to refer to the more remote and longer-disposed-of figure than to the "Owen Glendower" of "our indentures tripartite" and the Pennal Dispatch. Today we do not have to exercise much imagination to see how necessary this discretion may have been. Glyn Dŵr was a bit near the knuckle for the English officials.

There is again the hackneyed story of the abbot meeting Glyn Dŵr in the early morning on the hill slope. The fugitive leader remarks on the abbot's early rising, and receives the reply "It is you who are about early—too early, by a hundred years." It will seem that in one way and another the same "he shall come again" persists. As late as the early last century ballad-singers, it appears, had a jumbled and broadsheet version of this theme in which every age was concertinad. It is a fascinating subject but we must leave it for a moment.

That the Welsh princes were willing to admit the suzerainty of the English Kings, was not always and entirely because theirs was a Hobson's choice, for there was a lingering tradition of the *ameraudur*, the emperor.

After the death of Cadwaladr and the assumption by Edwin of the bretwaldaship (he had the *tufa* carried before him, according to Bede, like a Romanised official) the break comes. As the first entry in the *Brut y Tywysogion* says: "Henceforth the Britons lost the crown and the

[1] It may be remembered that Cronus, like the more local deity with whom Arthur's name may have connection, was also originally a god of agriculture.

kingdom and the Saxons gained it." From then on the
welsch, by an impertinence of history, "the foreigners,"
dug in behind a line vaguely corresponding to the modern
Welsh Border, for their six hundred years' war with England. That is to say the highland zone, with its particular
traditions and way of life was again in opposition to the
lowland zone with its new prestige and continental connections. Actually that losing battle, in various forms,
continues. Whitehall, Wall Street, the cinema, the wire-
less, are inevitably the allies of the lowland thing, as
surely as were the Court of Rome, and the rising civilization of Europe, in the early Middle Ages.

Nevertheless, on the Celtic fringe the vision of the unity
of the island was never entirely lost. That the barbarized
Romano-Celtic *sub-reguli*, increasingly less Roman and
increasingly more Celtic, never found unity among themselves, was no doubt mainly due to the inability to sink
local prestige, characteristic of societies in certain stages
of development and decline—and perhaps particularly
characteristic of Celtic societies. But over and above all
this there was present an aggravating cause: They could,
none of them, admit real allegiance to any among themselves, but "the head of the princes of this island" (so
Kulhwch addresses Arthur in the tale of Kulhwch and
Olwen). Yet the office implied in this and similar expres-
sions was at the best shadowy, indeed the shadow of a
shadow, for the *Comes Britanniae* office was hardly that,
and now even that shadow was cast in the shape of a
Northumbrian war-chief. As the troubled centuries drew
out that shadow gained substance and in the process assumed a more compelling aspect, until the metamorphosis
was complete, in the crowned and anointed figure of an
English and Christian King; and the lords of the ancient
remnant, the last representatives of Rome and before
Rome, "Sought Edward as Lord."[2] That the reality be-

[2] The Tenth Century West Saxon King, Edward the Elder son of Alfred
the Great, sometimes regarded as the first to whom the title "King of
England" could be applied.

hind the shadow had been inaugurated and maintained
by the Roman administration and idea—that this was the
origin of British unity was not for long of propaganda
value to the aggressed—in fact the tendency was all the
other way, to get behind the Roman thing and to think
in terms of a primitive Celtic greatness. In the Welsh
tales Arthur conquered Rome, not Caesar Britain. In the
somewhat late story of the *"Dream of Mascen Wledig"*
the emperor of Rome, the lord of the world, dreams of
the charms of Helen of Britain, Elen of "the hosts," Elen
of the "army paths." "Not more easy to gaze upon the
sun when brightest, was it to look upon her by reason
of her beauty . . . a frontlet of red gold was upon her
head, and rubies and gems were in the frontlet, alternating with pearls and imperial stones . . . she was the fairest
sight that ever man saw." And his embassage coming to
find the object of his dream, arrived, by way of Snowdon,
in Anglesey and "they beheld the maiden sitting on a chair
of red gold" and went upon their knees, saying "Empress
of Rome, all hail." That's the way round it was in the
Welsh mind. We are inevitably reminded of William
Camden, "It (Britain) is the masterpiece of Nature, perform'd when she was in her best and gayest humour;
which she placed as a little world by itself, by the side
of the greater, for the diversion of mankind" (*Britannia,*
1586).

The loves of Britain and Italy are a long standing affair.
Were India to become abandoned by the present administration, and were a period of chaos to supervene, and
were a Mongolian adventurer, of some sub-Stalinist dynasty, to sit in the vice-regal seat at new Delhi, he might
for the inhabitants of Kashmir, have a just sufficient whiff
of the British Raj to command some sort of respect, and
in these days, Lord Curzon might be sung of as a native
ruler of fabulous pretensions, and even Warren Hastings
might be metamorphosed into an indigenous cult-hero—
so strangely does myth weave its meander.

The tradition of Arthur is a subterranean one, it emerges to have significance, sometimes here, now there. An example of its significance in actual affairs may be cited from the tradition of David, brother of the last Llywelyn. Hunted from one fastness to another, he was finally secured, it is said, by the treachery of his own people, to whom he had been so great a traitor; and with him were taken the heirlooms and regalia of his house, among which, and chief of which, were a relic of the true cross and the "crown of Arthur." Edward, it is said, had these exposed at Westminster.

Whether elements in this story are factual or apocryphal, it serves to show that for both conquered and victors there was significance in such spoil. The loss of Arthur's crown and Christ's cross together would indeed be symbolic of the final overthrow of the pretensions of the princes of the highland zone to represent the tradition of rule in Britain, and for the English there could be no better symbols of the passing of the *imperium* to themselves. If these events occurred, they did but set the seal on the events of the late Seventh Century.

The other story of Edward ordering the head of Llywelyn to be crowned with ivy and set up on the Tower has a similar connotation. It is supposed that this was done in derision of part of a vatic tradition that a Welsh prince should ride crowned through London. West Cheap is mentioned as a district through which this mock was enacted, but it was at the White Tower that the spectacle had most significance, and most interest for us in our present study.

"The Towers of Julius," "The White eminence in London, the place of fame," these were familiar to Welsh tradition, the mound by the river, where it was said that the head of Brân the Blessed was inhumed to secure the land against invasion and unfertile crops, the place of the cist that Arthur opened because he would secure the land "by his own might alone" was indeed appropriate to the

ivy mock (at least one chronicler mentions a silver coronet
—but the ivy crown seems more common to the legend) at
the expense of the last representative of a dynasty that
had origin in the Roman collapse and which men then
held had roots more ancient still, roots indeed in "windy
Troy."

Both Archbishop Peckham and the Welsh leaders in
their stormy correspondence before the breaking off of
negotiations, refer to the Trojan tradition. In this connection the Archbishop raised issues of a moral nature, to
the detriment of the other party, a recurrent tendency
when Governments are decided upon the extinction of an
opponent. A few years later, Edward, in his correspondence
with Boniface VIII urges his claim to the Scots' Crown,
in virtue of the Troy-Brute-Britain myth and the sub-
jugation of the "whole people of Scotland" by "King
Arthur" all set forth, as though it were sober history. I
seem to remember a story about the holding of a tournament at Nevin, to round off the conquest, but I can't
put my hand on any reference to it. If, however, it took
place it would have the same signification and intention.

There could be no doubt, who in fact bore most outward resemblance to the Arthur of the *clerwr*, the itiner-
ant story-teller, who entertained the tribesmen in wooden
hendref and *hafod*[3] with tales of silken pavilions, auburn-
headed pages, caparisoned steeds, Cordovan shoes. These
descriptions have come down to us in such stories as
Peredur, the *Kulhwch*, the *Rhonabwy*, all of which, I
understand, were in their present form before the close
of the thirteenth century.

Any tournament or display of chivalry in thirteenth-
century Wales would muster among those "whose bright
eyes rain influence and award the prize," the Evas of
Tracy, the Sybils of Neufmarché, the Isobels of Cadurcis,
the consorts of Warrenne, Breos, Mortimer. These could

---

[3] *hendref* and *hafod*, winter and summer habitation, indication of movement from lower to higher pasture with the seasons.

of course better dress the parts of the ladies of the old tales.[4] But what about the Senenas, the Angharads, the Gwenllians?

They all were fled; perhaps to seek communication with Hawais and Hunydd and Generys, the century-dead mistresses of Hywel the Poet-Prince, or to call to remembrance Creirwy the daughter of the enchantress, and Tegau of the Golden Bosom, who flit mysteriously across the path of the Arthur of the native deposits. If, from the hills they wove a magic of vengeance, it was to prove as ineffectual as the earlier female incantations, when Mediterranean transports first forced the Menai shallows, twelve hundred years before. Not since Suetonius Paulinus had anything so totalitarian been possible. Sea power was again one of the deciding factors.[5] The embryo British Navy blocked Menai; and the Celtic sea, the ancient liaison with Ireland, which more than once had been useful to the Welsh political exiles, and vivifying to Welsh poetry and metric,[6] was severed; the game, at long last, was up.

At all events, all was a rubbing-in of the final passing of the *imperium* from the impoverished "dregs of the Trojans"[7] to the surcoated, powerfully harnessed, *de facto* inheritors. Not for nothing did Gruffydd ap yr Ynad Coch sing in his lament for his dead prince:

[4] I may misinterpret the degree of discrepancy between English and Welsh cultural life at that date. The fusion between tribal and feudal societies was in progress; and the evidence as to how much the arms, clothes, conditions, common to England, France, Europe were in vogue among the Welsh upper classes is difficult to determine in the absence of any plastic or visual art to speak of, and the written records are not of the kind to assist us much.

[5] Professor J. E. Lloyd has pointed out the importance of sea control in the reduction of North West Wales.

[6] See *Ireland and Wales, their Historical and Literary Relations,* Cecile O'Rahilly, Longmans Green.

[7] Henry of Knyghton gives a latin verse, which refers thus to the dead Llywelyn: "the totem of the Welsh, the chief and barbaric assassin of pious men, the dregs of the Trojans," and he juxtaposes it to an expression of the Welsh sentiment regarding him: "the exemplar of culture, the jewel of his fellow-rulers, the flower of Kings past and gone, the pattern of those who are to come, the leader, the praise, the law, the light of the people"—*Dux, Laus, lex, lux populorum.*

"Do ye not see the oaks beating together?
Do ye not see the waves scousing the land?
Do ye not see the truth gathering itself together?
Do ye not see that the world is done? . . .
Why are we left to wait?"[8]

That precisely two centuries later the Welsh should
have regarded the coming in of the Tudors as a belated
fulfilment of their hopes was perhaps natural—the genealogical connection of Richmond with Ednefyd Fychan,
and so with the Welsh Kings was sufficient to excite a
people devoted to such credentials, bogus or true—but
in the event "the Breton Richmond" and the new order
he inaugurated, in spite of his propagandist unfurling
of the "Dragon of Cadwaladr," proved a mockery—a
treble-mockery, for it was insensitive to Welsh tradition,
to much of the tradition of England, and to the central
tradition of Europe—a bad sign for a resuscitated Arthur.
Anyone inoculated with the Arthurian virus is likely to be
proof against any appeal which leaves out of account the
complexity of our tradition. Such a person is likely to feel
unfortified on those later, thinner, nourishments which
may be offered.

The *matière de Bretagne* (if one may borrow an expression used very early of the literary and romantic
Arthurian deposits and apply it to the island myth) is a
very mixed affair—not Celtic, nor Teutonic, nor classical,
nor national, nor Christian, but all these. Any tradition
is wanting which springs, for instance, from any one of the
pivotal landings, separately insisted upon, whether that of
William, Augustine, "Horsa," Caesar; or any tradition
resting solely, let us say, on the impressive events suggested
by the date 1588; and as for the tradition of 1688, it were
better not mentioned if we are to tune our ears to:

". . . ditties highly penn'd
Sung by a fair queen in a summer's bower"
or if you will:
". . . drunken prophecies, libels and dreams"

[8] Cf. The Development of Welsh Poetry, Ch. 111, H. I. Bell, Clarendon
Press, 1936.

for the texture of the thing we are examining is shot through with all this, and much more. Its composite weave is its essential characteristic, and its hues change under the changing lights, and we tire the eyes of the mind regarding it.

The Welsh Arthurian story of "The Dream of Rhonabwy" ends thus:

> "This Historia is called *The Dream of Rhonabwy*: and this is the reason why no man, be he bard or *cyvarwydd*, (story-teller, or seer, as opposed to court poet) knows the tale without a book—because of the many colours that were upon the steeds, and those of many a surpassing hue, and on the arms and their trappings, and the scarves, and on the virtue-bearing stones."[9]

We feel ourselves in similar plight, sometimes, with regard to the whole of this tradition. But in considering the tradition of a folk and a locality we must be prepared for a tortuous journey. The zone we search is traversed and Troia'd, we stumble from sections of well-revetted entrenchment, upon old workings fallen-in and shapeless, bombarded by the creeping-barrage of successive traditions. This comparatively intact duck-board track ends abruptly in a no-man's-land where fertility symbols jut up from craters made as recently as the twelfth century, and the female bear-deity of pre-history is seen swaying under the last star-shell, curiously uncertain of how to behave in full mediaeval mail.

But we must keep our heads down and creep toward; we have been ordered to secure identifications. Its papers are long since rotted, but perhaps under its steel hat we shall find bound a classical fillet, or beneath its rusted cuisses, the female thigh-bone of Artio. Across the waste land the growl of the creature—sacred, perhaps, to the inheritors of the La Tène culture (the workers in bronze,

[9] This translation is given by W. J. Gruffydd in his essay on *The Mabinogion*, Transactions of the Hon. Soc. of Cymmrodorion, Session 1912-1913.

the creators of a true abstract)—breaks against fragments of Gothic crenellation, and startles the ornaments of a Christian altar. The "bear of the Island" is inestimably old, its visage reflects millenniums of change. It knows sex-transmogrification, as it knows ploughshares can become swords, as it knows the waters of baptism can find a valid subject in the most elemental of creatures, as it knows that totems can be susceptible to chrismal acts.[10]

It can be seen that we are in a place of deep recession and super-imposition, of booby-trap and trip-wire. There are the oral and written folk-lore deposits, the slim "Nennian" material, the genuine Romance documents, the Ossianesque inventions, the tentative findings of the better scholars, the too easy conclusions of the lesser ones. In these circumstances we who feel the power of this thing, but who possess no specialist knowledge, and can so easily be caught out, can at least avoid one error. We must not be as those Christians who say of their composite tradi-

[10] I may have hung a very heavy package on a very insecure and possibly "condemned" peg. But it appears that there is evidence, from Gaulish inscriptions, of the existence of a male god of agriculture called Artaius, later on a war-deity, and behind that, evidence for a female deity called Artio found in association with a bear symbol, and as there seem to be philological connections between the Gaulish word for bear, and the names of the goddess and the god, it is suggested that the bear was possibly used as a totem among the still earlier Celts, although, as far as the plastic remains are concerned, other animals figure with prominence, horses, lions, boars, birds, whereas this cannot be said for the bear. It is further suggested that Artaius, the hero-god, may later have become associated with Arthur the man-hero. In historic times the rhetoric of Gildas bestows the title *Ursus* on one of those leaders he felt it necessary to admonish, but the suggestion that this has reference to Arthur is entirely conjectural. Bear—Goddess—God of the soil—God of weapons—Romano-British general—Christian King, the sequence at least may be suggestive for both those who adhere to the notion of inevitable progress and to those also who do not set proper store by the Doctrine of Development. Certainly we are today familiar enough with the actualities of an economic system being painfully re-geared so as to serve military necessities, and of "open cities" becoming "walled"—so that the frequent phenomena of agriculture deities becoming war deities noted by students of mythology. (Mars himself went through some such transformation—at least of emphasis) does not surprise us. In fact we seem to be experiencing in actuality in many ways what the myths of mankind have already mapped-out for our "information and necessary action."

tion: "The Old Testament means nothing to me—I am not concerned with the disgusting God of the Hebrew tribes, not yet with the tradition of the Synagogue"—or again "Greek thought only obscures the Gospel message" or again "True Christianity has no connection with mystery cults—we do not want Mediterranean Sacraments, or primitive eatings of the god." We know what a solvent all this can be—the same is true of the myth of Arthur. Blougram's

> "Clearing off one excrescence to see two,
>   There's ever a next in size now grown as big"

has some application here.

We must be careful with our rejections or these will be a disintegration—all will fall apart—he will be, not there, as surely as when, after Camlann, he suddenly was gone, with howling queens and barge and all—no king then—but "waters wappe and waves wanne"—for Bedivere. We must be careful not to isolate one part of his tradition, especially not to both isolate a part and then to develop and embroider it, so that at length it loses all affinity to, and all contact with, the complex of the ancient deposits.

This was Tennyson's trouble—what he left out. The objection that he invested his subject with the values of his own age, is in itself a most unsound objection—the poets have always done that—that is indeed their job, but all the time we should feel, along with the contemporary twist, application, veneer, or what you will, the whole weight of what lies hidden—the many strata of the thing. It would require a master of detection indeed, to sense in his Tristram "one of the three stout swineherds of the island of Britain," or to suspect in his Guenever the Welsh Gwenhwyfar, "bad when little, worse when big," one of three of Arthur's wives, neither is there in his Arthur himself any reverberation of the formidable totem of Celtic antiquity.

It may be objected that, after all, the genuine romance literature is equally swept clean of the primitive origin, but that would be a most superficial notion, for in Chrestien, Malory and the rest, we are aware of unplumbed deeps and recessions below and beyond the mediaevalised and christianised story. Gusts drive down upon us through sudden rifts in the feudal vaulting; up through the Angevin floor, we stumble upon twisted roots of primaeval growth among traceries of Gothic and Christian workmanship. Behind the contemporary "sets" the ever recurring "passing meek gentlewoman" complete in the paraphernalia of mediaeval high life—at the frame in the bower, at "matins and mass" in the enclosure at the lists (for us it is all almost Wardour Street by now), we scent things of another order. "She was put to school in a nunnery, and there *she learned so much that she was a great clerk of necromancy.*" Could we loosen the jewelled girdle and remove the rich cloth of vair, the figure beneath would be very other than that of "a fair lady and thereto lusty and young." Rather we should see displayed the ageless, powerful, vaticinal, mistress of magic, daubed with ochre, in the shift of divination, at the gate of the labyrinth—the spellbinder of some earlier society, where, though *Teste David cum Sibylla*, it was the latter who had most to say.

The Chapel of the Grail discloses a symbolism and ritual which a Sacred Congregation of Rites would find hard to define in purely Christian terms, but twelfth century allegory and French genius made superb use of the material. Never was the unicorn more subtly tamed, never was there a more fruitful baptism. The mustard seeds sown in remote times and places (how remote and what places we must leave to the specialists) had tough and tangled roots, tendoned deep down, but the French husbandmen pruned and grafted to some purpose, so that that herb cast its branches over many lands, and the singing birds of half Europe came to rest in its branches. They have sung in many modulations and harmonic recessions and with disparate intention. That full-plumed Faustian-throated bird that sang the *Parsifal* as late as the eighties of the last century was another fowl altogether from that which

chirped on west hill the *Peredur* (Percival of Welsh tradition,—called "Peredur of steel arms" in the earliest
poetry.)

To pursue the simile of the root and the branch; what
the romance writers did (and the cigar must here be
handed to the French nation) can be expressed as cultivat-
ing and developing the above-ground growth, the flower-
ing rod—as for the roots, they are another matter (although to-day they intrigue us most) they were enduring
long before. The Frenchmen did not plant the tree, but
they did have the intelligence and artistry, as might be
expected of them, to "produce" the fruit in a style and
taste corresponding with the demands of their market, and
that market was to be found in the smart society and courts
of West Christendom.

All the roots were by no means under the French ro-
mancer's forcing-frame, his Christian pruning knife and
chivalric fertilizer could not be universally applied. Tough
and ancient, deeply embedded fibres, shot up other ten-
drils to star like the saxifrage among the fissures of the
native hill-sites, to be cultivated as part of the tradition of
Western sea-board valleys. Those growths were impreg-
nated, we may suppose, with pollen blown from over the
new baily wall. The sophisticated strain shows itself in
the wild species. So much so that whether certain stories
possess much or any original element, in spite of the native nomenclature, and conversely how much others,
wholly courtly in terminology, hide a genuine early
tradition, are questions which a person without specialist
knowledge would be advised not to discuss.

But it is zero hour for the proper scholars, and also, alas
for the partizans. It is the moment both for the sparse
monograph, and for the letter to the journal, for: "Dr.
Nodens is most certainly mistaken if," and "it seems un-
believable at this date that," and "as I have already
pointed out, in" and "the available evidence tends, perhaps." There as laymen we must leave it, taking note of
the enormous complications of the theme. In the

Kulhwch ac Olwen (well known to English readers
through Lady Guest's *Mabinogion*) the giant task-setter,
Yspaddaden, says to the hero on the achievement of the
many and difficult feats necessary to the obtaining of the
bride: "She is thine, but therefore needest thou not thank
me, but Arthur who hath accomplished it for thee." There
are similar passages suggestive of the binding and loosing
power of Arthur. Sometimes one seems to detect in his
attributes things analogous to attributes of the Son in
Christian theology; and in the Taliessin poem, called
The Spoils of Hades, he raids the cold recesses of the
Celtic underworld, in his ship *Prydwen*, to bring to mor-
tals, it would seem, the valuable spoils held by the prince
of that place:

"Before him no one had entered it. . . . beyond the
glass fort they had not seen Arthur's valour." There was
the cauldron with the jewelled rim, that would boil no
"coward's food," there was the brindled Ox with the fabu-
lously long halter, the "fairy" city with the eight gates.
The setting is amphibious, a place of islands, and necks of
land, of crystal towers, of transparency and extreme cold,
unstable, with lights shining, which (like those familiar
Véry lights slowly gyrating over a 1916 or, I suppose, a
1940 Flanders field) coldly illumine, but do not clarify the
scene. He achieves his quest with great loss of men: "Seven
alone did we return" although his expeditionary force was
"three freights of *Prydwen*," his ship.

As in the case of Aeneas, it may be said we emerge from
this labyrinth through the ivory gate, whence issue "false
dreams"—not much the wiser, except to have grasped the
great wisdom that the iceberg of existence is vaster, by
many times in its hidden bulk, than what appears on the
mid-day ocean, and that, after all, is the lesson of any
"initiation"—from the most technically religious experience, to the better-knowing of a friend's mind.

If we are altogether impatient of what is seen darkly in
a mirror we shall have little use for the myth of Arthur.
We must not have too great a passion for continuous
definition—we must not look for an Ingres when Pascin

paints—the lady is apt to be fox just when we have got her appropriately placed.

Whatever tangle of myth is in this obscure material it is evident that here as in the romances, and as historical figure, Arthur is the conveyer of order, even to the confines of chaos; he is redeemer, in the strict sense of the word; he darkens the Lombard threshold only with his weapon; his potency is the instrument of redemption, the pawn-ticket that he presents is called *Caledfwlch, Escalibor, Caliburn,* with which he killed the black sorceress, the daughter of the white sorceress, and with which he mastered Palug sea-cat, is in Môn. Always the consolidator, the saviour and the channel of power, the protector and gift-giver, and more significantly for us "the Director of Toil." Treachery is his undoing, in all the deposits and, as is suggested in Collingwood and Myers' *Roman Britain and the English Settlements,* it is not unreasonable to conject that this tradition echoes an historical probability. That the romances should have made that treason and undoing centre round the *affaire* of Lancelot and Guenever and of course the "ill-vassallage" of Mordred,[11] is not surprising considering their period, bias, and intention; but we will return to that in a moment. It is of interest to remember that Lancelot is of late introduction, he seems not to occur in any of the Welsh or other folk-tales, he is a romance figure, and as romance figure he has altogether ousted Gawain in importance; whereas in the early stories, it is Gawain who is the most famous, Gawain, the Welsh Gwalchmai, "one of three golden-tongued Knights," notorious for his courteous behaviour in both Welsh and English tradition, as for instance in Chaucer's *Squire's Tale*:

> "As well in speech as in his countenánce,
> That Gawain with his oldë courtesý
> Though he come again out of Faërie,
> Him couldë not amendë with a word."

But it is notable how in Malory, Gawain, taking second

[11] The Medraut of tradition, always a figure of treachery and plot.

place to Lancelot in every virtue, is sometimes far from courteous, his bravery is still on the whole allowed him, but his character has certainly changed for the worse.

Although Lancelot seems to be an introduced figure, nevertheless, in the earliest known form of his story, the *Lanzelet*, a Middle High German poem by Ulrich von Zatzikhoven, he is called the son of King Pant of Genewis (identified by some as Gwynedd, that is, North West Wales).[12] There seems to be some very primitive material in this story which the romance authors dropped or modified, but that he was fosterling to a lake-fairy (hence his name) has remained. This connection with water-maidens and wonder-cities under pools is at least suggestive of Celtic affinities. The theme is common to so many lakes, meers, mountain-pools and places of sea encroachment throughout the Welsh lands.

The folk tradition of the insular Celts seems to present to the mind a half-aquatic world—it is one of its most fascinating characteristics—it introduces a feeling of transparency and inter-penetration of one element with another, of transposition and metamorphosis. The hedges of mist vanish or come again under the application of magic, such as Geraint ap Erbin encountered, just as the actual mists over peat-bog and tarn and *traeth* disclose or lose before our eyes drifting stumps and tussocks. It is unstable, the isles float, where was a *caer* or a *llys* now is a glassy expanse. The young herdsman offers his barley cake to the yellow-haired girl, "a ransom in her comb,"[13] who rises from Llyn y Fan Fach;[14] his ecstasy is

---

[12] See Sir Lancelot of the Lake by Lucy A. Paton, Introduction, Broadway Mediaeval Library, Routledge, 1929.

[13] See Mr. René Hague's poem *Green Christmas*, privately printed.

> "She counts her hair for gold
> The silver-footed one
> A ransom in her comb"

There is an associative interest in Mr. Hague's image; it so happens that it was conceived in connection with purely personal affairs which by chance had for their background a district not far removed from Llyn Safaddan (Llangorse lake) notorious for its lake-legend associations.

[14] See *Welsh Folk-Lore and Folk-Custom*. T. Gwynn Jones, Methuen, 1930.

short-lived, but a second time and third she appears—
there is courtship and marriage—but nevertheless "the
three inadvertent blows" are given, and water-bride and
all her dower of fairy-kine, the waters claim again, just
as Arthur's power dissolves with the disappearing, in dark
water, of *Excalibur.*

But to return to Lancelot, whatever be the remote
origin of his tradition, those, somehow very moving words,
in the French prose story (*Le Livre de Lancelot del Lac*)
"I know that he is of the land of France, for right well
he speaketh the language thereof," expresses, one feels,
his position in the main; it was under the aegis of Romance
that he assumed his importance, and that means under the
French aegis, that means his importance as "lover," for,
like the modern American film makers, the courtly writers
were concerned to establish the love interest above all else.
They "rationalized" the dark struggles of a folk-mythology
which they could not understand, and changed the emphases of possibly historical, military and political in-
trigues to fit the love game. The themes of Christian
mysticism and passion between the sexes was cast over the
whole material at their disposal—it was a vulgarization
as well as a refinement.

Matthew Arnold in his *The Study of Celtic Literature* has something to say about this: "how evidently the
mediaeval story-teller is pillaging an antiquity of which
he does not fully possess the secret; he is like a peasant
building his hut on the site of Halicarnassus, or Ephesus;
he builds, but what he builds is full of material of which
he knows not the history, or knows by a glimmering tradition merely; stones 'not of this building,' but of an
older architecture, greater, cunninger, more majestical."

From the rise of Romance literature until just recently,
the love interest has dominated the field in all our story-
telling; there are signs that the tide is turning—both in
literature and in life, which is the raw material of literature. The war of cultures and ideologies has returned,
our individual passions are already taking a modified

position in relation to affairs of race and myth and idea. In Europe to-day "men march, they keep equal step" to "death's sure meeting-place the goal of their marching," they follow "a laughing leader, going down into the host, into the loveless battle."[15] If the press reports are to be given credence, young men in the armies of those who oppose us, die in hospitals, refusing alien blood-transfusions in obedience to a fanatical devotion to the mystical body of the tribal *ecclesia*. They die kissing the portraits of their leaders rather than that of Alde or Emma, or the Queen of Heaven. But by no means only among the enemy is there indication of the change, there is much among ourselves and among all peoples to suggest a veering of the wind. Perhaps we are entering again upon a period when the love story may give place to the story of the heroic and of heroics—both.

It is to be hoped that this masculine emphasis is at all events tempered by the saving scepticism of the female mind; there is a danger of Juno being put into a concentration camp, of her being liquidated. There is danger that the deprivation of the Romans may be ours also, that deprivation which Jackson Knight, in his *Cumaean Gates*, explains and clarifies:

"There is a difficulty in seeing what the personality of Juno means, and why a goddess, honoured in Rome, should be so hostile. The answer is that Juno is fiercely feminine. She was not among the principal early deities of Rome, and was never one of the greatest. Rome worshipped male gods first. Rome began, because Juno acknowledged defeat.

"Virgil knew the cost of Empire; the cost in suffering, and the cost to conscience and to so many graceful things. . . . In so far as he accepted the resignation of so much that he loved before the destiny of a greatness sometimes hard, he accepted it seeing and feeling. The male principle, which is seen in Fascism now, is

[15] These quotations are from the *Gododdin* verses,—they are of very early date—attributed to the sixth century poet, Aneirin.

always fighting the female principle, which has found its way into Communism, and lost much of itself as it went. Virgil found some consolation in courage and national honour and in the generosity which a conqueror can reach. To such things poets will return. T. S. Eliot has returned to them, in 'stone, bronze, stone, steel, oakleaves, stone, horses' heels.' He trusts 'in hands, quiet over the horse's neck.' But still like Virgil, he has to cry 'O hidden under the dove's wing, hidden in the turtle's breast. . . . At the still point of the turning world. O hidden.' "

It is an idle question whether this change is a retrogression or an advance, for man does not determine these things, nor the temper of the world into which he is born. He can at best suffer the circumstances of his nativity and tradition. But there is something that he does determine, which it is his nature to fulfil. Whether on pre-history hill-camp, or in city-state, or in mediaeval manor, in the world of the primitive migrations or of Imperial collapse, in Victorian security or in our own Neo-Georgian predicament, he can, must, and does, "make a song about it." If not in praise of Clarissa's forehead, then in praise of the vallum successfully defended, if not of the successful resistance, then of the Waters of Babylon. In due time, there rises above the cotton-field whips a body of song of great poignance and of real inventive interest. Who would have guessed that in the African transportations to the American Continent, the theme of Salvation, as conceived by certain Christian sects, would, by contact with something in the Negro genius, have given "Evangelicalism" its intensest art-form, and given to the world a very remarkable folk expression of abiding interest—a true, poetic-metric expression? In some way or other these things, perhaps, may always be, unless the temporary triumph of those conditions which are dictated by the primacy of material values so enervates man, that his native inclinations are numbed at the roots.

Spengler had some insight into the cyclic character of the periods of decline, and certainly the trend, as far as we can see of the contemporary world, verifies some of his conclusions. But in our confusion and complexity we dare not commit ourselves to any water-tight explanation. We know that within our own time more and more communities of men have abandoned, or been deprived of, long-standing cultural ways of life. We have seen them released and emancipated from hard and ancient economies and rooted conditions, and we have seen them adopt, or be assimilated by, a very different rhythm of life. We have seen their large measure of disillusionment and have heard many causes blamed for this state of things and many remedies propounded. The truth is we do not know in what fashion a new synthesis will be effected, how the gains will be consolidated and the ills overcome —if either. We do not know what songs may yet be possible or what shape our myth will take, but it looks as though the waste land before us is extensive; and it is certain that in our anabasis across it we shall have reason to keep in mind the tradition of our origins in both matter and spirit.

Tudor Aled, the Welsh fifteenth-century poet, who died in the Franciscan habit, says: "Clear token does man give of what sort is his root."

If we doctor the flowers and cut away the foliage to suit our particular age and prejudices we shall fail to recognise the nature of the root. "To Arthur the pot, to Gwenhwyfar the pan" must be remembered when we are reading of the great feudal figure, surrounded by his peers, in the mixed material sumptuousness and spiritual awareness at the "high feast of Pentecost," in all the circumstance of the Malorian story. The primitive division of goods between man and wife of the Welsh Codes brings us back to the realities of the economic basis of all society. We seem to see in that traditional saying, the hearthstone, the griddle, the herds, the twined wattle and the circular unmortared huts within the enclosing earth-works,

the berried rowan planted to ward off the damaging magic
—all the down-to-earthness, and intuition of powers-not-
earthly, of the primitive scene.

The clues are many and varied and cover large fields
of enquiry. Does any one know for instance why Arthur
is called "one of the three useless bards"[16] in one of the
Triads? There remains much for those who are competent to do, and all things connected with this tangle
should be of interest to people of this island, because
it is an affair of our own soil and blood and tradition,
our own "inscape," as Hopkins might say—it is the
matière de Bretagne. We have said enough to indicate the
intricate nature of this thing, and the necessity of preserv-
ing the many elements. "All must be safely gathered in,"
as Mr. Stanley Spencer said to me, with reference to the
making of a picture (a more apt expression of the artist's
business I never heard). *"Restaurare omnia in Christo"*
might be said to be on the labarum Arthur carries as
indicative of *one* of the *many* emphases in this changing
role from Agriculture Deity to Mediaeval King.

To conserve, to develop, to bring together, to make
significant for the present what the past holds, without
dilution or any deleting, but rather by understanding
and transubstantiating the material, this is the function
of genuine myth, neither pedantic nor popularising, not
indifferent to scholarship, nor antiquarian, but saying
always: "of these thou hast given me, have I lost none."

We have attempted an amateur exploration of some few
of the many thickets (and we have only touched on the
fringes) that compose Arthur's wood. We have stopped
to speak of a gnarled bole here and of a bright shrub there,
with no liberty to speak except for a deep affection for this
forest of Brociliande (the scholars must forgive our tres-
pass, as they must excuse our confounding, for want of
knowledge, the ancient perennials with the changing de-

[16] I do not know from which series of Triads this comes, or whether it
represents a genuine early tradition, or is of late invention.

ciduous boughs that make up the tangle). But now I should
like to say something of the book which is the main channel of this thing for the English reader.

For English-speaking people "this noble and joyous book
entitled *Le Morte Darthur*"—"ended the ninth year of
the reign of King Edward the Fourth, by Sir Thomas
Maleore, Knight, as Jesu help him for his great might,
as he is the servant of Jesu, both day and night," must
remain the normal and national "source"—rather as the
Authorised Version of the Bible remains so for them,
whatever its deficiencies and excellencies, among the many
versions of the Christian Scriptures, and in some ways for
comparable reasons. Incidentally, the Malory has points
of resemblance to our Vulgate, in the sense that it can be
called a true version, the precise originals of which are
no longer available to us.

Malory wrote his book only just in time—a little later
and it might well have been a romantic rather than a
romance document. He was just in time to be part of that
decaying world that knew the shadow of feudalism, to be
at all events familiar with its outward accidents and to
appreciate something of its inward idea. The Middle-age
in England was not quite dead, though the self-destruction
of the Wars of the Roses, in which the author was, perhaps, himself involved, was the outward sign of the breakdown of the old synthesis—the conflict from within, of
the Marxists, that makes inevitable the new order. However that may be, he could still write authentically of
"knighthood." His data—his visual, felt, data I mean—
were accurate and experiential—contactual—a necessity
to the making of a genuine writing—there can be no
getting round that, in the long run. The imagination
must work through the what is known and known by a
kind of touch. Like the Yggdrasil of northern myth, the
roots must be in hard material though the leaves be con-
ceptual and in the clouds—otherwise we can have fancy
but hardly imagination.

When Malory has reason to describe the quarterings

on a shield, it is work-a-day, and as a police constable might describe the number-plate of an automobile. Whereas a hundred years later, in Spenser, whose gifts as a maker of writings no one would question, the charge on the surcoat of the Knight of the Red-Cross,

". . . pricking on the plain
"Y-clad in mighty arms and silver shield"

has already lost liaison with the concrete. The whiff of gunpowder was already in the nostrils of horse and rider, fire-locks are opening the visors, the "jousts and tournays" are already "Ye olde"—and no degree of artistry can overcome the fact.

But Malory was on time in other senses. Had he written a century and a half earlier his English would have been sufficiently archaic to require translation; as it is, anyone can read him with little effort. Admittedly Sommers' facsimile of Caxton's edition is a very different thing to read compared with the punctuated and modernly spelt version published by Dent, but the latter is on the whole satisfactory for the ordinary reader, and I have used it in the quotations in this essay.[19] People have told me how they are discouraged from persevering in Malory because of the endless clichés, the repetitions, the feats of arms, the knight and lady situations all of one pattern, in fact discouraged by the facade of chivalric literature, and others find the supposed lack of construction, the pieced-togetherness of the whole work, a difficulty, but these irritations are superficial and once overcome, the reader is rewarded.

Not only is this book a repository of ancient, essential, integral things, not only is it what some call a "human

---

[17] The whole question of "modernized" versions of the earlier English writers is one about which no two persons will agree, and about which any one person will have contradictory feelings. In some moods, and I think in one's more clear-sighted moods, one would oppose any tampering of any sort what so ever with the spelling and punctuation of the originals, for the convenience of the modern reader. But in the case of Malory the modernization is less damaging than in the case of Chaucer.

document"—and indeed it is sympathetic to and has correspondence with, the deepest of our emotions—but it has also unique qualities as a writing in the English language, and I often wonder why its uniqueness is not more discussed by those whose business it is to compare and assess the different influences in the development of the English prose style. For those who may be less acquainted with it, I shall quote one or two passages that seem to me to convey some idea of its quality as writing. Book ii, ch. 18.

> Book ii, ch. 18.
> "Then said Balin le Savage, What knight art thou? for or now I found never no knight that matched me. My name is, said he, Balan, brother unto the good Knight Balin. Alas said Balin, that ever I should see this day, and therewith he fell backward in a swoon. Then Balan yede on all four feet and hands and put off the helm of his brother, and might not know him by the visage it was so ful hewen and bledde; but when he awoke he said, O Balan, my brother, thou hast slain me and I thee, wherefore all the wide world shall speak of us both."

Book iii, ch. 14.

> "Is the knight that oweth this shield your love? Yea truly, said she, my love he is, God would I were his love. So God me speed, said Sir Gawaine, fair damosel ye have right, for an he be your love ye love the most honourable Knight of the world, and the man of most worship. So me thought ever, said the damosel, for never or that time, for no knight that ever I saw, loved I never none erst"

Book vi, ch. 15.

> "And then he saw a fair sword lie by the dead knight, and that he gat in his hand and hied him out of the chapel. Anon as he was ever in the chapel yard all the

knights spake to him with a grimly voice, and said, Knight Sir Lancelot, lay that sword from thee or else thou shalt die. Whether that I live or die said Sir Lancelot, with no great word get you it again, therefore fight for it an ye list. Then right so he passed throughout them, and beyond the chapel yard there met him a fair damosel, and said, Sir Lancelot, leave that sword behind thee, or thou wilt die for it. I leave it not said Sir Lancelot, for no entreaties. No, said she, an thou didst leave that sword Queen Guenever should thou never see. Then were I a fool an I would leave this sword, said Launcelot."

In each of these passages, although the mood is varied, we have the characteristic emphasis by double-negatives. This runs throughout. The formal strength of the sentences seems to have a relationship with the degree of determination required by the content. Malory frequently conveys this feeling of men doing things, good or bad, "to the uttermost." They say "no" with unmistakable intention. This feeling is not appreciable in the Celtic tales, and perhaps we can, in this, see the spirit of the Northern thing, (which Professor Tolkien describes in his Beowulf essay as: "the theory of courage, which is the great contribution of early Northern literature") and possibly fused with something of the Pauline conception of the Christian armed man—"and having done all, to stand."

Of the recurring poetry of so much of Books xiii to xviii which deal with the Sangreal, it is not easy to select a passage. In those chapters a world is created. As in the world of dreams the objects are natural and sharply defined, but their juxtaposition is of the mind and of the imagination. We are reminded for much of the time of Paul's "whether in the body or out of the body I cannot tell." As in the Celtic mythology previously mentioned, the episodes move against a background of isthmuses, is-

The Myth of Arthur

205

lands, peninsulas, deserts. It is indeed the Western Thebaid; it is the Paradise of the Fathers and Hieronymus Bosch transferred to the Anglo-Franco-Celtic sea-board, but a naive relationship with the animal creation has crept in.

"Often they arrived in isles far from folk where there repaired none but wild beasts." Percivale sides with the lion against the serpent because of its being "the more natural beast of the two."

Book xiv, ch. 6.
"And the lion went always about him fawning like a spaniel, and he stroked him upon the neck and shoulders. And then he thanked God of the fellowship of that beast." "Then he went up unto the rock and found the lion which always kept him fellowship, and he stroked him upon the back and had great joy of him."

In this same Sangreal section, we get the meeting of Lancelot and Galahad, his son, each on the quest.

"And there was great joy between them, for there is no tongue can tell the joy that they made, either of other, and many a friendly word spoken between, as kin would."

The notion that the *Morte Darthur* lacks construction has always seemed to me somewhat superficial, for it gathers depth and drive as it proceeds toward the final disaster, as few writings do. Individualistic works of great genius, such as *Moby Dick* or *Wuthering Heights,* notorious for this quality, hardly excel it in this particular, but of course it *is* composite and not an individual creation, but a selected and dislocated translation; nevertheless we move on through many changes of mood to Book xx, chapter i, in which the smouldering begins to break flame. We almost feel late frost blight bud and steel wind strip tree, in:

"So in this season, as in the month of May, it befell

a great anger and unhap that stinted not till the flower of chivalry of all the world was destroyed and slain."

In the closely-packed chamber of the king, the nephews jostle each other as nearly as rivals at a sherry-party. The malignant Agravaine can stand it no longer: "Then Sir Agravaine said thus openly and not in no counsel, that many knights might hear it"—the scandal is given vent.

"Then spoke Sir Gawaine and said, Brother Sir Agravaine, I pray you and charge you move such matters no more afore me, for wit you well, said Sir Gawaine I will not be of your counsel. So God me help said Sir Gaheris and Sir Gareth, we will not be knowing, brother Agravaine, of your deeds. Then will I, said Sir Mordred. I leave well that said Sir Gawaine, for ever unto all unhappiness brother Sir Mordred thereto will ye grant; and I would that ye left all this and made you not so busy, for I know, said Sir Gawaine what will fall of it. Fall of it what fall may, said Sir Agravaine, I will disclose it to the King."

The three dissentients depart, "making great dole." The King is informed. The tension snaps, and from then on to the end of the book the recitation hurries forward with the split loyalties, the taking of sides, the unforgettable words between Lancelot and the queen, the mêlée at her chamber-door and his escape. Mixed with profounder things is an excitement almost akin to a Broadway shoot-up, or a Wild West boy's tale. For all the mediaeval accidents and accents, Tommy-guns seem to be racking the enclosed space, the hero unscathed—"so Jesu be my shield." Any conflict at an egress, or collision of wills in the narrows, at stair-head or at door, (as Gordon's was, and remember Herbert of Cherbury's "Come down, Welshman") have, as in the case of confined struggle at trench-block or crater-lip, a particular quality of tension,—this the *Morte Darthur* here conveys.

This incident of the trapped and unharnessed Launce-

lot, the stout resisting door, the fourteen informers without, "armed at all points as though they should fight in a
battle," the breakaway, and Mordred's tail down, who
"fled with all his might," creates a visual image not easily
forgotten. That door of the Queen's chamber, by the
imaginative power of Malory's narrative (bare as it is of
elaborate "descriptive writing"), is made a concrete symbol of the idea "door," and of those age-long dramas to
which door-posts have been the inanimate witnesses;
the closings and the openings—fast, ajar, set wide; the
enterings-in and the final goings-out of good things and
bad, the burstings-open and the silent withdrawals, the
comedies and the tragic errors. If we let our minds rove
in imaginative, rather than "free," association in this matter of the door of the Queen's Chamber, from:

> "She took out her little forty-four,
> Rooty-toot-toot, three times she shot
> Right through that hard wood door"

to the *Pax Vobis*, which "when the doors were shut,"
broke in upon the apostolic assembly in the 20th chapter
of John's Gospel, we shall just about appreciate the varia-
tion in range of Malory's gunnery. While his fieldpieces
divert the forward positions with light stuff of the Sir
Dinidans and their "light ladies," of the petty jealousies
of the Queen and the sallies of Sir Kay, his longrange
and emplaced siege-pieces leave the back areas in no doubt
but that this is no subsidiary raid, but heavy with the
story of final disaster and with the burden of the Sangreal.
He attacks in depth, all is gathered in, baptised if need be,
somehow incorporated.

This is the final test. Does a work of art not only gather
recession from the past, but does it project itself forward
so that other works of art and of nature, however trivial,
and of only remote association, are conditioned by it, in
our minds, as this tree or bit of sky evokes the exclamation
"Pure Constable"? (Though here of course the association is obvious and the conditioning direct.) At all events,

things can be "Pure Malory" for those acquainted with him.

One may laugh in reading him, but more I suppose for the wry understanding and sudden turns of mood, than for humour or wit. There are such incidents as that of Sir Kehydius (brother to Isoud La Blanche Mains, rival to La Beale Isoud, in the Tristram section), and how he explained himself to King Mark, when he leapt from Isoud's "bay-window" in dread of Tristram and landed at the King's feet as he sat playing at chess, below.

"And when the King saw one come hurling over his head he said: Fellow, what art thou, and what is the cause thou leapest out at that window? My Lord the king, said Kehydius, it fortuned me that I was asleep in the window above your head, and as I slept I slumbered, and so I fell down. And thus Sir Kehydius excused him."

But whether grave or gay, if profane or sacred, of the contingent or the absolute, all is held within the restraint of the diction. The explosiveness of the content never cheapens the form nor destroys the shape of the writing. The liturgy proceeds toward the inevitable disintegration of the realm and toward the "most piteous history of the morte of King Arthur." In the twenty-fourth and last book, there is a passage we may find profitable.

"For then was the common voice among them that with Arthur was none other life but war and strife, and with Sir Mordred was great joy and bliss. Thus was Sir Arthur depraved and evil said of. And many there were that king Arthur had made up of nought, and given them lands, might not then say him a good word. Lo Ye all Englishmen, see ye not what a mischief here was: for he that was the most knight of the world, and most loved the fellowship of noble Knights and by him they were all upholden, now might not these Englishmen hold them content with him. Lo, thus was the old custom and usage of this land; and also men say that we of this land have not yet lost nor forgotten that custom and usage. Alas, this is a great default of us Englishmen, for there may no thing please us no term."

The kind of epilogue which follows on the disaster of Camlann, has a quality of its own—it is full of tenderness and of what Chaucer expresses in "the wrestling of this world asketh a fall." There seems no wind to stir the pennons, the shivered lances lie unsalvaged, the long-legged squires slip away, there is unemployment among the hangers-on, the *jongleurs* and the stewards. The calamity is of a sobering nature; the "fair pavilions" have vanished with the spread beds for joyous unions; Dame Brisen's work is done and a magic more powerful than that of Morgan le Fay, or even Merlin, begins to operate. —The political, romantic, and military strivings fade out altogether. Another initiation is in process. Even the highly-placed clerics take to Religion—the "Bishop of Canterbury" is in his hermitage "between two cliffs";

> "and there was none of those other knights but they read in books and holp for to serve Mass and rang bells, and did bodily all manner of service. And so their horses went where they would, for they took no regard of no worldly riches"

Those straying riderless horses gone to grass in forest and on mountain, free of their paraphernalia of war, seem as their masters to have acquired a new yet aboriginal liberty. We seem to have seen their descendants, shrunken in bulk, as happens to all creatures that the highland zone assimilates, but holding themselves with breeding, black in colour, and primitive in contour, on a Brecon hill-slope, and once, white under a rowan tree, above Hartlington Hall in the recesses of Warfedale. Guenever also "wrapped in cered cloth of Raines, from top to toe in thirty-fold" is placed in her "web of lead"

> "And when she was put in the earth Launcelot swooned,

and lay long still, . . . for when I remember her beauty
and her noblesse, that was both with the King and with
her, so when I saw his corpse and her corpse so lie
together, truly mine heart would not serve to sustain my
careful body. Also when I remember me how by my
default, mine orgulity and my pride, that they were both
laid full low, that were peerless that ever was living
of Christian people, wit you well said Sir Launcelot,
this remembered, of their kindness and mine unkind-
ness, sank so to mine heart, that I might not sustain
myself. So the French book maketh mention"

Launcelot also "they laid . . . in the body of the choir"
at Joyous Gard, "and sang and read many prayers over
him."

"And right thus as they had done their service, then
came Sir Ector de Maris that had seven years sought
all England, Scotland and Wales, seeking his brother,
Sir Launcelot.
"And when he beheld Sir Launcelot's visage he fell
down in a swoon. And when he waked. . . . Ah Launcelot, he said, there thou liest, that thou were never
matched of earthly knights' hand. And thou were the
courteoust Knight that ever bare shield. And thou were
the truest friend to thy lover that ever bestrad horse.
And thou were the truest lover of a sinful man that
ever loved woman. And thou were the kindest man that
ever struck with sword. And thou were the goodliest
person that ever came among press of knights. And
thou were the meekest man and the gentlest that ever
ate in hall with ladies. And thou were the sternest
Knight to thy mortal foe that ever put spear in rest.
Then there was weeping and dolour out of measure."

Characteristically the Bishop is recalled from his seclu-
sion by the new king—but for the men of arms

"they all lived in their countries as holy men. . . .

"And some English books make mention that they went

never out of England after the death of Sir Launcelot,
but that was but favour of makers. For the French book
maketh mention, and is authorised, that Sir Bors, Sir
Ector, Sir Blamore, and Sir Bleoberis, went into the
Holy Land thereas Jesu Christ was quick and dead . . .
and these four knights did many battles upon the mis-
creants or Turks. And there they died on a Good Friday for God's sake."

So ends the *Morte Darthur*.

"But that was but favour of makers," might well be kept
in mind with regard to the whole.

The flavour left with us by the concluding sentence is
so exclusively Mediaeval that we feel altogether divorced
from the underlying traditions of the story. Here the traditions of the Celtic West and perhaps of Classical antiquity, and of the warfare between Romano-Briton and
Saxon are lost in the world of Roland and St. Louis. In
this connection it would be interesting to know about the
inception into these stories of the Saracen knights, like
Sir Palomides, Priamus, and Sir Safere, and others.
Palomides is an important character in the Mark-Tris-
tram-La Beale Isoud episode, where his hopeless love for
Isoud, his constancy and prowess are notable, and if I
remember rightly, he refuses baptism until he has accomplished a specified number of feats. This has sometimes reminded me of that tough and elusive man, Penda
of Mercia, representative of the last of the northern pagans,
who is said to have refused baptism until he should find
a Christian who kept the Christian rule, and who died
unchristened.[18]

But in this flattening-out after the power-drive, this,
so to say, Dickensian "conclusion," this tidying-up after
the explosion—the requiems done and the lived-happy-

---

[18] I suppose this notion originated with Bede's statement that Penda
"hated and despised those whom he perceived to be without works of
faith . . . . . . saying that they were contemptible who scorned to obey
their God, in whom they believed."

ever-afters sorted out, it is possible that we are once again, obliquely and by analogy, confronted with a reflection of actual events. The loss of the "Crown of Britain" and the political and military eclipse of the Roman-British provincials, and the cutting off of the Celtic West, was accompanied by one of the most remarkable and enthusiastic movements in history. If the Battle of Camlann and those other "Camlans" and "Catraeths"—Deorham, Chester, Winwaedfield,[19] and many lesser setbacks—have left a tradition of successive and inevitable defeat in face of Germanic infiltration, the same period that knew these ruinous events witnessed also the phenomenon of Celtic coenobitical enthusiasm. The *clas*[20] of "David the Waterman" in South Wales, Padern in Ceredigion, Iltyd, Teilo, Trillo Beuno, Cadfan, with his mother, "the three-breasted Gwen," Nonn the mother of David, Tudno, Tyssilio, that spread the gospel in the districts of St. Malo,—the men and women of the wattled *bangors* and of the naive Penitentials, those complex figures who apepar to have combined a Pauline zeal for the gospel, a fanaticism like that of the Thebaid, with a consciousness of the beauty of the created world not always found in ascetics.

There seems some indication that side by side with this asceticism there was a love of the shapes of their desolate retreats, and of the animals who praised God with growl and cry in these places. Some of this feeling may have found its way into our later literature. Perhaps long before St. Francis, the islands of the West may have "had great joy" of the brute creation.

[19] The battles of Deorham and Chester, respectively ,severed the Britons of Wales from those of South West England and from those of North West England. The defeat of Winwaedfield, forty years later, smashed the alliance between Mercia and the Welsh. Catraeth and Camlann are more of tradition than of history, perhaps, and are symbolic of disaster, the former more glorious, where three hundred, after the mead feast, are destroyed by a superior enemy force—this exploit is given permanence in the *Gododdin* poem. Camlann is symbolic, not only of disaster, but of betrayal, and Arthur's death.

[20] *Clas*   community, enclosure.

It has tentatively been suggested that the early Celtic nature-poetry is not unconnected with the solitaries who left their colleges and enclosures to seek more isolated encounter. "In hill and plain, in the islands of the sea, there is no escape from Christ" is a fragment attributed to one such. Whatever the hair-splitting, the severities, the taboos, the background is the flora and fauna of Thule, where the contours are lost and found, where intuition refracts the shape of definition, where men speak true only when they speak as poets. "The dreaded Infant's hand" strokes the forest cat and the cat in the cell of the Irish solitary evokes a poem—just as, centuries late, Kit Smart from his asylum wrote in praise of his cat, Jeoffry.

A glance at the Irish and Welsh[21] Penitentiaries, canons, and Tables of Commutation is sufficient to dispel the idea, sometimes put forward, that the Celtic coenobites, hermits and missionaries practised a religion more in harmony with the liberal evangelicalism of modern times in contradistinction to an ecclesiastical "Roman party." Whatever differences there were, both were equally sacramental and ascetical. In many ways the modern Englishman would have found the western enthusiasms the more trying of the two, although perhaps in the latter he would recognize affinities, springing not from congruity of belief and practice, but from congruity of soil and blood and climate.

They were of their age. Sacrament jostles magic; codes of severe penance, primitive taboo, local cult-practice, were no doubt as entwined in their *lived* word as are the still to be seen abstractions and monsters interlaced, on the scripts of their *written* word. It was a complex of enthusiasms that blazed up from the ashes of the lost west. The strayed horses of the *miles*, going "where they would," became very fiery indeed by sea and by land. They neighed

[21] McNeill and Gamer say in *Mediaeval Handbooks of Penance* of the exclusively Welsh documents "the penalties in their canons are mild in comparison with those prescribed in most penitential literature." They suggest that later a greater severity is recognisable.

against the warriors from the woods, and from among the
tumuli bid them remember:

> "After blows and bloodshed
> And white steeds caparisoned
> This grave holds Cynddylan"[22]

and they, like the Fore-runner, cried:

> "If the son of man perish
>   without atoning
> To God for the sin he hath
>   committed
> It had been better no soul
>   entered his flesh"[23]

This was their main plank, and by "atoning" they meant
"atoning," not "being sorry." But they built their habita-
tions where:

> "Cold is the lair of the fish under
> The shelter of the ice, emaciated is the
> Stag, short the twilight, trees bend."[24]

Arthur's ship *Prydwen* of the *Spoils of Hades*, the galley
of Artorius the *Comes*, this no longer rides the *Mare Occi-
dentale* or the *Fretum Gallicum*, the pharos at Bononia is
long extinguished—but the trimmed and tarred coracles
push out for "the love of God" from western sinus and
island to drift without chart or helm-control (like the
open boat in the *Anglo-Saxon Chronicle*) "By adven-
ture and by grace," as Malory would put it, to beach on
the flats of estuaries, to be moored under the deserted
harbour-moles, where the Roman anchorage-stones litter
at low tide, and the disintegrating Roman iron corrodes

---

[22] From the *Stanzas of Graves* as given in Skene's *Four Ancient Books of
Wales,* from a twelfth century MS. in the *Black Book of Carmarthen.*

[23] From the ninth century Cambridge Juvencus MS.

[24] Also from the *Black Book of Carmarthen.* So that in each case the
verses cited are later than the period we are thinking about,—but they
express all that age. They are among the oldest literary remains we possess
in the Welsh language.

and streaks tawny the crumbling Roman cement, where
west wind and west tide prey on the carcass of Empire;
or over-land between the "army-paths," carried on back[25]
where the inland streams change level, to be tethered under
bank in upland reaches—for the watermen of God must
bring their rule to the evacuated, and to where the ancient
hill-forts are being feverishly re-conditioned for internecine
war—for the long long decline and winter of the West.

> "The snow falls, the plain is covered,
> Warriors hasten to battle, I go not,
> My wound will not let me."

> "Long is the night, bare the moor,
> Grey the hill, green the banks, the
> Sea gull is inland, a heavy sea runs,
> There will be rain today."[26]

And by the watch-fires, at the boundary-mounds:

> "I fondle no maiden to-night, my retinue is not large
> Myself and my frank around our cauldron.
> I smile not, I kiss no *canella* to-night, though we
>   should drink new mead;
> Myself and my frank around our pan.
> Ask of me no mirth to-night, my lay is a wail,
> One word two ills doth cause."[27]

To those so encamped, and the age was, as ours threatens
to become, one of encampments, of distressed and up-
rooted urban populations, thrown back among the tribal
and enduring rustic communities, the whole unhappy mass
being subject to what Mr. Churchill would call the "swoop

[25] As might be seen recently, and perhaps can still be seen, in South
West Wales.

[26] This is also from the *Black Book of Carmarthen*. Skene's translation.

[27] A more recent and very different version of this is given in H. I.
Bell's *Welsh Poetry*, so different that it is clear how obscure this material
is for the specialists. The translation given here is from Rhys' essay:
Origin of the Welsh Englyn. He gives it as a tentative attempt. The word
canella he leaves untranslated, being unable to nail down its meaning
within the context.

and scoop" of military manoeuvre, where everyman's hand was against everyman, and men sat wondering what was brewing over the hill or across the neck of water, those apostles of the West did not bring to those so situated, a message of freedom from encounter or lessening of tension; they were naïve men, but not so naïve as to suggest a "better time coming." On the contrary they proposed a more arduous warfare and more fearsome privations as necessary to the taking-on of Paul's adversaries and theirs, "the prince of the power of the air" and the "cosmocrats of the dark aeon," and as necessary incidentally to the living of a possible life in this world, for only within their enclosures was there normal order in that age.

In conclusion let us return to the strayed horses of Lancelot and his companions, become, as we have presumed to fancy, the Creatures of the "New Law."

In the eleventh-century *Life of St. David* by Rhygyvarch of Menevia, St. Brendan, the navigation saint, "leading a wondrous life on a marine animal" meets in the middle channel of the Irish sea, the Irish abbot Barre[28] returning from his pilgrimage to the Tomb of the Apostles, by way of St. David's community in South Wales. He, Barre, is riding on David's abbatial horse, now become by marvel sea-horse. Brendan hails his fellow countryman and fellow athlete with these words: *Mirabilis Deus in Sanctis suis.*

The mythological deposits seem to say to us: God is wonderful in his masters of illusion, in the transmogrifications, in the heroes who sustain the folk and the land.

The historical fragments perhaps say to us: God is wonderful in the Dux and in his mobile tactic, in the defence of the province.

The Romance authors say, but what they say is complex: God is wonderful in the achievements of feats, in lover and beloved, and in the bond between lord and

---

[28] St. Finbar of Cork.

vassal. But after the deluge, after the severe fasting, when the realm is "wholly mischiefed" and all the armament is all "to-brast," their tradition drops a hint of where man would say the next wonder is to be felt, and suggests the nature of the recovery, no recovery at all in the immediate sense: the *status quo* is not restored, the wrongs go un-righted, the aggressed are aggressed to extinction, the "noble fellowship" is dissolved for ever, no recovery at all—"No electress at all but old Moppa Necessity" as Joyce says, but out of that necessity which left no choice, there were forces that electrified the succeeding order. We do not yet know how narrow our own choice may be, or what news our strayed horses may bring, or in whom or what the wonderfulness may be shown, or which way the winged-cat, when the wind blows where it lists, may jump.

In some moods those repeated words of Turpin in the *Song of Roland* "Sirs, you are set for sorrow," would seem to be our text, and often times, as Lancelot says, what we do for the best, turns out for the worst, but we have heard with our ears and our fathers have told us the mar-vels done in their time and in pre-history, so that, one way or another, *Deus ex machina* may have for us another than its usual connotation. From the machine-age the strayed machine-men may create a myth patient of baptism. Arthur may return from "faërie" in the least expected of guises.

It so happens that I write this concluding sentence on the day when David (*Dewi Sant*) is confessed by all the western church. There is a tentative, and I suppose an invented, traditional association between him and the sub-ject of this essay, which association has at least a concep-tual validity. Arthur, the *Comes*, the man who led the "loricated hosts" in the defence of the island, the fabulous lord of the world, gives place, in our minds, at least for today, to the confessor within his wattles at Mynyw among the Irish-Welsh of the extremity of what is now Pembrokeshire, training his shock-troops in the technics of an offensive which had for its objective a true *lebensraum*, the *limes* and boundaries of which march with and impinge upon mundane lands, but which had extending frontiers the other side of time.